# DRACULA
## WAS A
# WOMAN

## Other books by Raymond T. McNally

*A Clutch of Vampires*
*In Search of Dracula (with Radu Florescu)*
*Dracula: a Biography of Vlad the Impaler (with Radu Florescu)*
*The Essential Dracula (with Radu Florescu)*

# DRACULA

## WAS A

# WOMAN

In Search of the Blood Countess
of Transylvania

---

## *Raymond T. McNally*

Book Club Associates
London

*To Carol*

This edition published 1984 by
Book Club Associates
by arrangement with Robert Hale Limited


Printed in Great Britain by
St Edmundsbury Press, Bury St Edmunds, Suffolk
and bound by Hunter & Foulis Ltd

# Contents

# *Illustrations*

Cachtice Castle: the castle most often associated with the Blood Countess (*Raymond T. McNally*)

Map of Eastern Europe, *c.*1500

*Between pages 126 and 127*

Carol Borland as 'Luna', the vampire girl (*From the MGM release 'Mark of the Vampire'* © *1935 Metro-Goldwyn-Mayer Corporation. Copyright renewed 1961 by Metro-Goldwyn-Mayer Inc.*)

Theda Bara, the first screen vamp, hunching over a male skeleton

Christopher Lee as Count Dracula, *Dracula A.D. 1972 (photograph by permission of Hammer Film Productions Limited)*

A victim of a vampire's attack, from *The Vampire Lovers* (*Hammer Film Productions Limited*)

Three female vampires lean over the fallen body of Jonathan Harker, from Tod Browning's *Dracula*, 1931 (*Universal*)

Dr Van Helsing's dead decaying daughter, John Badham's *Dracula* 1979 (*Universal*)

A female vampire on the attack, *The Vampire Lovers*, 1970 (*Hammer Film Productions Limited*)

Sandra Harrison as a teenage vampire on campus, *Blood of Dracula*, 1957 (*American International Pictures*)

John Van Eyssen as Jonathan Harker prepares to drive a stake through the heart of a young Vampire, Valerie Gaunt, *Horror of Dracula*, 1958 (*Hammer Film Productions Limited*)

Ingrid Pitt as Countess Bathory, *Countess Dracula*, 1972 (*Hammer Film Productions Limited*)

Countess Bathory prevents her lover from leaving (*Hammer Film Productions Limited*)

The procurement of girls for Countess Bathory (*Hammer Film Productions Limited*)

The Countess readys herself for the kill (*Hammer Film Productions Limited*)

The aged Countess Dracula with her accomplices (*Hammer Film Productions Limited*)

Two vampire girls in *The Brides of Dracula*, 1960 (*Hammer Film Productions Limited*)

In tombs of gold and lapis lazuli
Bodies of holy men and women exude
Miraculous oil, odour of violet.
But under heavy loads of trampled clay
Lie bodies of the vampires full of blood;
Their shrouds are bloody and their lips are wet.

—W. B. Yeats
"Oil and Blood"

# Introduction

AFTER having written four books revolving around the historical Dracula, the Dracula novel, and vampirism, I was reasonably certain that I had succeeded in unearthing most of the facts on the subject of Count Dracula. However, I continued to be haunted by several unanswered questions: There were no associations between the historical Vlad Dracula, known as "The Impaler" (1431–1476), and any acts of blood drinking either in the documents or in Romanian folklore, so how did Bram Stoker, author of the novel *Dracula*, come to make Count Dracula into a drinker of human blood? Was it all simply the product of Stoker's wild imagination? Or his reading of some books about Transylvanian superstitions? Or his chance meetings with the Hungarian orientalist Arminius Vambery? The historical Dracula, about whom Stoker knew a great deal, was actually a prince, so why did Stoker present him as merely a count? Vlad Dracula was a Romanian not a Hungarian, so, in the novel, why is Count Dracula portrayed as a member of an ancient Hungarian race tracing a bloodline all the way back to Attila the Hun? Where did Stoker possibly get his information about Count Dracula's hands and fingernails, which according to Stoker's description resemble those of a werewolf rather than a vampire? And where did Stoker get the idea of presenting the count as looking younger after he had imbibed human blood, a notion not prevalent in folklore? Furthermore, there is a great deal of eroticism in the novel, yet little in the life of the historical Vlad Dracula—from where did this eroticism come?

I went over Bram Stoker's unpublished personal journals again and again until I hit upon the clue: Stoker had definitely taken notes on the story of the infamous Blood Countess, Elizabeth Bathory from Hungary in *The Book of Werewolves*, written by Sabine Baring-Gould (the author who is most remembered for having composed the words to that rousing hymn "Onward, Christian Soldiers!"). In Baring-Gould's book on werewolves Stoker became engrossed in the following legend:

In Hungary once lived a countess who killed her young female servants in order to bathe and shower in their blood, because she felt that these blood treatments halted the aging process and restored her skin to youthful vigor and freshness. This practice started when a maid accidentally pulled the countess's hair while combing it; Countess Elizabeth Bathory instinctively slapped the girl on the ear, but so hard that she drew blood. The servant girl's blood spurted onto Elizabeth's hands. At first the countess was enraged at this and reached for a towel to wipe off the blood. But suddenly the countess noticed that as the blood dried, her own skin seemed to take on the whiteness and youthful quality of the young girl's skin. After that, Elizabeth Bathory was driven to acquire and use the blood of some 650 young maidens for cosmetic purposes. Elizabeth was reported to have been a werewolf as well, because she reputedly also tore human flesh with her teeth.

I determined to find out all that I could about this strange Countess Elizabeth Bathory and her descendants and the role her image played in the creation of Count Dracula by the Irish author Bram Stoker. Unfortunately there was no reliable biography of Elizabeth Bathory in any language, and I discovered that there was a great deal of misinformation written about her.

Up until now the best biography about Elizabeth Bathory was by the German scholar R. A. von Elsberg entitled *Elisabeth Bathory: Die Blütgräfin* (The Blood Countess) published at Breslau in 1904. This book, long out of print, is very rare. Fortunately, I was able to locate and xerox the copy at the Widener

Library of Harvard University. Valentine Penrose's *Erzsebet Bathory. La Comtesse sanglante* is a romanticized version with no historical evidence.

I am especially grateful to the excellent Hungarian specialist in the seventeenth century, Dr. Laszlo Nagy, for his materials on the Bathory family and especially for his correspondence with me concerning controversial issues. He and I disagreed often, but the arguments were always stimulating. His short article "The Chronicle of an Old Criminal Trial" (*Egy Regi Bünper Kronikaja*) printed in *Inter Press Magazine* (No. 5, 1974: Budapest, pp. 133–140), is one of the best on the topic.

When tourists express an interest in Elizabeth Bathory, they are generally directed to the Cachtice fortress where, they are told, Elizabeth tortured and killed girls. This point of view was made popular in Czechoslovakia by a modern horror novel entitled *The Lady of Cachtice* written by the Czechoslovak author Jozo Niznansky (1903–1976). Largely because of the popularity of that novel, Elizabeth Bathory is known there as "the lady who bathed in human blood."

In our own day the most recent book in English on the subject is by the Hungarian refugee Gabriel Ronay, entitled *The Truth About Dracula*. He repeats the legendary bathing for cosmetic purposes without critical analysis or appraisal.

In the first part of this book I piece together all the available biographical information about Elizabeth Bathory. This material is, necessarily, "straight" history. The second part is an exploration into the central three taboos which rumors attributed to her, i.e., vampirism, werewolfism, and necrophilia, and the ways in which these themes have been treated in literature, theater, and movies.

I start out by trying to find out whether she actually was a "living vampire," a modern medical term referring to a patient morbidly fixated upon human blood. Did she really bite some of her victims? Did she eat their flesh? Or was she herself innocent of all the accusations and simply the victim of some conspiracy?

I also try to answer the questions: Are there such things as modern vampires, or is the vampire belief all traceable back to the folklore of superstitious peasants? How has the vampire image changed and developed over the years? Can one succeed in understanding the accusations against Elizabeth of biting human flesh and love for the dead by placing them in historical perspective?

It is time to put an end to the legends and rumors about Elizabeth and to analyze openly the taboo aspects of the subject. The biography that follows is based upon newly found source materials in Bytca, Czechoslovakia, the records of the court trials (copies were provided to me by archivists in Budapest and Vienna), and the various documents assembled by the German historian R. von Elsberg.

In the interests of simplicity for the average reader I have not included the diacritical marks common to the Hungarian and to the Czechoslovakian languages in transcribing such words into English. In the Czechoslovakian language, for example, "č" is pronounced like the "ch" in *church*, and "š" is pronounced like the "sh" in *shady*. A brief guide to Hungarian spelling and pronunciation is included below:

| archaic spelling | modern spelling | pronuncia- tion |
|---|---|---|
| cz | c | ts |
| ch | cs | ch |
| y | i | i |
| gh | g | g |
| th | t | t |
| eö (oe) | ö | ö (as in German) |
| ue | ü | ü (as in German) |
| | sz | s |
| | s | sh |
| | gy | dy |
| | j | y |

The so-called accent mark over certain Hungarian vowels indicates a lengthening of the pronunciation of that vowel. For example, "Báthory" would be pronounced "Baathory."

# 1

## In Search of the Blood Countess of Transylvania

I learned that the particular part of Transylvania where Elizabeth Bathory lived most of her adult life is located today in Czechoslovakia. I decided I had to go there.

Transylvania is a Latin word meaning "the land beyond the forest" (as Pennsylvania means "Penn's woods"). The term "Transylvania" suggests to most people a strange, far away, unknown place—much as one would say "that land beyond the clouds." Transylvania was not simply made up by some Hollywood filmmakers, as some Americans believe, but is a real geographical location with its own history linked to the Bathory story.

The name of the castle that Elizabeth Bathory frequented is Cachtice today, in the modern Czechoslovak language, pronounced "Chákh-teetsay." (Its old Hungarian name was pronounced "Chéyteh.") Prior to the end of World War I, the largely Slovak local population was dominated by a Hungarian nobility. Elizabeth's Castle Cachtice, I found, could be reached by car from Bratislava, the capital of the Slovakian part of Czechoslovakia. (The Federal Republic of Czechoslovakia has two main sections—the Czech area with Prague as its center and the Slovak part with Bratislava as its center.) I made reservations to go to the area and began a diary-type account of my search for the countess in the literary tradition of Bram Stoker and Wilkie Collins.

**Wednesday, October 1, Munich:** My wife and I first arrive in Munich by airplane; we stay at the famous Four Seasons Hotel (Vierjahreszeiten Hotel), which Bram Stoker had cited in the unpublished notes to his classic novel, *Dracula*. We also visit the old main art museum called the *Pinakothek*. According to Stoker's handwritten notes to the novel, the author had originally planned that Jonathan Harker go to the Four Seasons Hotel during his fictional stay in Munich in 1893 in a part of the novel which was not published in the original 1897 edition. We are intent upon traveling the hitherto unexplored paths of the Dracula trail, leading to the infamous Blood Countess of Transylvania.

**October 3, Vienna:** We leave Munich on the evening airplane to Vienna and arrive there at night. Immediately on arrival we go to see the street known as "Blood Street," which some sources have wrongly associated with Elizabeth Bathory, and also the house on Augustinian Street opposite Lobkowitz Square, the verified location of many of Elizabeth Bathory's flesh-biting and torturing atrocities. In the dark Viennese night these places seem ominous and foreboding.

**October 4 and 5, Vienna:** We had written ahead to Dr. Anna Benna, director of the Vienna archives, for reliable historical source materials about the Countess Elizabeth Bathory and photos of the places associated with her. During our visit to the archives, Dr. Benna kindly provides us with microfilms of the Vienna documents, some of which had been transferred to Budapest after World War II. She also arranges to have reproduced relevant photos of the places and personalities connected with Elizabeth's life. It is an auspicious beginning to our on-the-spot investigation.

**October 6, Bratislava:** We depart from Vienna for Bratislava, actually a mere one-hour bus ride, but we must pass through the Czechoslovak customs at the border between Austria and Czechoslovakia. This delays the trip for over two hours. Czech officials seem rather touchy. Early at night we finally reach Bratislava; arriving close to the castle of Countess Elizabeth Bathory.

**October 7, Bratislava:** We spend the day visiting parts of the old city where Elizabeth walked and lived during her visits there. Our appointment with the director of the archives of the Slovak Academy of Sciences proves to be most important: there the director tells us about the unpublished research done by Josef Kocis, director of the Bytca archives up the Vah River where the trial of Elizabeth Bathory had taken place in the year 1611. No one has done any serious research on this event since the turn of this century. [Little did I know at that time that this new research was destined to change much that had been previously written by historians about Elizabeth Bathory.]

**October 8, Trenscin:** We hire a Rent-a-Car in Bratislava and head out highway E-16 for our first stop—Elizabeth's castle. At the town of Trenscin we are obliged to spend a rainy night, since the road to Castle Cachtice is, reportedly, washed out. There appears to be no way we can get to it: only one old dirt road leads from the main highway up to the castle. Is this Elizabeth's way of warning us to stay away? Or is it just chance?

**October 9, Castle Cachtice:** Instead of riding up directly to the castle, we take the road to the nearby town of Vishine just below the castle. One of the Slovak peasants has told us that one could get a good view of the castle from there. The road to Vishine winds around the base of the mountain on which Castle Cachtice is perched. At Vishine we halt to get a clear look at the castle. The massive walls are still standing. The twisted battlements look like huge, black-stained jagged teeth cutting across the sky. It is in much better condition than we have anticipated, certainly better than the sad ruins of many other old castles. There stands the vast mausoleum where Elizabeth had reportedly murdered so many young girls and where she had died, walled up in one of the rooms.

**October 10, Castle Cachtice:** In the morning, with the help of some local peasants, we get the road repairmen to fill in one of the huge, muddy holes in the road with dry dirt and place wooden planks over it temporarily, so that we can begin the ascent to the castle. There is no question of trying to go all the way on foot; the place is too far and too high up. It is still raining hard. The road seems to get poorer and poorer the further we go; it is no longer a real road for cars but has turned into a muddy, rough path with deep furrows. Several times we are afraid that we will get stuck in the mud. Finally we come upon a section that makes further transport by car impossible and we are obliged to proceed the rest of the way on foot. Thunder and lightning amid the livid gray clouds above make us aware of the wildness and uncanniness of the place.

We can already see the broken castle entrance looming ahead like the screaming mouth of some dark angel whose wings have been pinned to the ground. We make it on foot. A local Slovak watchman is there to take us around. We enter the main gate and investigate the tower and its dungeons, the places where many of Elizabeth's crimes are said to have been committed. At the ascent to the pinnacle of the inner castle complex I stop; I cannot bring myself to walk up into the ruins of Elizabeth's private quarters. They seem to shoot up all alone into the sky. I cannot feel the ground beneath my feet (but then I am a victim of acrophobia). My wife and the Slovak watchman go up alone to take photographs of the ruins of Elizabeth's private chambers. I stay below to investigate the main castle tower. They descend and the Slovak tells us stories.

The watchman at Castle Cachtice is well informed. He does not repeat the usual legends about Elizabeth bathing in the blood of young virgins. He knows that the countess bit the girls on their shoulders and breasts. He gives us a running commentary as he shows us through the three main sections of the castle with its triad of gates leading to the holy of holies, Elizabeth's private torture chambers. The first gate leads into the semipublic part of the castle. There the common people used to meet in order to petition the lord or mistress of the castle for settlement of their grievances. Elizabeth's manservant, nicknamed Ficzko, meaning "lad" in Hungarian, used to bring the girls in quickly through that area and then into the second courtyard where Elizabeth's castle servants lived. From there the girls were usually taken through the third gate separating the servants' quarters from the private rooms of Elizabeth. The girls were then led to the main tower room, where they were instructed to strip, supposedly in order to wash themselves. From the upper rooms in the tower Elizabeth looked down on the nude girls and selected ones suitable for her night games.

We finally see and hear enough for one day and head back to the village of Cachtice.

**October 11, Beckov:** Before proceeding to Bytca, the town where Elizabeth's trial took place, there is one other castle in the area which we wanted to see; it is called Castle Beckov, pronounced "Bets-kof." There Elizabeth had reportedly also tortured and killed many servant girls. We had already seen the castle from a distance across the Vah River, along the main highway E-16, but we wanted a closer look. By a minor road that skirts the river we reach Castle Beckov. It is almost as stark and impressive as Castle Cachtice. The ruins stand on the top of a massive rock formation that looks as if it had been thrust out of the ground by some violent eruption. One can easily see why it was used by the countess as an inaccessible place to indulge in her lurid obsessions.

**October 12, Bytca:** In the morning we set out for the town of Bytca, pronounced "Byt-cha." We hope to find out about the new documentation on Elizabeth that, according to the archival authorities in Bratislava, the director of the local archives in that town, Josef Kocis, has discovered. A heavy rain is falling as we pull alongside the old Thurzo palace where the Bytca archives are now located. I stop a fiftyish-looking gentleman and ask him where I can find Mr. Josef Kocis. He tells me that he is this same Kocis and invites us into his office. There for the entire afternoon we talk about Elizabeth Bathory and especially about his discoveries of certain unpublished manuscripts. He tells me about what he has found and shows me the manuscripts. After talking with him, I feel that the English-reading world should know about this legend-smashing, newly found documentation, especially about its first-time revelation regarding the real life of Elizabeth Bathory.

**October 13, Bytca:** I spend another day with Mr. Kocis in his archives where he shows me some more new documentation. It is fascinating; I decide that the entire history of Elizabeth Bathory must be rewritten. Kocis promises to send me microfilms of all the documents through diplomatic channels.

**October 14, Bytca:** I copy down some of the relevant citations and the texts from some of Kocis's documents, but there is simply too much material to digest in the short time I have. I will have to wait for the time to study them all later, and in depth, upon my return to the States.

**October 15, Castle Cachtice:** Before leaving the area and returning to Bratislava from Bytca, we feel the need to have another last look at the castle and the town of Cachtice itself. It is raining hard again when we return to Cachtice. Elizabeth's castle looks even more grim than it did a few days before. We wander around the town and find that little Cachtice has a small museum of its own. It is closed, but we meet and persuade the director to open it for us. There we find the one portrait of Elizabeth that we had been searching for—a true-to-life rendition of her famous "beauty."

In the last major biography of Elizabeth in any language, entitled *Elisabeth Bathory (Die Blutgräfin)* (The Blood Countess), the German author R. A. von Elsberg published a copy of a portrait of Elizabeth Bathory in which she looks beautiful. This same portrait once hung in the gallery of Count Zay from Castle Zay-Ugrocz and was, evidently, a highly idealized portrayal. The style of her dress and jewelry is typical for the Hungarian aristocracy of the late sixteenth century. A proud impressive lady with a high forehead, small hands, her hair pulled up in a bun, gazes from the picture. She does not look at all like the "tigress in human form," that legend has made her.

R. E. L. Masters and Edward Lea in their book, *Sex Crimes in History*, evidently saw something different in this same portrait, reproduced in the Elsberg book, for they wrote:

> None of these women approaches, so far as depth and sophistication of sadistic sexual perversion is concerned, Elizabeth Bathory . . . [with her] astonishingly white flesh, almost translucent, through which one could see clearly the delicate blue veins beneath; long shimmering silken hair, black as the plumage of the raven; sensual, scarlet lips; great dark eyes capable of doelike tenderness, but sometimes igniting into savage anger, and at other times glazing over with the abandoned somnolence of intense sexual passion.

[I am especially fond of the "doelike tenderness."]

My wife and I excitedly discuss this newfound portrait over dinner. How different from what the well-known one in the Elsberg book shows. [Rumor had it that she was one of the loveliest women in all of Europe. If so, standards of beauty have changed radically since then.] In the Cachtice painting her skin is sallow, her ears big, and the expression on her face dull. She looks more like an overgrown, ugly boy than an attractive woman. The museum also has a portrait of Elizabeth's husband Ferenc Nadasdy, as well as valuable historical sketches that depict Castle Cachtice in earlier times.

According to the director of the Cachtice museum, Elizabeth's Iron Maiden once stood in the museum, until it disappeared in the turmoil following World War II. It is impossible to substantiate this claim. It is true, however, that Iron Maidens were used in Europe in the sixteenth century.

The Iron Maiden is a mechanical device that opens somewhat like the Venus flytrap and has hidden spikes on the inner surfaces. There is a famous one in the torture chamber in Nurenberg, Germany. Made in a female form, when closed it looks like a harmless, though huge, statue. But the Iron Maiden is rigged with a secret spring device that opens and closes it around a victim in a deadly embrace.

Elizabeth reputedly had her own special series of Iron Maidens made by a German locksmith for her various residences, including the house on the Augustinian Street across from Lobkowitz Square in Vienna, and, of course, for Castle Cachtice. Professor Paul A. Keller, who now owns Lockenhaus Castle in eastern Austria, which once belonged to Elizabeth, claims that this was the first of her castles to house an Iron Maiden. Elizabeth's Iron Maiden usually was rigged up to look like a real woman. It had human hair on the head and in the pubic area. The statue was clothed in rich garments and bedecked with jewels. Elizabeth customarily ordered a girl to fix the jewels on the Iron Maiden. At first, supposedly, some of the girls would resist, since they had heard rumors that there was something evil about the iron statue. Under stress of orders directly from the countess, however, the servant would usually comply. At first nothing would happen as the girl went about her task of polishing the jewelry on the breast of the Iron Maiden—that is until the girl happened to touch that part of the jewelry on the breast that was secretly connected to the inner mechanism. (One can easily imagine Elizabeth watching all this in breathless anticipation.) The top part of the metal statue grabbed the girl suddenly in a tight embrace; sharp spikes came out of the statue's breasts and pierced and tore the victim's flesh; blood flowed copiously; and death quickly ensued.

**October 16 to 19, Piestany:** After leaving Cachtice in the morning we make another major stop on our journey through Bathory country—the health resort at Piestany, pronounced "Piesh-tany." Shortly before the trial of 1611, Elizabeth, who had fallen very ill, had gone to Piestany to seek a cure or "to take the waters" as one used to put it. We wanted to see what it may have been like for Elizabeth. Of course, the place has changed over the past three hundred years.

The claim in the official guide book that the ancient Romans knew it as a famous spa with medicinal sulfur springs is false. In fact, Piestany was unknown in antiquity. Only in 1551 did a Viennese physician, George Wernher, draw attention to it in his book *Hypomnemation de Admirabilis Hungariae Aquis*. By 1571 Johann Crato von Graftheim, personal physician to Ferdinand

I, Maximillian II, and Rudolf II, prescribed treatment at Piestany.

Several hundred years ago, patients like Elizabeth Bathory bathed in pits dug out of the warm sandy mud banks formed from abundant deposits of the River Vah, which flooded periodically. Elizabeth would have bathed right outside near the river, since there were no indoor facilities in her day. Many of her contemporaries complained in letters about the lack of comfort at Piestany. It was only at the outset of the nineteenth century that the place acquired its popularity. Ludwig van Beethoven and Franz Lehar, two illustrious composers, "took the waters" there, as did the famous Russian basso Feodor Chaliapin and the Mahrajah of Hyderabad.

Today, Piestany is an ultramodern health resort with up-to-date equipment. The phrase "Arise and Walk!" is engraved in bold bronze lettering over the front of the colonnade bridge joining the town to the spa island. The statue of a young man breaking his crutches is the symbol of Piestany. The present visitors included many reputedly oil-rich Arabs who have come for the intensive cure under supervision of the spa's doctors.

The basic treatment was and is drinking from the hot sulfur springs and bathing in the muddy, sulfuric waters, supposed to be beneficial for all sorts of diseases. In order to try it, we arrange to take the plunge into the thermal waters. The result was that we smelled of sulfur for days. (It is not one of our favorite odors.) Undeterred by the odor, we drank some of the sulfuric waters available at the spa fountain, where we had noticed countless people going to fill up bottles of the stuff. The water is disgusting in taste to us, but it seems that many people assume that if something tastes or smells bad enough, like sulfur, or garlic, then it must be good for them.

**October 20, on the road from Piestany to Slovensky Grob:** We need a respite from the intense Bathory search and especially from our experience with the sulfuric treatment at Piestany. Off Highway E-16 is the town of Slovensky Grob, famous for its wine and goose. We dine in a peasant house on superb goose and new potent wine.

**October 21, Pezinok.** We stay over in an inn in this small Slovakian town, since it proves impractical to push on to Bratislava, given the bad weather conditions on the roads.

**October 22 to 24, Bratislava:** We go back to the main state archives to talk with the director and make certain that the documents promised by Kocis will be forwarded to us through the proper channels at the Slovak Academy. It is time to leave Czechoslovakia on the only bus that departs from Bratislava to Vienna. It is nighttime and there are delays again at the border. But this time we do not mind—we have found new evidence leading to the discovery of the true history of the Blood Countess of Transylvania.

One important example of what we found out on our trip to Transylvania is that we can completely discredit the belief that Elizabeth tortured and killed girls only at Cachtice Castle. During the official court trial of Countess Elizabeth Bathory held in 1611, in answer to Question Nine, "Where were they tortured?" (see Appendix Trial Documents), Helena Jo, Elizabeth's accomplice and former servant, replied that wherever the mistress happened to come, everywhere she immediately sought a suitable place to torture the girls. Elizabeth's manservant Ficzko informed the judges that at Bytca the girls were tortured in the pantry, at Sarvar Castle in the tower where no one was permitted to enter, at Cachtice in the cellars and in the clothes washroom, at Keresztur Castle in the closet, at Lezeticz in the castle dungeons. Even when she visited friends and relatives Elizabeth did not hesitate to continue with her torturing of young girls. According to further court testimony, at Prince Eszterhazy's Frakno (Forchenstein) Castle she utilized a huge underground chamber which had been cut out of the rock by hundreds of Turkish prisoners of war who had been imprisoned there under terrible conditions for some thirty years. During her visit to Prince Eszterhazy's castle she had five girls killed and hidden there in its vast underground labyrinth. So the evidence proves that the countess killed not only at Castle Cachtice but in Vienna, Bratislava, Beckov, and even at the

Nadasdy family seat of Sarvar twenty kilometers from Szombathely, and also at Keresztur about ten kilometers from the town of Sopron. In short, she did it everywhere she could.

In the official tourist information in Slovakia the town of Bytca is described as the place where Elizabeth Bathory was kept in prison. The publication *Slovensko-strucny sprievodca* (Concise Guidebook of Slovakia) (Bratislava, 1955) specifically states that "Elizabeth Bathory served out the sentence for her crime as a prisoner in Bytca" (p. 232), but this assertion is not true. The trial took place in Bytca, but Elizabeth was held under house arrest in Cachtice and served out her sentence in Castle Cachtice.

For over a hundred years after her death in 1614 the true story of Elizabeth Bathory was hushed up. The scandal had in fact rocked upper-class Hungarian society. On King Matthias II's command it was even forbidden to bring up her name in polite Hungarian society. The record of her court trial, including letters from those seeking to intercede on her behalf, were locked away. The record of her court trial was copied by the priest Karl David of Saint Peter's Church, who brought it to the cathedral chapter town of Esztergom. There the top-secret record was put in a folio closed to public perusal. Most chronicles do not even mention her existence. A conspiracy of silence about Elizabeth's activities ruled upper-class Hungarian society. Naturally, all of these precautions backfired; lack of proper information gave rise to a vast rumor mill about what "that infamous countess" had done.

Only during the early 1720s, over one hundred years after the death of the countess, did a Hungarian Jesuit named Father Laszlo Turoczy stumble upon copies of the original trial documents in an attic at the castle of Bytca, the place where the court proceedings had taken place. Though he did not publish the trial documents, Father Turoczy wrote a book in Latin entitled *Ungaria suis cum regibus compendio data* (Hungary, A Dated Compendium with Its Kings), in which he referred to parts of the trial documents and also to the stories about the countess which he had heard from the peasants in Cachtice village. He called Cachtice Castle "the scene of the infamy of a cruel tragedy" (infamia crudelis tragaediae funt theatra), because it was there that the illustrious Bathory name fell into ignominy due to the atrocities of Elizabeth Bathory. He described how, in the year 1610, Count George Thurzo had been sent to Cachtice to investigate and had found the body of a young girl who had been tortured and recently killed (ecce puellam ex flagris et ustulatione recens emortuam reperit), along with evidence of the torturing and killing of other girls. Thereupon, he reported, Elizabeth's helpers were put in chains and she was taken into custody and sent "to a secret cell room" in Cachtice fortress. Turoczy put the number of girls killed at six hundred from the testimony of the three culprits, Ficzko, Helena Jo and Dorothea Szentes, and the maid Zusanna. There was also mention of Elizabeth Bathory's blood bathing. One should recall in this context that during the 1720s when Turoczy's book appeared, the heyday of a vampire craze was spreading all across Europe. According to the tales which Father Laszlo Turoczy heard from the villagers around Castle Cachtice, Elizabeth used the blood treatments because, as she reportedly said, "It is my duty to be good to my husband and make myself beautiful for him. God showed me how to do this. So, I would be unwise not to take advantage of this opportunity."

It was the German scholar Michael Wagener who in the late eighteenth century popularized this legend in the West; in his publication *Beiträge zur Philosophischen Anthropologie* (Articles on Philosophical Anthropology) he wrote:

> Elizabeth used to dress up well in order to please her hus-
> band . . . On one occasion, her chambermaid saw something
> wrong with her headdress, and as a recompense for observing
> it, received such a severe box on the ear that blood gushed from
> her nose and spurted on her mistress's face . . . When the blood
> drops were washed off her face, her skin appeared more beau-
> tiful; whiter and more transparent on the spots where the blood
> had been. Elizabeth, therefore, formed the resolve to bathe her
> face and her entire body in human blood, so as to enhance her
> beauty. Two old women and a certain Ficzko assisted her in her
> undertaking. The monster used to kill her luckless victim, and
> the women caught the blood in which Elizabeth used to bathe

at the hour of four in the morning . . . She continued this habit after the death of her husband in the hope of gaining new suitors. The unhappy girls, who were lured to the castle under the pretext that they were to be taken into her service there, were locked up in a cellar. Elizabeth not infrequently tortured the victims herself; often she changed her clothes which dripped with blood, and renewed her cruelties. The swollen bodies were cut up with razors . . . She caused, in all, the death of six hundred and fifty girls, some at Csejthe [Cachtice] where she had a cellar constructed for the purpose, others in different localities; for murder and bloodshed became a necessity with her.

Sabine Baring-Gould in his *Book of Werewolves* based his account of the Elizabeth Bathory story on that of Michael Wagener, suppressing the last name of the countess, referring to her simply as "Elizabeth _____" and merely quoting from the Wagener text.

The noted German historian Fessler in his ten-volume work *History of Hungary and Its Lands* repeated the legend that she "daily washed in human blood" to maintain her beauty. The author evidently got carried away, because he claimed that Elizabeth killed aristocratic girls *en masse.* He did not realize that any mass shedding of blue blood would have been halted. In fact Elizabeth murdered mostly peasant girls and, only later in life, ones from the lesser nobility.

The Hungarian author Deszo Rexa, who had himself been born in the shadow of Cachtice Castle, wrote at the beginning of this century in *Bathory Erzsebet Nadasdy Ferencne,* that the local villagers still recalled the deeds of the notorious "Vampire Lady" who had lived in that castle. Rexa also claimed that at Elizabeth's trial in 1611 the main instigator, Count George Thurzo, acted "properly" in his decision not to bring Elizabeth herself to the stand for prosecution. Deszo Rexa stated emphatically that "the decision of Thurzo was very objective" (p. 36). But Count Thurzo was far from being "very objective" in this case; he had his own ax to grind, as we shall see later in detail. Rexa decided also that Elizabeth was unaware of any guilt, because she was, he felt, insane. However, recent research, which I present in this book, has thrown doubts on that hypothesis.

# 2

# Historical Background: The Bathory and Nadasdy Families, 1560–75

IN Vienna, the capital city of Austria, there is a small dark street called "Blood Street," very near the famous St. Stephen's Cathedral. It is believed locally that the street was so named because it was where "the Blood Countess from Transylvania," Elizabeth Bathory, stayed when in Vienna. Another story (found in old books) is that an unidentified maniac once set up an Iron Maiden in one of the houses and the resultant stream of blood from his victims gave the street its name. One of the oldest references to Blood Street in Vienna calls it "the Blood or Milk Street" without explaining exactly why the use of "blood" and "milk" designations. Today it is still clearly called Blood Street.

Disappointingly, it is a documented fact that Countess Elizabeth Bathory never lived on Blood Street. Instead of Blood Street, the reader in search of Countess Elizabeth's Vienna residence should wander over to Augustinian Street to the spot where an eighteenth-century house now stands on the corner across from Lobkowitz Square. (Augustinian Street leads to the very edge of the royal Austrian Palace.) This house is now the French Library of Vienna. At one time, however, on that same corner, stood an old princely arsenal owned by the fifteenth-century Catholic Hungarian king, Matthias Corvinus, who donated the building to the Augustinian monks who then lived on adjacent Dorothea Street (Schlimmer, *Ausführliche Häuser-Chronik der Stadt Wien* (Detailed Chronicle of Houses in the City of Vienna, p. 225). That is how the building came to be known as "the Hungarian House." In 1531 the monks sold the house (moving to larger quarters across the street), and it later changed hands several more times. It is not known exactly when the Nadasdy-Bathory family acquired it, only that around 1650 the house already belonged to an uncle of Elizabeth Bathory, Count Ferencz Nadasdy, who had the same name as her husband. The actual transfer, however, must have occurred before the end of the sixteenth century, for the court testimony at Elizabeth Bathory's trial in 1611 provides us with a valuable clue. In answer to the question concerning the murdered girls, i.e., "Where were they tortured?", Elizabeth's accomplice Helena Jo replied: "In Vienna, there the monks hurled their pots against the windows when they heard the lamentations [of the girls being tortured]." These monks could have been those from the old Augustinian monastery across from the house where the gruesome sounds of torment would have been easily heard. (None of the present-day traffic was there in Elizabeth's day to muffle such noises.) Having heard these cries, why didn't the monks do anything more about it? First of all, Elizabeth was a Protestant and they were Catholics. Secondly, she was a countess and thus under special jurisdiction over which they had no influence.

In the cellar of this Viennese mansion, Elizabeth had a blacksmith build a cylindrical cage with long iron spikes in it. The cage, attached to a pulley, could be raised or lowered at will. The countess would choose a big-bosomed girl from among her seamstresses, who would be stripped and forced to enter the cage. Elizabeth's assistants would then hoist the narrow cage upward, and Elizabeth's maid Dorka (Dorothea Szentes) would stab the girl with red-hot pokers. As the girl writhed and tried to avoid being burned by the hot poker, she would impale herself upon the spikes, while Elizabeth shouted sexual obscenities at her from a stool beneath the cage.

Who was the Elizabeth Bathory behind these horrible stories?

Elizabeth Bathory was born in 1560 and grew up in the era of Queen Elizabeth, Süleyman the Magnificent, and Ivan the Terrible, a period known in history as Early Modern Times. She was destined to live a longer life than most people of that time, as few of the era reached her fifty-four years of age, because of bad hygienic conditions, disease, and pestilence.

Countess Bathory was a Hungarian. It was once thought that the Western name for Hungarians derived from the word "Hun," the name given by Europeans to Attila the Hun's famous horsemen who invaded Europe during the fifth century. But current philologists at the Hungarian Academy derive the word *Hungar* from an ancient Turkish word meaning "ten tribes" (*on-ugur*). Hungarians call themselves "Magyars" (pronounced "Mad-jar") and are ethnically members of the Finno-Ugric tribes that originally came from East Asia.

Hungarians have an old Latin proverb: *Extra Hungaria non est vita et si est vita, non est ita* which translates as: "Outside of Hungary there is no life and if there is life, it's not the same." The proverb reflects the attitude of a people with a language that has no common basis in any country west of Turkey except perhaps Estonia. Hungary is even today a strange land. Few Englishmen or Americans know it all and many merely associate it with the Danube River beyond Vienna, the old border between Germany and Hungary.

The original Hungarian tribes overran present day Hungary under their king Arpad in the late ninth and early tenth centuries. The first crowned king from the line of Arpad was the famous Stephan the Great (r. 997–1038). Stephan, who had been born a pagan, broke with his Eastern heritage, turned his eyes towards Rome and, for better or worse, linked the destiny of his land with the West. Stephan married a Bavarian princess named Gisela and became a Roman Catholic, calling in Roman Catholic churchmen and monks and endowing them with huge tracts of land. On the basis of that act the Hungarians joined European civilization. Pope Sylvester sent Stephan a crown with which Stephan was crowned king in the year 1001 (that illustrious crown of Saint Stephan was spirited away from Hungary after the Second World War and only recently returned to Hungary). Stephan became revered among Hungarians as Saint Stephan; he was formally canonized as a saint in 1083.

Hungary developed quickly until, by the second half of the fifteenth century, the people were enjoying their golden age during the reign of Matthias Corvinus (r. 1457–1490). A contemporary of the historical Vlad Dracula (whose main rule in Wallachia was from 1456 to 1462), Matthias Corvinus encouraged culture and Renaissance humanism by building libraries and inviting prominent scholars from the West to live and work in Hungary. Corvinus also made Hungary into a well-ordered modern state built on European Renaissance models.

After the death of Matthias Corvinus at the age of forty-seven in the year 1490 a great decline began in Hungary. The country was faced with a host of severe problems: the power of the central government eroded due to a series of ineffectual kings who occupied the Hungarian throne; as a result the unstable power of the constantly infighting local lords or magnates grew. Most serious of all, however, the Turks were making inroads into Hungarian territory.

In mid-1526, the Turks were on their way to Vienna, the seat of their archenemy, the Hapsburg monarchy. Along the Turkish road to Vienna lay Hungary, the conquest of which became one of the primary objectives of Sultan Süleyman the Magnificent. The Hungarians suffered their Waterloo at the fatal battle with the Turks at Mohacs, a place downriver south of Budapest on August 29, 1526, when the cream of the Hungarian nobility, no match for the sultan's forces, was cut down by the swords of the sultan's soldiers. The Hungarian king, Lajos II, drowned in a stream during the battle. Mohacs was truly a national catastrophe, for Hungary became, in effect, a Turkish-controlled province. Budapest itself fell to the Turks ten days later. The Hungarians retained control of only southern and western strips of their country; the Ottomans ruled most of its most vital areas.

The country was split up into three parts: the Great Plain, consisting of northern Hungary and a large section of Transdanubia, was ruled by the Turkish sultan's satraps; the western and some northern areas were under Hapsburg rule; and finally Transylvania itself, which managed to survive as a fairly independent state. The Transylvanian rulers usually had to side either with the Hapsburgs or the Turks in the main struggle between those superpowers.

In the midst of this Turkish onslaught, beleaguered Hungary was also caught up in an inner religious struggle between the new Protestant converts and the Catholics. The Protestant cause had been enormously successful among the common people and also among segments of the nobility, although most of the kings and the great lords remained technically Catholic. Protestantism had been particularly victorious in Transylvania, even among the nobility.

One of the best observers of sixteenth-century Europe, the seasoned diplomat and traveler Sigmund Freiherr von Herberstein, reported to the Holy Roman Emperor, Maximilian, about the state of affairs in Hungary: "I cannot report without sighing and great pain how this kingdom, shortly before so very rich, powerful and held in high esteem has very quickly sunk so painfully low before our very eyes . . . The upper aristocracy of the realm from spiritual prelates downwards live in unbelievable luxury . . . these magnates could in Parliament get anything or pass any law they wanted to with the nobles' votes and common acclaim . . . justice is hard to come by and the poor are very oppressed. And in the meantime, all the good laws have fallen into disuse and have been undermined . . . the kingdom has fallen into a sad state of decline."

Elizabeth Bathory was born into one of the richest and most powerful Protestant families in all Hungary. Her family was to provide two of the most important ruling princes of Transylvania, a number of war heroes and church officials of Hungary, and even a great empire-builder, Stephan Bathory, prince of Transylvania and king of Poland.

Wenzelin, the ancestor of the Bathory family, had come from Swabia into the service of King Stephan the Great in the eleventh century. When Wenzelin died, he was able to leave a large estate to his heirs. By the fourteenth century the Bathory family was divided into two main lines: the Somlyo and the Ecsed branches. Their children inherited not just one but three last names: Csaky, Dragffy, and Bathory. (Ivan Nagy, *Magyarorszag Csaladai* [The Great Families of Hungary] Vol. 1.) There is some genealogical evidence that the Bathory clan was related by marriage to that of the infamous ruler Vlad Dracula, the Impaler.

Both of Elizabeth's parents were members of the Bathory family: her father, George, was a high-ranking lord from the Ecsed branch of the family, and her mother, Anna, was from the Somlyo line. Anna had had two husbands (Antal Drugeth and Gaspar Dragffy) before marrying George Bathory. Elizabeth was raised at Ecsed, the Bathory family seat in Transylvania.

The constant intermarriage among the few Hungarian noble families evidently caused the blood to run a bit thin. One of Elizabeth's uncles was reputedly addicted to rituals and worship in honor of Satan, her aunt Klara was a well-known bisexual and lesbian who enjoyed torturing servants, and Elizabeth's brother, Stephan, was a drunkard and a lecher. Many members of Elizabeth's family complained in their private letters of symptoms which showed signs of evident epilepsy, madness, and other psychological disturbances.

Another uncle of Elizabeth's, Gabor, lived a retired existence on the family estate in Ecsed. According to the reports from his domestic servants, Gabor used to get dressed up in the middle of the night, and, crying out in an incomprehensible language, he would struggle with nonexistent attackers. Or, his mouth foaming, he would fall to the ground and roll around. When his servants tried to help him up, he bit their arms and hands. During his rare moments of relative lucidity, Gabor, like Elizabeth, complained about suffering from very severe headaches.

Elizabeth herself suffered from childhood with a disease which was called epilepsy at the time. One cannot place too much credence in that appellation, however, since in the past the word "epilepsy" was used very loosely to cover a great many mental and physical illnesses. The evidence simply demonstrates that Elizabeth was subject to periodic fits during which she was overcome by seizures of rage and uncontrolled behavior.

In 1566, when Elizabeth was six years old, Sultan Süleyman the Magnificent died and the great Ottoman system began to sink into a slow decline. The Turks' hold over Transylvania weakened; sultans began to spend more time in the bedrooms of the harem and less on horseback leading their armies. Süleyman's successor Selim (r.1566–74) became known as "The Sot" because he preferred bottles to battles. News of some of the strange goings-on at the Ottoman court undoubtedly reached the ears of the young Elizabeth.

As a child, Elizabeth appears from records to have been very intelligent and was said to have impressed most of her contemporaries by the depth of her learning and culture. Unlike many noble girls who received a bare minimum of "household education" and training, Elizabeth was well educated not just in comparison with other noblewomen of her age but with her male peers as well. At a time when most Hungarian nobles could not even spell or write, Elizabeth became fluent in Hungarian, Latin, and German. Her letters, several of which have been fully quoted in the Elsberg biography, prove this. Even the ruling prince of Transylvania at the time was barely literate.

Once when a band of gypsies were invited to Ecsed Castle in order to perform some music for a wild party, one of them was accused of selling his children to the Turks. Elizabeth hid behind some columns in the hall to watch the proceedings. The accused gypsy, his hands tied behind his back, was brought forth. He defended himself by claiming that the Turks had actually stolen his daughter. However, the police had found a large amount of money in the gypsy's pockets, and he was unable to explain how he had come by so much money. His judges found the gypsy guilty and condemned him to death. Elizabeth recalled his long cries in the night, bemoaning his upcoming demise, which evidently made a lasting impression on her. At dawn Elizabeth escaped from the surveillance of her governess and ran outside the castle to witness the punishment. There she saw a horse held fast to the ground as some soldiers slit open its belly. Three of the soldiers then grabbed the guilty gypsy and shoved him inside the horse's belly until only his head stuck out of the dying animal. Another soldier armed with a huge, long needle and coarse ropelike thread sewed up the culprit in the belly of the horse. He was condemned to die along with the putrefying horse. At first Elizabeth noted the horrible stench coming from the victims, but, to her surprise, she also found herself giggling over the bizarre execution, according to the French writer Maurice Périsset in *La Comtesse de Sang*. To her this horrible scene appeared to be just an example of black humor. She apparently enjoyed the process of punishment. At an age when most children learn to control their aggressive tendencies towards others, Elizabeth was under no such constraints.

So powerful was Elizabeth's family that, in 1571, when she was only eleven years old, one of her cousins, who, like her brother, was named Stephan, became ruling prince of Transylvania. Two years later, when the Transylvanian peasants rose in rebellion, Prince Stephan had the noses and ears cut off fifty-four culprits under the shadow of the gallows. Elizabeth learned at an early age that one can deal ruthlessly with disobedient peasants.

Her cousin Stephan had ambitions that went far beyond Transylvania. He hoped to become the first Bathory to be not only the ruling prince of Transylvania but also the king of Poland. Stephan Bathory secured election as King of Poland in 1575 and one year later was crowned. There were competitors for the crown, however, especially the Hapsburg Maximilian II.

Stephan married Anna Jagellon, the last descendant of an old Polish dynasty, and proved to be a strong ruler. He made many plans to unite Eastern Europe against the Turks who were then threatening his native Transylvania. During the last phase of the Livonian War (1579–82), Stephan, at the head of an army of peasants from his royal estate, routed the forces of Ivan the Terrible and put an end to Russian encroachment in the northern White Russian region. As a result, Stephan Bathory's rule, in Transylvania from 1571 and in Poland from 1576 to his death in 1586, achieved renown.

During her cousin Stephan's rule, Elizabeth was betrothed and married to Ferenc Nadasdy, who came from a somewhat less established family than that of the fabulous Bathorys. A bit of historical background is necessary in order to understand why Elizabeth considered her standing to be superior to that of her future husband.

The Nadasdy family was an old aristocratic one, but one with little wealth and thus unable to support grand careers for its members. The family seat of the Nadasdys was located not far south of the Hungarian town of Sarvar, (pronounced "Sharvar") on the left bank of the Raba river. From there the Nadasdy family had moved to Sarvar itself, where the Raba and Güns rivers flow together along the old communication lines from Graz to Budapest. A castle that was not then very old stood at Sarvar. A long bridge connected the town to the inner castle. Today only the bare ruins of a pentagonal castle built in the sixteenth century remain. (In the past the area was sometimes called Sziget and Csepreg, names derived from the surrounding villages.)

After the defeat of the Hungarians by the Turks at Mohacs, Sultan Süleyman the Magnificent decided not to attempt any wholesale annexation because of problems he faced in the East; instead the sultan accepted the offer of John Zapolya, leader of the lesser Hungarian nobles, to leave them in control of the country provided that they acknowledge Ottoman suzerainty and pay tribute. A Hungarian assembly finally met on October 15, 1526, in order to choose a new, "proper" monarch. But the nobles seemed to be in no hurry to appoint a king of their own. There were two main competitors for the crown: John Zapolya, the Turkish-backed candidate; and the Hapsburg Archduke Ferdinand, brother of the Holy Roman Emperor Charles V. Archduke Ferdinand was a strong contender, since he had married Anna, sister of the former Hungarian king Lajos II and, as the widowed queen's brother-in-law, he stood next in line for the throne. But the powerful Ottoman Turks opposed the Hapsburgs. Ferdinand chose as his close adviser a young, intelligent, seasoned diplomat, a noble named Thomas Nadasdy, the man who was to father Elizabeth Bathory's future husband, Ferenc Nadasdy.

Thomas Nadasdy, who had been born in 1493, stood head and shoulders over most of his colleagues. As a young man, he had studied in Rome, Bologna, and Graz, and had been deeply influenced by Renaissance scholarship. He had already distinguished himself in various diplomatic negotiations in 1521. But Thomas, though belonging to the old nobility, was poor. He supported Ferdinand in hopes of furthering his own situation. Other nobles hoped for German aid against the Turks.

Ferdinand's main competitor for the Hungarian crown, John Zapolya, leader of the national party, volunteered to marry the widowed Hungarian queen in order to boost his chances for the crown, but was firmly turned down, because the queen did not consider him a worthy mate. But Zapolya had the backing of the Hungarian nobles, because they admired his forceful handling of peasant revolts. It had been Zapolya who had suppressed the peasant uprising of 1514 in a sea of blood. A member of the lower gentry named George Dozsa had led the peasant revolt; and he had been roasted alive on an iron throne and his followers forced to eat his flesh before they themselves were broken on the wheel and hanged. Support for Zapolya grew day by day, whereas that for Ferdinand began to weaken. Ferdinand was too preoccupied with establishing his rights in Austria and Bohemia to assert his rule in Transylvania.

The fate of the Nadasdy family hung in the balance. Finally in the summer of 1527 Ferdinand acted. He entered Hungary at the head of a large army. His trusted adviser, Thomas Nadasdy, commanded the advance troops with a retinue of some three thousand knights. Nonetheless, a majority of the Hungarian nobles elected Zapolya king of Hungary at the Tokay diet (the formal deliberative assembly of the nobility) on September 16, 1527. Zapolya spent a good deal of his time in Transylvania trying to secure his position there. But he lost his nerve; his supporters turned coward and Ferdinand defeated Zapolya at Tokay on September 26, 1527. So, on December 17, 1527, Ferdinand was proclaimed king at Bratislava and

rewarded Thomas Nadasdy handsomely, making him commander of the entire Buda district (Klein, *Geschichte von Ungarn*
[History of Hungary], Vol. 3, p. 425).

But Zapolya was still actively plotting behind the scenes; he
secured renewed support from Sultan Süleyman on February
28, 1528, and headed towards Vienna accompanied by a Turkish army. Along the way his army had to pass through the
territory of Buda under Thomas Nadasdy's control. Rather than
make a stand to try to hold back the sultan's troops, Nadasdy
went into hiding and emerged with a sudden change of heart
in favor of Zapolya. So much for loyalty! Süleyman's forces
occupied Buda on September 3, 1529, and subsequently mounted
the first Ottoman siege of Vienna (September 27 to October 15,
1529). But Vienna held out against the Turkish onslaught. Much
of Europe was shocked at the sight of a Turkish army outside
the gates of Vienna itself.

In 1530 Zapolya, the Turkish vassal, appointed Thomas Nadasdy Master of the Treasury. Although Thomas had gained
public honor, it is evident from his private letters that he suffered: he knew that many nobles considered him an untrust-
worthy vassal, a traitor to his former lord, Ferdinand, who had
befriended him. Thomas Nadasdy even sought some way of
finding an honorable death.

At the head of an army of ten thousand, Thomas Nadasdy
besieged the castle of Szigetvar, where he scored his greatest
military victory. In recognition Zapolya gave him the region of
Fagaras in Transylvania. (Horvath, *Grof Nadasdy Tamas elete* [The
Life of Count Thomas Nadasdy], p. 9). The struggle between
Ferdinand and Zapolya raged on and it was tearing Hungary
apart. Thomas contacted other nobles, who issued an ultima-
tum for both sides to come to terms, and the turmoil subsided
for a time.

Thomas, who now had some property and status, went in
search of a rich girl to marry—and in 1530, at the age of thirty-
seven, Nadasdy became engaged to a fourteen-year-old child
named Ursula Kanizsay, the second daughter of Ladislas von
Kanizsay. When Thomas married Ursula in 1535 she could neither read nor write, and she spoke only Hungarian. But she

was enormously rich. One stretch of her land was nearly two hundred kilometers long. But, to secure all that property, Thomas was obliged to change his political alliances once again. He left the service of Zapolya and gradually moved over to Ferdinand once again on the condition that he would be allowed to hold onto his new wife's properties.

At last, Thomas Nadasdy was able to live in luxury. An ardent Protestant, Thomas invited Lutheran scholars of note to Castle Sarvar: the "Hungarian Luther," Matyas Devay, and another theologian, Janos Sylvester, both of whom had known Luther and the famous Lutheran scholar Melanchton personally. Sylvester began to translate the Bible into the Hungarian vernacular. Castle Sarvar became a kind of second Lutheran Hungarian Wartburg.

Sarvar was one of the properties Thomas Nadasdy had acquired by his marriage to Ursula Kanizsay. It was in the middle of the communication line from Graz to Budapest. A castle that was then fairly new once stood there. Thomas Nadasdy filled it with works of Italian and German artists, a result of his humanistic upbringing. He set up a printing press and was one of the first to publish books in Hungarian. Two rivers, the Raba and the Güns, which flowed together there made the castle an "island," as the scholar Sylvester called it. In 1532 the castle had successfully withstood a Turkish onslaught.

During July and August 1532 when Süleyman's forces were marching through Hungary, they also attacked the former royal free city of Leka (Lockenhaus), a Nadasdy possession located in Burgenland, part of Austria today. Luckily the small local troops were able to defend the city—considered a kind of miracle. People there spread the rumor that their patron, Saint Martin, himself had helped in the defense of their city against the Turks.

Peace negotiations between the Hapsburgs and the Ottomans resulted in a temporary peace settlement in June of 1533. Ferdinand acknowledged the sultan as "father and suzerain," and abandoned his claims to Hungary other than those border areas that he had occupied since the original Ottoman conquest. In return he agreed to pay the annual tribute to the sultan. The Turks had thus achieved their major objective: to establish a friendly vassal as a buffer state against possible Hapsburg expansion in the future. Zapolya was installed as king of central Hungary under Turkish tutelage.

But Turkish relations with the Hapsburgs were strained because of raids and counterraids across the borders of the two great empires. Even Zapolya, vassal king of Hungary, began to fear some complete Ottoman occupation, so he made a secret agreement with Ferdinand at Grosswardein (Varadin, Oradea, Varad) in February 1538 in which the childless Zapolya agreed to will all of Hungary to Ferdinand in return for a promise of assistance against any future Ottoman attack. This move by the Hapsburgs ran counter to the ambitions of the Polish King Sigismund concerning Hungary. He subsequently arranged for the marriage of his daughter Isabella to Zapolya. A son, named Sigismund John, was subsequently born to Zapolya, who then tried to get Polish help to nullify his previous agreement with Ferdinand. Zapolya was also relying especially upon Ottoman help to counter Hapsburg power in his own land.

When Zapolya died on August 22, 1540, Ferdinand asserted his claim; he declared Zapolya's marriage null and void in accordance with his previous agreement with Zapolya, and proclaimed in addition that Zapolya's son was not in fact a natural son. Hapsburg soldiers invaded and occupied Pest, while Ferdinand's agents promised that he would acknowledge Ottoman suzerainty if he were allowed to rule the area. But Süleyman refused to tolerate this expansion of Hapsburg rule. The Porte (the government of the Ottoman Empire) recognized Zapolya's infant son as King Sigismund Zapolya (1540–71). This led to new clashes with Ferdinand, who then launched another invasion into eastern Hungary.

In 1541 Süleyman himself led a major expedition into Hungary. Realizing that it would not be wise to leave the country in the hands of the infant prince Sigismund Zapolya, he sent the boy off with his mother to "rule" as prince of Transylvania. Hungary was formally annexed to the Ottoman Empire as the Turkish province of Buda, though Ferdinand continued to hold onto the highlands west and north as vassal. A western crusade mounted against the Turks in 1542 failed.

In the end the Hapsburgs held only a narrow strip of land in western and northern Hungary, and even then were obliged to pay tribute to the Turks. Warfare continued unabated in the frontier lands, while Ferdinand tried to rule either from Prague or sometimes from Vienna. Thomas Nadasdy spent the better part of each year in Vienna at court, but he hurried home to his beloved wife in Sarvar when affairs of state allowed it. Despite the great difference in years between Thomas and his teenage wife Ursula Nadasdy it appears to have been a happy match. In his letters to her he called himself "your old gray vulture" and "your old piece" and fondly referred to her as "my sweet, loving little Mary."

Meanwhile Thomas was making a name for himself. By 1554 he won the title of Prince Palatine, which conferred on him the extraordinary right to act directly with the authority of the king himself in Hungary like a viceroy. But evidently something was still missing from his rather full life. Already in his fifties he had no male children to inherit all that he had fought for. Just as he had about given up hope, his wife gave birth to a male child. The boy was born on October 6, 1555, but Thomas would learn about it only later at Christmas when he was able to get home to Sarvar. The child was named Ferenc (pronounced "Ferents") and he was destined to become a Hungarian national hero and the husband of Elizabeth Bathory. On June 2, 1562, seven years after the birth of Ferenc, Thomas Nadasdy died.

Thomas Nadasdy's widow Ursula was publicly so grieved at her husband's death that she had a special monument built in his memory. Her boy Ferenc grew up mostly at the family estate in Sarvar. But in the hot summers Ursula usually took the boy to the cooler mountain air of the castle at Leka (Lockenhaus) near the city of Köszeg in an isolated corner in the eastern part of the Leitha mountains.

Growing up in these border regions between the Hungarian lands and those under Turkish control was somewhat like living on the frontier between Israel and Lebanon today. One had to be constantly prepared for the possibility of attack from the outside. People took their rifles with them wherever they went. It is little wonder that the boy Ferenc developed a war-like style of living. His home life as an adolescent resembled an army barracks always at the ready. Even the new agreement between the Ottomans and the Hapsburgs, concluded on June 1, 1562, did little to lessen the actual hostilities in these frontier areas. But toward the end of the reign of Süleyman, signs of Ottoman weakness became apparent and with Süleyman's death in 1566 the long, great decline in Turkish power began to set in.

The wealthy widow Ursula packed the fatherless twelve-year-old off to school in Vienna. There are some eighty-two documents which attest to Ferenc's record at school for the years from 1567 to 1569. Ferenc was not a good student. He barely learned how to write some Hungarian and to speak and read a little German and Latin. His mother kept notes about his shoddy performance in school. Ferenc, who had apparently not inherited his father's intelligence, developed into an athlete, but little else. His mother wondered in her diary what would happen to him later in life when his physical prowess would fail. Nonetheless she did not discipline the child; she continued to pamper and spoil him. Although he acquired little academic education, he was evidently popular among his peers.

Ursula was getting old and weak; it was necessary to find someone to run the vast estates. She wanted the same type of happy marriage she had enjoyed for her son Ferenc and did some careful matchmaking. Sixteen-year-old Ferenc was engaged to eleven-year-old Countess Elizabeth Bathory in 1571.

The Turks were at this time still sweeping all over the Nadasdy lands. Ursula Nadasdy had given some of her land to the Hungarian king for protection from the Turks before her death, but Castle Cachtice and the seventeen villages surrounding it remained hers and were inherited by her son Ferenc. The old days of Ottoman dominance, however, were numbered. Sultan Süleyman's successor, Selim "the Sot," was noted mainly for his drunken orgies, enjoying the pleasures of the harem, and leaving government to his ministers. He died in October of 1574 from injuries incurred by a fall in a Turkish bath. Some contemporary sources claimed that this fall resulted from dizziness when the sultan tried to stop drinking. His son and successor, Murad III (r. 1574–95), loved the harem almost as much as his father had. Together with his forty concubines Murad produced some 130 sons and countless daughters (daughters didn't count for much in those days), but even the most ardent devotees of the sultan's male prowess agreed that he had taken too much advantage of a good thing.

Meanwhile, Elizabeth Bathory, engaged to Ferenc Nadasdy, was developing into an emancipated young lady. She enjoyed her independence. She liked to dress in men's clothes and play men's games. Unfortunately, while engaging in sexual play with one of the local peasants at the chateau of her future mother-in-law (whom she secretly hated, as is evident from Elizabeth's private letters), Elizabeth had become pregnant. So, under the official pretext that Elizabeth had contracted some "illness," she was spirited away to a remote Bathory castle in Transylvania, where Elizabeth gave birth to a daughter. The bastard daughter was given away to a peasant, along with plenty of money to pay for the upbringing of the child. The peasant, who took the baby off to live in Wallachia (part of southern Romania today), had to promise never to return with the child during Elizabeth's lifetime. The private correspondence of Ursula shows that the entire affair was hushed up in anticipation of Elizabeth's coming marriage to Count Ferenc Nadasdy.

# 3

## Elizabeth's Married Life: Ferenc Nadasdy; the Hungarian-Turkish Conflicts, Castle Tortures, 1575–1604

THE formal marriage of Count Ferenc Nadasdy and Countess Elizabeth Bathory, a lavish, gala event, took place a few months after Elizabeth had secretly given birth to her bastard. Ferenc had invited the Holy Roman emperor Maximilian II (r. 1564–76), son of his father's old ally Ferdinand, to attend the official marriage party held on May 8, 1575. Emperor Maximilian was staying in Prague at the time, and considered the trip to Varanno, where the marriage was to take place, too dangerous. Instead he sent a delegation to represent him and an expensive wedding present.

The young couple were formally married as scheduled at Varanno Castle. Elizabeth was only about fifteen years of age; Ferenc was twenty-one. Such marriages between young people were, of course, quite common then, especially among the nobility, where property considerations and proper bloodlines were so very important. In this case two prominent Protestant families were joining forces. The bearded young Count Ferenc Nadasdy henceforth added her last name to his. But Elizabeth, fully emancipated as she was, chose to remain a Bathory, rather than take his name, since she considered that her name was much older and more illustrious than his.

Holy Roman Emperor Maximilian II died one year later after a twelve-year reign, and his son Rudolf II (r. 1576–1612) became Holy Roman Emperor. Historians have been unduly critical of Ferdinand and his son Maximilian II; actually both had been quite gifted in statecraft, and had even sought compromise when necessary (a rarity in that era). But Rudolf II, emperor during the entire period of Elizabeth Bathory's marriage, and her trials and incarceration, was quite different from his father and grandfather.

Rudolf was more interested in alchemy and magic than in running his empire, and after receiving his royal post in 1576, he retired to his Castle Hradschin in Prague and rarely left it. His uncle, the famous Spanish Hapsburg King Philip II, was fully occupied in Western European struggles against the English, Dutch, and French, so the governance of the central European empire was left largely in the hands of local lords. It was not until after the Ottoman sultan Murad III defeated Persia by the year 1590 that Rudolf began to interest himself in the empire. He started to worry that the Ottomans would turn westward against him.

The young bridegroom Ferenc Nadasdy made war his "career." But three years after his marriage, in 1578, together with the other Hungarian heroes Erdödy, Zrinyi, and Batthany, he was able to capture the Bajcsa fortress from the Turks, thereby opening the way to Sziget. Two years later, again with help from Zrinyi and Batthany, he clashed with the Ottoman Empire again at Gubernoker Field, where the leader of the Turkish troops, Iskender Beg, died in battle. In the next ten years he figured prominently in the campaigns against the Turks. By 1587 Ferenc Nadasdy was given the title of "High Stable Master." Not only the Hapsburg king but also the Turkish sultan took account of his prowess. This meant that Nadasdy had to be on his guard constantly against an attack on Castle Sarvar.

There was no natural frontier between the Hapsburg and the Ottoman empires such as the Pyrenees mountains that separate Spain and France. The "frontier" was an extremely fluid line floating around networks of fortresses. Sarvar was part of the exposed border. In May 1588 Nadasdy began to refortify the castle towers and walls to secure it further against Turkish incursions. The castle at that time was surrounded by water, which formed a natural barrier against attack, though today those waters are gone, having been diverted at the outset of the nineteenth century.

Subsequent events proved that Nadasdy had been wise in his efforts to prepare for further conflicts with the Turks.

While Ferenc was spending most of his time at war, Elizabeth was not idle. She had taken on the task of handling the day-to-day activities at the Nadasdy family seat, Castle Sarvar—especially the task of disciplining the servants. The countess carried her "disciplining" to a point that would be considered sadism today.

The Countess not only beat her girl servants with a heavy cudgel, she also stuck pins into the upper and lower lips of the girls, according to the eyewitness testimony of her female servant, Dorothea Szentes. Elizabeth Bathory also stuck needles into the girls' flesh and pins under their fingernails. She also dragged some girls out into the snow and then had her women servants pour cold water on them until they froze to death, according to the testimony of the Countess's manservant Ficzko.

During their first ten years of marriage, Elizabeth and Ferenc had no children. This was not unusual in those times. Her husband was off at war so often and for so long, it is no wonder that they had little time together. Around 1585 Elizabeth gave birth to a girl whom she named Anna, possibly in memory of her own deceased mother. Over the course of the next nine years Elizabeth bore two more girls, named Ursula like her deceased mother-in-law and Katherina.

In one letter dated at Sarvar Castle, Anno Domini 1596, 8th day of the month of July, she wrote: "My much beloved Husband, I am writing to offer my services to you, my beloved lord and master. As for the children, thanks be to God, they are all right. But Orsika [Ursula] has eye pains and Kato [Katherina] has toothaches. Thanks be to God, I am feeling fine, even though I have headaches and eye pains. May God protect you and be with you." So, the bestial woman known from documented history was also the concerned wife and protective mother, as this letter reveals her to have been. Such apparently contradictory behavior patterns were not unusual. A noble generally treated immediate family in a totally different way from his or her servants.

While Count Nadasdy was off at the endless wars, when Elizabeth was not busy writing loving familial letters, she suffered from boredom and tried to amuse herself. She reputedly engaged in sexual horseplay with one of her manservants, Istvan Jezorlay, a male of reputedly exceptional sexual prowess. She also often chose to visit her aunt Klara, an open bisexual. Wealthy and powerful, Klara always had plenty of available girls around. Elizabeth presumably enjoyed herself with her aunt Klara, since she visited her aunt's estate frequently.

Elizabeth's only son Paul, the youngest of her children, was born in 1598. The peasant woman Helena Jo, one of the "accomplices" charged in the 1611 trial, was chiefly responsible for taking care of the infant Paul. Helena Jo was Paul's *dajka*, a term meaning "wet nurse" as well as "child nurse." This Helena Jo had been married to a certain Stephen Nagy, and, after the death of her husband, had continued in Elizabeth's household service. According to contemporary chroniclers, she was a small peasant woman of extreme ugliness. But then all of the close servants of the countess have been depicted as being ugly, no doubt in an attempt to have their physiognomies better "match" their supposedly despicable souls.

Meanwhile, renewed warfare between the Turks and the Hapsburgs broke out in 1593. That year, at the battle of Sissek, Ferenc Nadasdy had helped set the Turks in flight. Thousands of Turkish soldiers were drowned in the River Kulpa as they sought to escape. But this was not enough to bring the sultans to a halt: the fighting lasted through the reign of Mehmed III (r. 1595–1603) and plagued his successor Ahmed I (r. 1603–17). Emperor Rudolf succeeded in persuading the Pope to mobilize and support an army of eleven thousand men who, along with some financial aid from King Philip II of Spain, enabled the Hapsburgs to take the fortress of Esztergom on the Danube River, an important link in the Ottoman defensive chain in central Hungary. With Hapsburg assistance, the Romanian principalities on the lower Danube rose in revolt against the sultan in 1594. Michael the Brave, ruler of Wallachia, alienated by the ever increasing financial demands from Istanbul, led this revolt.

Representatives sent by the emperor and the Pope had convinced the two other semiautonomous princes of the Balkans, Aron of Moldavia and Sigismund Bathory of Transylvania, to join with Michael. In 1595 Michael the Brave of Wallachia fought off the Ottoman army sent against him. Michael, who knew Greek as well as Romanian, presented himself as a champion of the Greek Orthodox Christian faith as well as of the Romanian nation, and so his revolt was one of the most serious threats to Ottoman domination in over two hundred years of domination of the area.

Sultan Mehmed III prepared an all-out invasion to smash Christian resistance in the Balkans. In 1596 at the head of an army of a hundred thousand men the sultan grabbed the stronghold of Eger thereby cutting communications between Austria and Transylvania. At a huge battle near Eger at Mezökeresztes on October 26, the Ottomans inflicted heavy losses on the Hungarian army. After the victorious campaign Mehmed III went home to his harem in Istanbul but kept a sharp eye out for renewed rebellion of the princes in the Danubian states, because it was evidently beginning to disrupt the important flow of Romanian grain to the Ottoman empire.

Luckily for the Turks, Michael of Wallachia and his allies had a falling out. Near the outset of the year 1599, a cardinal in the Roman Church, Andreas Bathory, Elizabeth's cousin, who had been raised in Poland, took over the rule of Transylvania from his cousin Sigismund Bathory. He tried to change Transylvanian foreign policy by abandoning the cooperation with the other Balkan princes and Emperor Rudolf II, substituting an alliance with Poland (Transylvania and Poland had previously been united under Sigismund's uncle Stephen Bathory from 1576 to 1586). Infuriated, Rudolf II encouraged Michael of Wallachia to invade Transylvania. By November 1, 1599, Prince Michael the Brave managed to take Transylvania, but he went beyond Rudolf's instructions and took Moldavia too, which had also risen against foreign rule. For a short time Wallachia, Moldavia and Transylvania were unified, presaging the modern boundaries of Romania.

In 1600 Michael the Brave officially proclaimed himself ruler of all three states, Wallachia, Moldavia and Transylvania. The Poles, who felt cheated out of their alliance with Transylvania, invaded; at the same time the Turks attacked Wallachia. Caught in a desperate situation, Michael sought help from Rudolf II; together the imperial army and Michael's forces drove the Poles out of Transylvania with their victory on August 3, 1601, at Guruslau.

When Sigismund tried to get his post of Ruling Prince of Transylvania back in 1601, Michael drove him out. But the assassination of Michael in that same year opened the road up to the Transylvanian throne for Sigismund again. Fearing that Michael would be powerful enough to break away from the Empire, taking with him the Balkan principalities, the imperial commander had had him murdered. The final outcome of all these battles, alliances, and intrigues, by the way, was that Europe delivered the Balkans into the hands of the Turks in 1601, where those lands remained until the nineteenth century.)

The interplay of the Ottoman and Holy Roman empires must be seen against the background of the increasing conflicts between Protestants and Catholics, especially in the Central European sections of the Holy Roman Empire, namely present-day Germany, Hungary and Transylvania. The wholesale siding of the Holy Roman emperor Rudolf with Catholicism lost him any support he might have had among the Protestant nobles. After 1594 he stopped even appearing before the German Parliament (the Reichstag). In fact, by the end of 1598 his mental state had become questionable (although he technically "ruled" until his death in 1612) and Hapsburg government—what there had been of it—ground to a halt.

Elizabeth's husband was by now a well-known war hero: he was one of five (along with Zrinyi, Erdödy, Batthany, and Palffy) sharp-sabred heroes known as "the unholy quintet" who inspired fear in the Turks. The Turks even dubbed him with a popular nickname to indicate their fear of him, the "Black Knight of Hungary." Archduke Matthias, the estranged brother of mad Emperor Rudolf II, turned to the Black Knight for help in his struggles to hold off the Turks. "We assume," he wrote to Nadasdy, "that a few days ago a person from the nobility by the name of Gaspar Hennici came to you from Transylvania; he can give a good deal of basic news about the current situation in this land. We would appreciate it if you would send him on to us as quickly as possible. He is supposed to be sent back home as quickly as possible." This letter was dated July 28, 1600, at the very time when the Hapsburg court in Vienna feared the worst for Transylvania.

Not far from the Nadasdy seat of Sarvar is the market town of Papa, which was an important fortress at the time. Here Ferenc scored one of his greatest victories. French and Flemish mercenaries were garrisoned there. They were generally good soldiers when all went well. But in 1600 no Turks were occupying their time and energy, and they recalled that the general staff owed them some sixty thousand ducats in back pay. The troops demanded immediate payment from their Hungarian overlords. No payment came. They even sent a delegation to a Turkish pasha, in which they promised to turn over the fort to the Turks, if the Turks would come up with all the back pay. The Turkish pasha was unfortunately only able to send ten thousand ducats to the soldiers at Papa. The soldiers then plundered the town and raped the local women.

Quickly the Hapsburg army commander Adolf Schwarzenberg gathered his troops and marched on Papa to quell the rebellion. Nadasdy went with him, and when Schwarzenberg was hit with a cannonball, Ferenc Nadasdy assumed command. The mutineers were besieged and surrendered on August 10, 1600. Nadasdy treated them without pity: those whom he captured were "hanged with inhuman cruelty" (Klein, *Geschichte*, vol. 4, p. 46). Nadasdy felt that he had to make an example of them. The Protestant factions greeted Ferenc's triumphs with particular enthusiasm. On December 30, 1600, he was called to Vienna for special honors, where he remained at least a week.

On March 23, 1601, Ferenc Nadasdy was in Pozsony (Pressburg, Bratislava). There he became sick. The Black Knight could hardly stand on his own two feet. He suffered strong pains in his legs, so much that he was unable to leave his room. But by spring he was feeling in better health, so emperor Rudolf entrusted him with a peace mission to the Turkish sultan. The negotiations fell through, however, because the emperor's demands were too high. Hostilities between the Hapsburg armies and the sultan's forces broke out again. Nadasdy returned to Sarvar Castle and began trying to fortify the surrounding castles. Körmend, St. Gotthard and Papa were given special attention.

Nadasdy got into an argument with the imperial chancellery about the amount of ransom for his main war hostage, Abdullah Pasha. Nadasdy had demanded twenty thousand talers for the release of Abdullah Pasha. But the imperial authorities had negotiated the figure down to sixteen thousand florins (a substantial reduction). They tried to minimize the lowered demands by pointing out to Nadasdy that it had to be paid in gold bars and not in goods. But Nadasdy was upset about the fact that he had not been consulted about those financial negotiations with the Turks. In addition, the crown already owed Nadasdy a good deal of money, which he had lent to the financially-strapped Hapsburg monarchy. This royal debt would in large measure become one of the main causes for Elizabeth Bathory's downfall ten years later.

During the spring of 1602 open warfare broke out again between the Turks and Hapsburgs. Although still actively soliciting the chancellory in Vienna for the monies due him, Ferenc did not let the outstanding debt undercut his loyalty to the Hapsburg monarchy, and he was not swayed in any way from his anti-Turkish sentiments. By August of 1602 Ferenc Nadasdy opened up a renewed campaign against the Ottomans in league with Count George Thurzo, one of Elizabeth's relatives through marriage. They were successful in setting up

Hungarian garrisons in several towns on the right bank of the Danube. Nadasdy and Thurzo in fact became close friends— ironically George Thurzo would later become the organizer of the famous raid on Elizabeth's castle and the main sinister force behind her subsequent trial. By the middle of November 1602 hostilities temporarily halted only to resume in the next year with minor results on either side. Toward the end of 1603 Ferenc suddenly became very ill, and died on the morning of January 4, 1604, as a heavy snow fell on his castle at Sarvar.

Dead before he was fifty, Ferenc was a typical warrior-noble of his time. He spent most of his time away from home in battle. His life there began when his general staff came to "lunch," usually around 10:00 A.M. They then proceeded to eat and drink, apparently until almost 4:00 P.M. Wine flowed freely. Most of them had to take naps after all that. Those that could still walk went off to make merry somewhere else. Unless they had to go to battle, they were drunk most of the time. It was every man for himself. Each took what he could. At those rare times when these veterans came home, they brought with them their battle-hardened way of life.

Although he never shared her infamy and may not even have known the extent of his wife's murderous activities during his long absences, it is known that, when he was home, he too enjoyed torturing servants. When Ferenc was on home– leave during rare respites from warring against the Turks, as we have seen, Elizabeth and he had spent some time together engaging in activities that would be characterized as sadistic today.

One summer when Ferenc was home on furlough, he showed his wife how to discipline the younger sister of Helena Jo, one of the female servants at Castle Sarvar. The girl was taken outside the castle. She was undressed until she stood stark naked before the on-looking Ferenc. Her body was then smeared with honey, and she was forced to stand outside for twenty-four hours, in order to suffer bites from flies, bees, and other insects. The girl was in so much pain that she fell to the ground afflicted with a mysterious "falling sickness" according to the court testimony of the manservant Ficzko.

One of the favorite methods for dealing with supposedly lazy servants was known as "star kicking." Paper was placed between the toes of a servant and then set on fire. The girl, screaming in pain, would "see stars" and kick. This "treatment" was used on one of Elizabeth's servants who suffered from the so-called "falling sickness" referred to above. Both Ferenc and his wife suspected that the girl was faking the illness. So Ferenc taught Elizabeth a more sophisticated form of "star kicking." He advised his wife to have the pieces of paper soaked in oil, as he felt that once oiled paper was set on fire between the girl's toes, she would get up even if she were half dead. According to the available evidence, however, Ferenc tortured servants, although he did not torture them to death, as his wife did.

Then, as now, funeral encomiums have little to do with the nature of the personality or lifestyle of the deceased. Listen to what the local pastor at Sarvar said at Ferenc's death:

> His Grace fought the good fight against the Devil, the World, the Flesh and Sin. He carried out the word of God with forethought and love; happy is he gone to the Lord's Table, and he did not spend his leisure time in idleness but was dedicated to the reading of the Bible. He was good like a father to his subjects. He passed out food and clothing to the poor and supported the youth in their studies. He ate and drank sparingly and never overburdened his heart with excesses. Saturdays and on all days before holidays he ate only once and then only sparingly. The more recognized and great he rose in the eyes of his king and country, the more humbly he conducted himself, because any pretensions were far removed from his inner character.

One would have thought that there was a saint in the coffin. Funeral speeches are not noted for their accurate portrayal of the deceased's flaws, but this speech was perhaps more outrageous than most.

A mere four weeks after the death of her husband in 1604, Elizabeth returned to Vienna to the Nadasdy mansion on what is now Lobkowitz Square. Evidently Elizabeth had assumed that she had fulfilled the proper time for official mourning and could enjoy the delights of Vienna life. The emperor Rudolf, however, was shocked that Elizabeth chose to appear at court so soon after the death of her dear, beloved husband, and he showed visible signs of irritability at the behavior of this brazen widow.

Most previous historians have written that it was Elizabeth's traumatic reaction to the death of her husband that triggered her legendary blood baths for cosmetic purposes. Her German biographer R. von Elsberg even claims that Elizabeth sought to preserve her beauty for a potential suitor after her husband's death. It is known that Elizabeth made only brief appearances at the imperial court. But on one of these relatively rare occasions she was apparently attracted to a young nobleman named Ladislas who had a large physique, and was handsome and strong. Elizabeth and he rode together often in the Vienna woods. According to legend, it was on one of those outings not long after Ferenc's death that the following incident is supposed to have happened: Elizabeth was riding through one of her villages in the company of a young admirer, Ladislas, and came across an ugly old woman. Elizabeth turned to her male companion and asked, "What would you do if you had to kiss that old hag?" The young man blurted out, "Ugh! God save me from such a hideous fate." Upon hearing that, the old hag shouted up at Elizabeth, "Take care, O vain one, soon you will look as I do and then what will you do?" This supposedly led Elizabeth to worry excessively about old age, and thence into bathing in the blood of young virgins. But there is no evidence anywhere in the documents for this tale, so it must be dismissed as yet another myth about Elizabeth.

Along the Vah River about a dozen miles from the city of Trenscin, Elizabeth had another home in which she liked to live, near the fortress of Beckov. The sources do not indicate exactly where Elizabeth's house stood in the town except that it once stood near the marketplace. People in Beckov refer to some ruins on the northwestern corner of the fortifications and indicate that the cellar there was used by Elizabeth for her torture chamber. But this is not likely, since the documents reveal that Elizabeth used not a cellar in Beckov but the laundry room of her townhouse there. The reason for that was simple:

she needed readily accessible water and fire for some of her "night games."

The fortress at Beckov, known as Blindoc in Hungarian (pronounced "Blindots"), is called "The Fool's Castle" locally. Legend has it that its name was derived from a favorite court jester who tricked his master, Lord Stibor, into building it. The story goes that upon returning from a hunt with a large retinue, Lord Stibor was so pleased with the antics of his jester, a dwarf named Butzko, that he asked the dwarf to name any favor he wanted. Butzko requested a castle on an impregnable rocky mountain. The fellow hunters supposedly broke out in laughter over this ridiculous request, because they thought that the request could not be fulfilled. But Stibor himself became angry at their laughter which seemed to hold him up to ridicule. So Stibor decided to fulfill this seemingly impossible demand. He had the castle built within a year, but, instead of letting the dwarf move into it, Stibor himself established his residence there followed by his wife, children, and the hunting dog that he loved more than his family.

Stibor's hunting dog provides another legend: The dog was faithful to its master but dangerous to other humans, because of its aggressive nature. One day, an old gray-haired servant whom the dog accosted saved himself from its jaws by breaking one of the dog's legs. Stibor was sitting at table when his beloved animal came hobbling along, howling in pain. Stibor became so angry that he grabbed the gray-haired servant and threw him from the parapets of Beckov Castle. The man died, his limbs scattered at the foot of the mountain fortress. One year later, however, the servant was avenged: Stibor was entertaining some guests with wine. Suddenly his mouth went dry; he went out into the castle garden to get some fresh air and to take a nap. He woke in pain, screaming that he saw the place from which he had thrown the old servant become blood red. He ran around blindly and accidentally fell from the parapet. His wife vainly tried to save him, but the guests held her back. Later, she took a knife and killed herself. Soon after this the Stibor family died out, and the castle was passed on to others.

Although the legends are probably untrue, Beckov is certainly one of the oldest Hungarian fortresses: it was cited in 1208 by an anonymous chronicler as one of the forts guarding the western frontier. Not even the Tatars were able to take it. And in the year 1388 King Sigismund really did give the fort to a Field Commander Stibor and his brothers. The aristocratic Banffy family owned it for a time until it was acquired by Ferenc and Elizabeth Bathory-Nadasdy. In Elizabeth's day Beckov fortress was in good condition and, indeed, not until 1729 did the fire break out that left the castle in the ruined state in which one finds it today. During Elizabeth's lifetime the strong fortifications and impregnable location again proved to be formidable: in 1599 when the Turks besieged the fort, they were compelled to retire without being able to seize it. Today the place looks very different from the way it did in Elizabeth's day. The fortress and the town were once connected together; Elizabeth's house was part of an entire fortified complex. The Vah River used to flow directly under the fortress.

Among the many tortures that Elizabeth inflicted on her servants at Castle Beckov, Helena Jo testified at the trial in 1611, one of the girls in Elizabeth's entourage was burned severely when the Countess set her pubic hair on fire with a candle (see Appendix A, Trial Document, Question Eight, Statement by Helena Jo). Also, according to the court record, if the girls did not complete their sewing by 10:00 P.M., which was the time when the maids were supposed to begin dressing the Countess for the night, they were at once taken away for torturing. In addition, if there were other infractions of house rules, the girls would be led off again to the torture chamber, sometimes as often as ten times a day. Elizabeth often made the girls strip, and, in that condition in full view of her male servants, four or five naked girls would stand in front of her Ladyship there and even in that state they would fix up her frills and goffer her ruffs. The sources also show that one day the Countess herself put her fingers in a sewing girl's mouth and pulled it until the girl's mouth split at the corners.

Such treatment of individual Slovak peasants by their Hungarian lords was perhaps a little extreme even for those days, but it would have aroused little comment even if it were well known. Peasants were in general treated quite harshly; servants were often recruited by force and usually subjected to bodily punishment by their Hungarian overlords. They were considered chattel and had no real rights. Judge Istvan Verböczy's Tripartium Bull of 1517 had, in retaliation for a violent peasant revolt in 1514 under the leadership of George Dozsa, tied even the free peasants to the land and reinstated old feudal restrictions. A peasant could sometimes leave the service of the lord, according to the law, but in practice this did not happen, since the lord could accuse the peasant of some crime and have him convicted by the courts. A noble such as Elizabeth could treat peasants as cruelly as she wished; they had no recourse against her.

The Slovak peasants realized that any direct resistance to Elizabeth's tyrannical rule would be futile, but they were able to engage in some cunning subterfuge. Realizing that Elizabeth's cruelties were somewhat fewer when she had visitors, they did all they could to lengthen the guests' stays: they let their horses go; they hid a wagon wheel.

Elizabeth often called herself simply the "relicta Nadasdyana" after the death of her husband, as did the chroniclers. She spent a good deal of her widowhood near Castle Cachtice near the Vah.

The valley of the Vah River in Transylvania lies between the towering ridges of the Carpathian Mountains to the north and west and the Tatra Mountains to the southeast. Southwest of the present Slovak town of Nove Mesto on the Vah River, the Little and White Carpathian Mountains on the right bank of the Vah River seem almost to fold into one another, and the Vah River suddenly opens up into a gradually widening plain. There at the top of two hills on opposite sides of the green valley stand the ruins of two fortresses. On the left side are the ruins of Castle Temetveny and on the right those of Castle Cachtice. The original Castle Cachtice had been built by local frontier lords some time after the Mongolian invasion during the middle of the thirteenth century. It had been added to by many subsequent owners until it fell into the hands of the

Nadasdy-Bathory family in the sixteenth century. (Below the castle are some caves which were discovered only in 1956.)

Elizabeth apparently hated the castle itself and so usually stayed in the town in a mansion which disappeared long ago. Only the remains of the outside walls of the old manor house are still barely visible. The townfolk used the stones to construct other buildings, since there was a scarcity of hewn rock for building. Only the little stone bell tower, which once gave access to the labyrinthine cellars underneath the manor house, remains. These cellars may still frighten the average visitor, some of whom have even lost their way within them. The local guide tells of the deaths of many maidens tortured and killed by the countess there. Local peasants avoid the cellars, parts of which are indeed dangerous, as some have caved in.

The cellars of Cachtice date back at least to the fourteenth century. They were first used as wine cellars, since the Cachtice vineyards once produced a very fine wine. Elizabeth, however, used the cellars to torture and kill her female servants.

Elizabeth, as was the custom, had a house master named Benedict Deseö, then an overseer Jacob Szilvassy, and Stephan Varga, Balthazar Fok, and other administrators to keep peasants in line. Closest to her, however, was Janos Ujvary, nicknamed Ficzko. Weak-minded and physically deformed, Ficzko came into Elizabeth's service in 1594 and is reputed to have been a dwarflike cripple. He was the only male servant ever permitted to take an active part in Elizabeth's "games."

It is clear from an examination of the court testimony, especially that of Ficzko and Helena Jo, both of whom had been with Elizabeth for many years prior to the death of her husband, that Elizabeth's torturing and killing girls did not result from any special reaction to the death of her husband Ferenc. One factor which made her practices quite unusual even in those times of casual cruelty is that she concentrated exclusively and excessively on women, a fact that she did not try to conceal. After torturing her own servant girls for years, she began to pick out aristocratic ladies for victims. That is the subject of the next chapter.

# 4

## The Plot Quickens: Suspicions and Investigations; Murder and Werewolfism, 1604–10

IF Countess Elizabeth could get away with almost any treatment of her peasants, then where did she go wrong? What mistakes did she make that led to her trial and incarceration? Elizabeth depended a great deal on the advice of her main confidante, a woman named Anna Darvulia, whom Elizabeth probably loved. All of the witnesses at the trial testified to the extraordinary influence and power which Anna Darvulia exercised over Elizabeth. From about 1604 to 1610 she served Elizabeth, and supposedly with her the real evil came to the castle.

Anna Darvulia remains an enigmatic person. No one at the trial was able to provide any extensive information about who she was, merely that she had lived in the town of Sarvar. All the witnesses did testify, however, that it was Darvulia who had taught Elizabeth many new torturing procedures and that she was one of the most active sadists in Elizabeth's entourage. She made it her business to know about everything and everyone in Elizabeth's service. Darvulia, who was closest to the countess, insisted on taking only girls "who had not yet tasted the pleasures of love" and, most important of all, only peasant girls. Darvulia, described as "a wild beast in female form," reminds one of the infamous Nazi Elsa Koch of Belsen.

Helena Jo, one of Elizabeth's accomplices, mentioned that

Darvulia was afflicted with a similar kind of epilepsy as that from which the countess herself suffered. Darvulia eventually had a severe stroke. Katarina Beneczky stated at the trial that Darvulia also went blind, evidently from the effects of her illness, and so Dorothea Szentes (who was called "Dorka") and Helena Jo had to do the beatings.

Darvulia had instructed Elizabeth in the cold water technique. Elizabeth's manservant Ficzko asserted that Elizabeth had several girls killed by having them dragged naked out into the cold winter snows. Then she had ordered her old women to pour cold water over the girls lying in the snow. (This event was to inspire a painting by the nineteenth-century Hungarian artist Csok.) Ficzko at the trial also stated that Elizabeth herself sometimes poured cold water over the girls, until the water turned to ice in the cold. The girls froze and died.

Sometimes a piece of money which lay around was stolen by one of the maids. Such a crime could not go unpunished so a search would be made and a culprit found. Elizabeth made her servant pay for stealing in a rather forceful way. The coin was taken from the girl, heated in a fire, and pressed glowing into her hand. She had to hold it until it sizzled a mark in her hand as a sign and warning against potential thieves among the other maids.

The style of the times required the countess to have well-pressed stiff white collars at her disposal, such as the one in her portrait. But if the collar was not white enough, or if it had not been goffered to perfection, the countess would grab the iron and thrust it into the face of the maid responsible. The maid's mouth, nose, and throat would become one great burning wound. According to the court records, this occurred not just once but many times.

On one occasion, it is said that four or five maids received orders to bind the straw lying around the court into bundles. The countess found their work inadequate, so she commanded that they do it all again, but, this time, they were to work naked. Since it was cold, it meant they would work better. Nakedness was at this time also a means of humiliation. In another circumstance, she stripped some maids and then called in the male lackeys to watch them sew and stitch naked in full view of the men.

In the winter of 1607 Elizabeth attended the wedding of one of the daughters of her neighbor Count Thurzo (who was later to become one of her most powerful adversaries). Along the way a maid servant tried to run away. The frost and the snow, plus the cold wind prevented the girl from making a successful getaway. She was caught by Elizabeth's cohorts. Near the small village of Predmer the execution took place. She was stripped naked and water poured over her head. The girl died when the water froze into ice on her.

Clearly, a servant's escape was intolerable to Elizabeth and the punishments were always death, although the method of execution varied. Another time, a twelve-year-old girl named Pola somehow managed to escape from the castle. But Dorka, aided by Helena Jo, caught the frightened girl by surprise and brought her forcibly back to Cachtice Castle. Clad only in a long white robe, Countess Elizabeth greeted the girl upon her return. The countess was in another of her rages. She advanced on the twelve-year-old child and forced her into a kind of cage. This particular cage was built like a huge ball, too narrow to sit in, too low to stand in. Once the girl was inside, the cage was suddenly hauled up by a pulley and dozens of short spikes jutted into the cage. Pola tried to avoid being caught on the spikes, but Ficzko maneuvered the ropes so that the cage shifted from side to side. Pola's flesh was torn to pieces.

The illness of her dear Darvulia, which occurred when Elizabeth was in her forties, affected the countess's behavior more than the death of Ferenc had (he had never been home much anyway). Elizabeth had generally followed Darvulia's clever advice to torture and kill only peasants who were, after all, fair game. The authorities would not worry about the disappearance of a few Slovak peasants.

But as the incapacity of Darvulia increased, Elizabeth lost all sense of aristocratic decorum. She felt alone and turned to the widow of a tenant farmer from the nearby town of Miava named Erzsi Majorova. (The last name is, by the way, a corruption of the Hungarian word *majoros* meaning "tenant farmer," with a Slovak feminine ending "-ova" added to it.) From the evidence presented at the second trial of January 7, 1611, it appears that it was this Erszi Majorova who encouraged Elizabeth to go after girls of noble birth as well as peasants. (Erszi Majorova was later in 1611 condemned to death and executed for complicity.)

It was at this point that Elizabeth made a major mistake. She probably could have gotten away with torturing and killing peasant girls forever, but noble ladies were taboo. The court documents aver that Elizabeth killed some girls of noble birth and so had to be brought to justice.

Around 1607, the elderly women in Elizabeth's employ began to function not merely as recruiters of peasant girls but as full-time procurers or "madams," as they would be called today. These women, as the court testimony shows, were mostly widows without any visible means of support and hence wholly dependent on the will and whim of the Countess.

The countess's manservant Ficzko affirmed at the trial that women in all the villages were eager to secure serving girls for her Ladyship. The daughter of one was killed and then she refused to recruit other girls. Mrs. Janos Barsony, who lived in the town of Gyöngyös not far from Taplanalva, went to engage girls. A certain Croatian woman of Sarvar and the wife of Matyas Detvös, who lived opposite the mansion of Zalai, also hired girls for service.

Ficzko also asserted that Mrs. Janos Szabo brought girls, among them her own daughter. She was killed, and Mrs. Szabo knew that she would be, but still she continued to engage many, many more girls. Mrs. György Szabo gave her daughter over to service at Cachtice Castle. The girl was killed, and she did not bring any girls after that.

Dorka named the wife of Janos Szilay from the town of Kocs who hired seamstresses and maidservants from the village of Dömölk where she lived. Katarina Beneczky stated that a Mrs. Liptai and a Mrs. Kardos also engaged in recruiting. Some of these procuresses even went to the Jewish quarter of Vienna in order to find girls. Katarina Beneczky lured girls away from other, far-off villages; some of these girls were still simple peasants, but others were of aristocratic background.

Helena Jo said in her court testimony that George Janosy, a nobleman, brought his younger sister to Cachtice. Two girls of aristocratic birth from Besce and two from Czegled were also brought; of the latter only one was killed. One girl from Polany was also acquired and Mrs. Barsony brought a big and beautiful girl, the daughter of a nobleman. Helena Jo also testified that she herself had participated in the killing of fifty or more girls.

During the winter of 1609 Elizabeth invited twenty-five daughters from the impoverished lesser gentry to spend some time at her Cachtice Castle. She eventually accused one of the ladies of having killed others for their jewelry and claimed that the lady in question had then committed suicide when caught out by the servants. Who could doubt the word of the great Countess? After all, Elizabeth was a member of the high nobility.

Elizabeth even had the audacity to kill the teenage Countess Zichy of Ecsed, that old Bathory family estate. Without enough servant girls available to torture and kill, Elizabeth more frequently sought out aristocratic girls.

But it was not easy to get aristocratic girls. The entire system worked against it. One could attract peasants into Elizabeth's service with the promise of a good job at more-than-decent pay, but one could not do that with noble ladies. One would have to convince the ladies, usually ones from the lower gentry, that a living experience alongside the highly placed and richly connected countess would bring with it incalculable rewards. Still, after word had spread about the strange goings-on, few noble girls would take the bait. So, according to the later court testimony, Helena Jo and Dorothea Szentes used to get peasant girls, have them washed down and scoured. They were then coiffured stylishly and dressed in fine flowing garments. At the appropriate moment Helena Jo would give the signal for the games to begin.

The girls would be ushered into a large dining hall where

they took their seats at the table in accordance with Helena Jo's strict instructions. All were expected to speak in a low voice and patiently await the main event, the coming of the countess. Eyes turned anxiously from time to time towards the doorway through which the countess was to appear. Finally, the countess, often dressed in a luxuriant red robe embellished with lavish pearls, made her grand entry. With an inclination of her head, she invited the girls to eat. They all knew what they were expected to do, since Helena Jo had schooled them beforehand, hoping that the countess might not notice the peasant background of these girls.

One accomplice testified that on some days Elizabeth had stark-naked girls laid flat on the floor of her bedroom and tortured them so much that one could scoop up the blood by the pailfull afterwards, and so Elizabeth had her servants bring up cinders in order to cover the pools of blood. A young maid-servant who did not endure the tortures well and died very quickly was written out by the countess in her diary with the laconic comment "She was too small."

At the trial of January 7, 1611, two witnesses from the village of Cachtice, Janos Khrapman and Andreas Butora, testified that a chambermaid who had survived the tortures told them that much of the bloodshedding was carried out by the Countess herself with the help of a woman dressed up as a man. When questioned, both witnesses were unable to identify this woman dressed as a man, only that she was evidently from high Viennese society. Who was this mysterious woman who dressed in man's clothing and joined in the sadistic games with Elizabeth? If it had been the notorious lesbian, Elizabeth's aunt Klara, surely they would have recognized her. But perhaps they were reluctant to reveal that.

The exact identity of the "mysterious woman" remains unsolved but it could have been a member of the Hapsburg royal family who frequently visited Elizabeth's house in Vienna. That unidentified woman habitually dressed in man's clothes and was announced by the servants simply as "Stefan." Elizabeth's servant Ericka, who was in charge of goffering her frills and preparing her perfumes, usually presaged the coming of Stefan with the words "It's on for tonight!" to the other servants in Elizabeth's entourage.

A castle chambermaid once came across Elizabeth and this noble lady of mystery as the two were torturing a girl with her hands tied and so covered with blood that one could not recognize her. This occurrence was confirmed by the testimony of Janos Khrapman and Andreas Butora at the January 7 trial.

The accused Helena Jo stated that the Countess heated iron keys and then coins red hot and forced the girls to take the hot objects in their hands. She also said that Dorka had cut the swollen bodies of the girls with scissors and Ficzko confirmed that Dorka had cut off their fingers with a scissors. He also added that the Countess put a burning candle to the pubic hairs of one of the girls.

One of the most shocking practices of Elizabeth Bathory was her addiction to biting human flesh. It may have been one thing to torture and kill servant girls, but, even for Hungarian nobility, it was quite another to bite their flesh. At one point in her life Elizabeth Bathory was so sick that she could not move from her bed and could not find strength to torture her miscreant servant girls. Helena Jo and Katarina Beneczky were obliged to take care of the bed-ridden patient. That must not have been much fun, because the Countess was not what one would call today a "good" patient. She fought against the whole idea of being sick, at the same time demanding constant attention. The court testimony confirms the following horrors.

Elizabeth turned and twisted in her sick bed madly in convulsive contortions. She demanded that one of her female servants be brought before her. Dorothea Szentes, a burly, strong peasant woman, dragged one of Elizabeth's girls to her bedside and held her there. Elizabeth rose up on her bed, and, like a bulldog, the Countess opened her mouth and bit the girl first on the cheek. Then she went for the girl's shoulders where she ripped out a piece of flesh with her teeth. After that, Elizabeth proceeded to bite the girl's breasts.

If there were only one person's testimony to this matter of flesh biting, it would be easy to dismiss it as yet another myth about Elizabeth. But Helena Jo as well as Dorka testified that

Elizabeth bit the girls and tore pieces of flesh from their faces and shoulders with her teeth. (See Appendix A, Trial Document, Question Eight, Answers of both Dorothea Szentes and Helena Jo.) Therefore, a modern accusation of extreme oral aggression against Elizabeth must stand as supported by the testimony of those on trial for their lives in 1611, as well as by testimonies at the preliminary investigations.

At the same time more and more people were becoming aware of the strange goings-on at Elizabeth's residences, the Hapsburgs were launching a vigorous Counter-Reformation movement which was to affect Elizabeth, as a Protestant, most profoundly. Under the direction and control of the Jesuits after 1604 and led by Cardinal Pazmany, their Counter-Reformation was making great strides. After a one-year interregnum (from 1605 to 1606) when Stephen Bocskay ruled with Turkish support, another of Elizabeth's Bathory cousins, Gabor Bathory, reigned as Prince of Transylvania (r. 1608–13). Elizabeth futilely placed her main hopes for survival in him. Unlike many of his predecessors, however, Gabor Bathory was not a sovereign ruler at all. The power of the Turks had increased considerably, and he in fact functioned merely as an administrator under Turkish control. The individual initiative that would have been needed to save his cousin was simply out of the question. Gabor Bathory had too many other things on his mind. Though he was techincally a Catholic, he hated Catholicism and drove the Jesuits out of Transylvania into Wallachia. Gabor Bathory also had the reputation of being a sex maniac; supposedly no man's wife or daughter was safe in his presence. He also liked bottles more than battles. When he was not completely drunk, he had a morbid fear and distrust of even his closest friends. It is thus no wonder that Gabor Bathory, known as "The Crazy Ruler," was incapable of rescuing Elizabeth from disaster.

Elizabeth Bathory's fate was also caught up in a mesh of political intrigue at the upper levels of governmental power. The Hapsburg lands in the early 1600s were divided into Lower Austria and Upper Austria, with Vienna and Linz as their respective capitals, ruled by the archduke Matthias, while northwest Hungary was ruled from Bratislava by the emperor Rudolf.

Personal relations between the two brothers, Rudolf and Matthias, were bad. Although a Catholic, archduke Matthias pursued a policy of toleration of Protestants, but Rudolf feared that such toleration would incite the nobility in Austria and Bohemia, who were largely Protestant, to hope for more concessions and would encourage the Hungarian nobles to bolt from his rule. In January 1608 the Hungarian parliament formally accepted Matthias as their king and in April of that same year by the treaty of Pressburg (Bratislava), Matthias and the parliaments of Austria, Hungary, and Moravia voted to force Rudolf to abdicate in favor of his brother Matthias. In June of 1608 Rudolf gave in and Matthias became ruler of Austria, Hungary, and Moravia.

During the summer of 1609 or 1610, in the midst of these political changes, Elizabeth Bathory had become gravely ill. She decided that her health had gotten so bad that she had to take the cure. She made plans to travel to Piestany to "take the waters" there. Piestany was a health resort in Elizabeth's day, but in 1599 the Turks had overrun the place, killed off some of the summer guests, and had taken others off as captives for ransom. So it must not have been an elegant spot when Elizabeth came there with her eldest daughter, now Anna Zrinyi, in tow.

According to Anna's letters, confirmed by the court record, shortly before taking her trip to Piestany, Elizabeth commanded Dorka to bring some of her household servants up to the Cachtice fortress. She also ordered that her female servants should go on an eight-day fast there in preparation for her cure trip to Piestany. Dorothea Szentes was charged with making certain that the girls would adhere to the strict fast. They were not to eat or drink anything. At night they were bathed in cold water and obliged to stand naked in the fortress courtyard to insure that no violation of the rules could take place. (Dorka was evidently experienced in preventing "in-house" assistance to sufferers.) But she apparently did her job too well. When Elizabeth was finally ready to make the trip to Piestany, she sent Katarina Beneczky to the fortress to fetch a servant because, of course, the countess would not think of making any trip without a servant. When Beneczky saw, however, how bad and run down the six servants were who had undergone her prescribed fast, she realized that she could not possibly even think of taking them along with her. Surprised at this turn of events, the countess was angry at Dorothea Szentes for carrying things too far. (See Appendix A, Trial Document, Question Five, Answer from Beneczky.)

Only one of the girls recovered enough to accompany the countess on the trip to Piestany. But this girl evidently underwent some evil treatment at the Piestany spa, because she died on the way back to Castle Cachtice. The official court testimony tells us that the girl from Dömölk died in the carriage taking Katarina Beneczky from Piestany to Csejthe. Even as this lady-in-waiting lay dying in the coach, Elizabeth continued to beat her. Her body was dumped from the carriage along the road for the wolves to dispose of. This particular victim had come from an aristocratic family in the town of Dömölk. Elizabeth herself was carrying things too far.

The sheer numbers of murders Elizabeth had committed by now were beginning to tally against her. Sometimes a mother of one of these victims would inquire about what had happened to her daughter. One such case was that of Anna Gönczy, who had heard from some of Elizabeth's servants that her daughter had died in service to the countess. The mother came to Elizabeth's castle at Cachtice and asked to see the dead body of her child. Elizabeth's servants, of course, refused to show her the dead girl's body, because it had the telltale marks of torture on it. The woman persisted until Elizabeth's castle officials finally silenced her with their threats. Only at the trial in 1611 did this mother finally dare to speak up.

Initially Elizabeth had seen to it that the dead girls were given a Christian burial by the local minister. But as the numbers of dead girls mounted, the local Protestant pastor, Pastor Janos Ponikenusz, balked and refused to cooperate. According to records, Ficzko had presented two new girls to the countess, who had had them stripped and tortured. The countess then ordered that the girls' veins be cut open. After they bled to death, Elizabeth ordered her servant Dorothea Szentes to in-form Pastor Janos Ponikenusz to give them a Christian burial. The minister was not satisfied by the explanation which the countess's servant gave him, however, and refused to give these girls an official burial service. This was the first time that the countess had encountered any significant resistance to her wishes. She met this embarrassing little difficulty as she had so many others. She simply went around the problem and had the girls buried clandestinely. Elizabeth subsequently stopped giving the girls church burials, and went on with the killings. She often disposed of parts of their bodies herself. Some bodies were buried in the mountains around her Cachtice estate.

The old servant women generally did not resist Elizabeth's orders. Only once did Katarina Beneczky try to counter her mistress's commands. When the countess ordered her to be more energetic, brutal, and cruel in handling the servant girls, Beneczky protested that it was against her nature to act like that. So Elizabeth commanded that Beneczky be beaten just as severely as the young girls were. As a result, the old woman was forced to spend an entire month in bed, recovering from the wounds she had received from the beating. Beneczky thereby learned how foolish it was to deny the countess's wishes (see Appendix A, Trial Document, Question Six, Answer of Beneczky). Considering Beneczky unfit for the main service of torturing and killing, the countess demoted her to the job of gravedigger.

But disposing of the bodies was developing into a major technical problem. At one point there were five bodies left under a bed in Cachtice to be disposed of while the countess went off on a trip. In order to throw off local suspicion, Elizabeth ordered that food should still be brought in for them, so that the other servant girls would think that the dead girls were still alive. To eradicate any possible identification of the mutilated bodies, a cover of lime had been strewn over the bodies. At night one corpse was dragged out for burial; several nights later, another. But Katarina Beneczky, who had been put in charge of disposing of the bodies, was too weak to haul out all the bodies by herself. Their flesh decayed after a while and began to stink up the whole house. The stench, in fact, got so pungent that no one could stand being in the house. Something had to be done about the rotting corpses. Finally Katarina Beneczky was forced to look outside the castle service for help. She was able to convince two peasants to aid her in getting these bodies out. The stinking lumps of flesh were thrown into a garden bed behind the castle where potatoes and rhubarb were grown. In this way a little series of strange cemeteries took root in the environs of Castle Cachtice. Ficzko admitted to having thrown the bodies of five girls murdered at Cachtice Castle into a wheat silo, and having put two others in "the little garden channel" at the castle; and to disposing of yet two more in the village graveyard at Leseticz at night.

In Burgenland (which is now in Austria, but once belonged to Hungary) in the town of Keresztur, the Reverend Pyrethräus refused to give a Christian burial to the many maids who had died of "unknown and mysterious causes" there, despite threats from Countess Elizabeth upon whom he depended for his living. He was unable, however, to stop the nightly secret burials in the village cemetery.

The Countess was apparently not worried about the denunciations from these local Christian ministers. After all, who heard about it except the local peasants, who did not count anyway? For a long time she was able to weather these minor difficulties. She was, after all, a pious person in the sense of that word in her day. She scrupulously observed official religious rituals; it was, after all, part of her situation in life. So for a time she convinced some seminary students to help her give the girls decent Christian burials. These seminary students dutifully sang the requisite funeral psalms and dirges and helped to bury the corpses. But such nightly burials gave rise to rumors about "black magic," which even the countess could not afford to ignore.

Reverend Majoros, the chaplain of her late husband, had denounced her from the pulpit, but Elizabeth had intimidated him. When the aged Lutheran pastor of Cachtice, Reverend Andreas Berthoni had questioned her about the deaths of so many maids, Elizabeth had ordered: "Do not ask how they died. Just bury them!" And the pastor did as he was told. He buried countless bodies secretly at night as he had been commanded. One entry mentions that on a single night he buried nine girls, all of whom had died of "unknown and mysterious causes."

His successor Reverend Janos Ponikenusz, following the secret notes left by Berthoni, investigated the subterranean passageway between the church and the castle, where the ancient crypt containing the tomb of Count Kristof Orszagh was located. He found nine boxes containing the mutilated remains of the recently murdered girls. No one had even bothered to nail the boxes shut. He reported the discovery to his ecclesiastic superior, the Very Reverend Elias Lanyi, and also noted that the stench was unbearable. But that report never reached his superior; the Countess's henchmen intercepted it. It was in this report that he wrote: "Oh such terrible deeds, oh such unheard of cruelties! To my mind there has not existed a worse killer under the sun. But I must restrain myself, for my heart is bleeding and I cannot say any more." Pastor Ponikenusz tried to flee, but Elizabeth's henchmen apprehended him and sent him back to his church. After these events, according to the trial witness Tamas Zima, the bodies of girls killed at Cachtice Castle were secretly spirited away to the neighboring village of Leseticz for burial.

Ficzko aided in the burial of one girl at Podolia, two at Keresztur and one at Sarvar. In his testimony he added that the others buried girls at Leseticz, Keresztur, Sarvar and Beckov castle and everywhere in the neighborhood. Dorothea Szentes also testified that the girls' bodies were dumped in wheat pits or secretly taken to neighboring Leseticz for night burial

Some bodies were dropped into the canal which ran behind the house through the garden. That process seemed to work fairly well, but only for a short time. Evidence started turning up in the oddest places. Here and there parts of dead bodies were unearthed. For example, when Elizabeth's son-in-law Baron Milos Zrinyi, Anna's husband, was paying her a visit, some of his dogs started digging around in the garden behind the castle. They accidentally turned up some obviously human skeletons. Elizabeth's servants eventually succeeded in driving off the baron's dogs—but not before his servants had seen the evidence which the dogs had dug up. (See Appendix A, Trial Document, Question Seven, Answer of Beneczky.) One wonders how Elizabeth explained the presence of human skeletons in her garden to her son-in-law. Prehistoric remains? . . . Turkish soldiers killed in battle? . . .

The baron was no fool; he had to know that something was rotten, but like so many others, he chose to ignore the evidence. But Elizabeth had a real reason for fearing her son-in-law Baron Zrinyi; he had seen something incriminating, and she was not certain that he would have sense enough to keep his knowledgé to himself. Letters between the two of them indicate that their relationship cooled.

Elizabeth preferred at the time her other son-in-law, George Drugeth from Homonna, who had married Katharina, her youngest daughter and favorite. (There is no word in any of the documents about Elizabeth's third daughter Ursula, who had been born after Anna, so one must assume that Ursula died young.) Both young men were, of course, aristocrats— and from families well-known in Hungary: Zrinyi's grandfather had defended the fortress of Szigetvar in 1566 and Drugeth's ancestors had played an equally important role in Hungarian history.

Her son Paul, who stood to inherit the majority of the family property and carry the Nadasdy name on, grew up independent of Elizabeth's control. According to the terms of Ferenc Nadasdy's will, Paul had been placed under the direction of a tutor and guardian named Imre Megyery. Megyery ran the huge Nadasdy estate at Sarvar, since Elizabeth herself had technically inherited only a small portion of the Nadasdy properties.

Elizabeth feared no man quite as much as she did this Imre Megyery. They had come into conflict many times over the years, so much so that a kind of mutual hatred resulted. They seldom even communicated with one another. He so controlled Castle Sarvar that Elizabeth felt compelled to move out of there, even though she had the right to live out her days there. However, the claim advanced in some books that Megyery threatened to expose Elizabeth's evil deeds is not backed by any evidence. Nonetheless, Elizabeth could not tolerate being in Megyery's presence. Perhaps she also felt that he had too much control over her boy Paul, whom she saw only rarely. Under the tutelage of Imre Megyery, Paul, not surprisingly, does not seem to have developed any strong affection for his mother.

Despite her great wealth and extensive properties, which she had inherited largely from her own Bathory family, as well as what she could wrest from her husband's estate, Elizabeth constantly complained about lack of money in her letters. In other households maids tended to live for a while, but in Elizabeth's service they died like flies. (When one is operating a murder factory, the costs can get quite high.) As the rumors spread about the evil doings at Elizabeth's houses, the job of maid to Countess Bathory assumed high risk proportions. Only the very brave, the very foolhardy, or the desperately poor could be lured into service. Ficzko testified that he was even forced to go with Dorothea Szentes off to some distant villages to do the recruiting, and that very high prices had to be offered to hire the girls. So it is no wonder that Elizabeth had her money problems.

Every time that Ilona Harczy, a choir singer with a beautiful voice, sang the psalms in the Church of Holy Mary in Vienna, people flocked there to hear her pure, lovely song. News reached Elizabeth's ears about this marvel and she demanded a command performance. The singer was brought before the powerful Countess, but the girl was unable to sing out of sheer fright or shyness. Elizabeth became irate and decided that, since the girl would not sing for her, then no one would ever hear her again in the Church of Holy Mary. Witnesses came forth to claim that Ilona was killed in the Vienna house on Augustinian Street.

Elizabeth evidently liked to have her female servants stripped nude in her presence. One of her servants named Tünde, who was big and solidly built, had the patience to work on making the Countess look beautiful. Often, so the court documents say, Elizabeth gazed into her mirror and ordered the girl to

strip naked as she performed the cosmetic treatments and coif-
feuring.

It had been common practice among the Hungarian nobles
to finance their knights, usually out of their own pockets. The
reason was simple enough; the crown usually did not have the
cash. In fact, Hungarian kings were generally forced to borrow
money from their own aristocrats—who often were richer than
the kings. Elizabeth's husband Ferenc Nadasdy had lent extensive money to the Hungarian king. When her husband died,
the crown had not paid up its debt to him. Elizabeth spent a
good deal of time and effort attempting to get that money. In
numerous letters to the Hungarian king Matthias II Elizabeth
reminded him of the debt owed to her dead husband's estate.
The king had owed Ferenc about 17,408 guldens, a king's ransom in those days. She not only wrote to Prague, where the
Hungarian king lived, about this outstanding debt of his, but
she also went there several times with the express purpose of
getting paid. She usually got the same answer to all her en-
treaties; she was told to be patient and wait yet a little while
longer (the former Finance Archives of the Empire, now called
the Haus-und Hof Archive in Vienna, contains these documents).

Elizabeth found herself in severe financial straits. She was
forced to put her castle at Theben up for sale. Theben Castle,
called Deveny in Hungarian, is located near the Danube River.
It formed a part of the Bathory complex of castles which the
Countess had inherited from her father. Today the castle lies
in ruins; the French had besieged and razed it in 1809. But in
Elizabeth's day it was a very important frontier fort. The crown
found the necessary money and in 1607 purchased Theben
Castle from Elizabeth Bathory. Yet Elizabeth was still in need
of money; in 1610 she pawned Beckov Castle for 2,000 guldens.

Count Thurzo stepped into this situation to play a critical
role. As the most powerful neighbor of the Countess he was
in a unique position. In addition, his relationship to Elizabeth
Bathory had been extremely close. There are extensive records
of their regular correspondence. She called him "cousin," and
he did likewise.

Late in the year 1610, Count Thurzo and the Bathory clan plotted strategy behind closed doors. Thurzo wanted to arrange for the countess to leave Cachtice Castle, sojourn in Varanno, and there be spirited off to a convent where she would end her days. But several days before Thurzo's plans had been formulated, he learned to his dismay that Imre Megyery had deposed a formal complaint against Elizabeth before the Hungarian Parliament. The Hungarian Parliament was to listen to the testimonies and accusations against the countess by witnesses for three long days. Thurzo's designs were thwarted, and he was forced to orchestrate a wholly new game plan.

# 5

## The Passion of Elizabeth Bathory: Bloody Christmas, 1610

TIMES were changing—and not in Elizabeth's favor. After 1606 when the Austrians concluded peace with the Turks at Zsitva-Török (where the Zsitva River flows into the Danube) the era of great turmoil was drawing to an end. The lawlessness and the extraordinary power of the local nobles were slowly coming to an end. Archduke Matthias, brother of the Holy Roman emperor Rudolf II, who had wrested control of Hungary from his brother's hands, was intent upon restoring order in the Hungarian lands. Matthias saw to it that the city of Bratislava (called Pozsony in Hungarian and Pressburg in German) became acknowledged as the new capital of Hungary. Rudolf retreated deeper and deeper into his castle in order to avoid learning about his hated brother's triumphs. He eventually went insane and died on January 20, 1612.

Matthias II started an investigation of his own into the allegations which had reached his court about the inhuman and ferocious acts of Elizabeth Bathory. The king expressed special displeasure that some of these acts had been committed against daughters of the nobility.

No previous historian has pointed out the existence of an important document which demonstrates that, as early as 1610, the king had arranged for a court of inquiry to be set up by Count Thurzo. From the end of March to the beginning of July the chief notary Andrei of Keresztur recorded the testimonies of thirty-four witnesses from the town of Novoe Mesto on the Vah River. Their statements were set down in a formal document dated September 19, 1610. (See Appendix for summary translation. The original document is in the State Archives in Budapest, which kindly provided me with a copy.) In short, we know now that there was abundant testimony by reliable witnesses, some of whom were nobles, to convict Elizabeth of murder. In particular, some witnesses stated that she bit the bodies of some of her victims. Such bestial behavior inspired legends to characterize her as a witch and a heretic, and more to our point, a kind of werewolf.

Some historians have wrongly assumed that the king went after Elizabeth because she was a Protestant and he a Roman Catholic. Although it is true that the Catholic Hapsburgs had stepped up their anti-Protestant campaign, Matthias II remained relatively tolerant in religious matters. His motives were largely economic, not religious in the Bathory case. If Elizabeth could be found guilty, her property would be confiscated and, most important of all, her claims to the debt which the crown owed her would be canceled.

The deceased Lutheran paster of Cachtice, Reverend Andreas Berthoni, had long suspected foul play at the castle. He had seen too many girls disappear behind those gray walls. He had denounced Elizabeth from his pulpit, and he had also composed an extensive report on what the countess had been doing. His successor, the Reverend Jan Ponikenusz, finally succeeded in smuggling the secret report written by the late Paster Berthoni to Count George Thurzo, Palatine Prince of Transylvania. The title "Palatine" allowed the Count to act with the full authority of the king himself in the absence of the king. This put the Lord Palatine, George Thurzo, in a very delicate position. As the widow of one of the leading lords in the realm, she could not be arrested without a special act of Parliament.

But evidence against Elizabeth was mounting; some of her crimes were serious enough to warrant the death penalty. Count Thurzo ordered a court of inquiry to be held at Bratislava, and the proceedings were duly recorded by the judge, Moiysis

Cziraky, on October 27, 1610. The evidence directly implicated personnel from Sarvar Castle (where more murders had taken place than anywhere else) in the killings.

In the winter of 1610 Elizabeth evidently still felt that her social position made her virtually untouchable before the law, since she had her servants toss four murdered girls from the ramparts of Castle Cachtice into the path of roaming wolves. This was done in full view of the Cachtice villagers, who reported this latest atrocity to the king's officials.

During the pre-Christmas season in 1610, Thurzo questioned Elizabeth herself specifically about the deaths of the nine virgins mentioned in the report of the late Pastor Berthoni. Elizabeth was undaunted; she explained to Count Thruzo that the nine girls had been victims of an epidemic whose spread had to be halted at any cost, so their burials had to have been held in secret in order to prevent further infection and panic among the common people. Rumors circulated among the local Cachtice villagers that the Countess was a witch. Though not formally ever officially convicted of witchcraft, like many of her contemporaries Elizabeth Bathory was very superstitious. During the late sixteenth and early seventeenth centuries superstition was widespread. For example, a work entitled *A Complete Home and Country Library* by Andreas Glorez, was published in Regensburg from 1668 to 1671. It was a best seller in its day. Glorez warned about the diseases caused by witches, and claimed that witches made wax figures with the faces of those whom they wished to make ill; they would then place the wax figures on meat skewers and roast the skewers over an open fire; the person depicted on them invariably took sick, and some died. The author asserted that almost all unexplainable illnesses were caused by witches, and he added a list of herbs and plants as antidotes.

As Mrs. Istvan Kovacs was to state under oath during Elizabeth's trial, the countess herself was very deft in poisoning and sorcery. In particular, she supposedly employed sorcery and incantations against the king, the Lord Palatine, Megyery and others. Ficzko also testified to one of Elizabeth's attempts at poisoning. Her female servant Majorova had acquired a reputation for being a great concocter of magic potions. During the Christmas season in 1610 Elizabeth set in motion her plan to poison the "plotters" against her.

She had Majorova mix up a batch of a potion with which to make a coffee cake. The peasant woman arrived with her concoction four hours ahead of the deadline set by Elizabeth. It was poured into a huge kneading trough. The countess herself took a bath in the mixture; part of the bath water was then taken down to the river; Elizabeth took a second bath in the remaining solution, out of which a special seed cake was made. Her plan was to serve the cake to the king and the Lord Palatine who were expected at Castle Cachtice. But first Elizabeth decided that it had to be tried out on some live subjects. Some of her retainers were forced to eat the cake, but evidently something had gone wrong with the secret formula, because all they got were bad stomachaches. For the moment Elizabeth abandoned her plans for the poisoning and did not dare to try it again, since the lords were becoming suspicious. (See Appendix, A, Trial Document, Question Eleven, Answer of Ficzko).

It was Ficzko who had apparently introduced Elizabeth to the occult. In an early letter to her husband after 1594 the Countess had written about her servant Ficzko whom she called Thorko: "Thorko has taught me a lovely new one. Catch a black hen and beat it to death with a white cane. Keep the blood and smear a little of it on your enemy. If you get no chance to smear it on his body, then get one of his articles of clothing and smear the hen's blood on it."

The local Lutheran pastor at Cachtice Jan Ponikenusz was convinced that Elizabeth had sent black cats and dogs against him by magic. He wrote to his religious superior Elias Lanyi that on the last day of December in the year 1610 after praying and talking with his wife at home, he heard the mewing of cats coming from the upper floor of his house. "This was not the noise made by ordinary cats," he asserted. He went upstairs to investigate and found nothing. Then his servants told him that the mice were squeaking in the boxroom. He ran there and again found nothing. As he was about the leave the house, six cats and dogs began to bite his right leg. The good pastor grabbed a stick and beat at them; they dashed into the yard as he shouted, "You devils go to hell!" His servant Janos ran after the creatures but could not see a single one. "As you can see," the minister wrote, "this was the doing of the devil." (The entire account reads like an immense fantasy; and I suspect that the clergyman simply came across a dog chasing some cats at night: obviously his feeling about the countess ran high.)

Elizabeth had her own special kind of charming prayer; it was not in Hungarian but in Slovak, the language of her peasants. According to Reverend Ponikenusz, Elizabeth had lost one of her most precious lucky charms, an incantation written on a slip of paper, the day before her arrest. So she hurried to the local forest sorceress Erzsi Majorova, the one who had helped her mix the potion for the ill-fated poisonous cake, to get a new incantation, which Ponikenusz quoted in one of his letters:

"Help me, O Clouds! O Clouds, stay by me! Don't let any harm come to Elizabeth Bathory, let her remain healthy and invincible! Send, O send, you powerful Clouds, ninety cats. I command you, O King of the Cats, I pray you, may you gather together, even if you are in the mountains, waters, or on the roofs, or on the other side of the ocean! May these ninety cats appear to lacerate and destroy the hearts of the king Matthias and of the Palatine Prince and in the same way the hearts of the red Megyery and of the Judge Cziraky, so that they many not harm Elizabeth Bathory! Holy Trinity, protect me!" (The text was published in Budapest on March 18, 1891 in a pamphlet by an author who only gave his name as Junius and did not mention the exact source of it; it was republished by George von Marcziani in another pamphlet entitled "Elizabeth Bathory" in Vienna on March 26, 1891. See the Foreign Pamphlets Section [Fremdenblatt], no. 87 in the State Archives, Vienna.)

The specific reference to the Judge Moysis Cziraky is worthy of note, because the countess's son Paul, who was evidently in on the deal to arrest Elizabeth, later on married one of the daughters of Moysis Cziraky. The reader may be perhaps surprised at the combination of pagan and Christian elements in Elizabeth's incantation, since the Christian Trinity took a back seat to the Clouds and the King of the Cats. But such practices were quite common at the time. Better to call up pagan support than to restrict yourself to Christian gods; better safe than sorry.

The Hungarians, who had originated in Asia, had once believed in an animistic religion known as Shamanism. The shamans were evidently some sort of augurs, magicians, soothsayers, and sorcerers. They had their secret incantations to the forces of nature. Inspection of the innards of slaughtered animals was part of their ritual, as it was in ancient Greece and Rome. Some of them believed in a Supreme Being called *Isten*, a word probably borrowed form the Persians, meaning "God." (In Bram Stoker's novel *Dracula* the reader may recall that one of the passengers in the coach bringing Jonathan Harker to Castle Dracula sees a tall mountain peak covered with snow and calls it *Isten szek* meaning "God's Seat," as Stoker points out in the text.) But besides this Supreme Being, ancient Hungarians also adored numerous other deities, such as those of the mountains, springs, rivers, clouds, fire, thunder, etc., and sacrifices were made to these lesser gods. In a way, Elizabeth represents an example of how the pre-Christian beliefs continued to persist for over five hundred years after the formal adoption of Christianity in the area.

Under pressure from the Hungarian Catholic nobles, most of whom envied the Protestant countess's land-holdings, Parliament was summoned to Bratislava, Hungary's temporary capital after the old capital of Budapest had fallen to the Turks. The nobles in solemn session listened to the complaints from the Cachtice villagers, presented formally by knights from the village. They also heard testimony from Imre Megyery, the tutor of Elizabeth Bathory's son Paul. In particular, Megyery offered evidence in the case of a girl whose murder he had seen. The Catholic nobles in Parliament especially registered their indignation at these acts of cruelty and bestiality by Elizabeth Bathory, and cited the fact that Elizabeth had tortured and killed girls of *noble birth*, not only peasant girls. The Protestant Count Thurzo was in a quandary. In the midst of his vain attempts to find some face-saving device and preserve

Elizabeth's family properties from possible confiscation by the Catholic king, an emissary from King Matthias II came to Bratislava with specific instructions for Thurzo to go to Castle Cachtice, ascertain the exact facts, and punish the guilty—under royal command.

Count Thurzo took the assignment seriously since, under the Hungarian constitution, he was second only to King Matthias himself and hence top executive of the Hapsburg power in Transylvania. This put Count Thurzo in a difficult position, however, as he was trying to come to terms with Gabor Bathory, the ruling prince of Transylvania, who was a relative of Elizabeth. He had hoped to avoid a confrontation between the interests of Protestant and Catholic noble families in this area.

But George Thurzo also believed, as did most people of the age, in witches. If Elizabeth were to be accused and to be found guilty of witchcraft, she would have to be properly punished. Only a few years before his raid on Elizabeth's castle, the count had had three of his own peasant women tried and convicted of being witches in league with the devil (who, by the way, was also condemned *in absentia*). One hundred and seventeen witnesses had been called up and had confirmed his worst suspicions about those women. All three were tortured and burned at the stake. It was the only way that God and justice could be served.

Count Thurzo planned his raid on Elizabeth Bathory carefully. He decided to act over the Christmas holiday while the Hungarian Parliament was not in session. With the Parliament not in session he figured that he might just be able to arrange things in the way that he wanted.

As Count Thurzo planned to make his surprise attack on Castle Cachtice, one of Elizabeth's servants reported to her that a girl named Doricza had stolen a pear. This incited Elizabeth's righteous wrath: imagine stealing a pear at Christmas time! This servant girl Doricza had only worked at the castle for only a month or so, and evidently did not know about the strict house rules concerning stealing.

Doricza, who was a buxom, powerfully built girl from the small Croatian town of Rednek, would prove to be one of Elizabeth's most long-lasting victims. The countess ordered the culprit to appear in the manorhouse laundry room.

Once the servant Doricza came to the laundry room, the usual "home justice" treatment typical of the countess was applied. The girl was first made to undress, then her hands were tied behind her back. Next her cheeks were slapped several times in preparation for the arrival of the countess with her club. The countess proceeded to beat the girl with the club, until Elizabeth became so tired that she could no longer raise her arms to strike. So Dorka had to take over the task. (Ordinarily Helena Jo would have done the job, but she was suffering from a stiff arm at this time.) After Dorka finished as much beating as she could, Elizabeth, somewhat refreshed, grabbed the club again and started in on the groaning Doricza. Elizabeth's shirt was so covered with blood that she changed into a fresh one.

But Doricza refused to die. Dorka then rose to the occasion. She grabbed a pair of scissors and stabbed Doricza again and again. By 11:00 P.M., according to the witnesses at the trial held on January 2, 1611, the girl at last expired; a twisted lump of flesh was about all that remained of her.

The famous raid led by Count Thurzo, which took place on the night of December 29, 1610 (in some accounts the date is given as December 30), has inspired a large number of legends incorporated in several novels. Most previously published works have claimed that the Palatine Prince surprised Elizabeth *in flagrante delicto* the night when she had just killed the young servant Doricza Szalaiova. One story goes that Count Thurzo and his raiding party arrived at Castle Cachtice shortly after midnight, just an hour after Doricza had died. The count supposedly leaped from his carriage and demanded to see the mistress of the castle at once. The servants were confused. Elizabeth had issued strict orders that no one should be allowed to disturb her "work." Whom should the servants obey? One of the frightened castle guards finally led the count's party through the castle. The group moved rapidly through the main courtyard and reached the room with its ten-foot thick impregnable walls. Suddenly Count Thurzo stumbled over something in the dark. He ordered the guard to bring his torch closer. In the dim light Thurzo could see the mangled body of a fair-haired girl about sixteen years old. She was lying naked in the snow. Her body had been cut and torn to shreds. It was still warm. Stepping over the body in the open courtyard, the count burst into the tower through its main door. Without waiting for the others, Count Thurzo quickly descended the winding tower staircase. Below he found yet another passageway. He went down about 150 feet. Then he heard muffled voices. He tripped, stumbled, and almost fell headfirst into a spiked door which would have probably killed him; fortunately his right hand caught the iron handle and the door swung open.

The air was damp and fetid, a combination of stale smoke and vapor. Through the haze he noticed a fifty-year-old woman crouching over a stool. She turned towards the count in a state of frenzy. It was Elizabeth. At first, not recognizing the intruder and thinking him one of the servants, the countess shrieked: "You shall pay for this intrusion!" The count noticed a female victim at the feet of the countess.

The girl's body had been mangled, and she was dead. In the far corner of the room the count discerned three other girls bound and gagged. "Not so, my lady," the Palatine Lord is said to have shouted back at Elizabeth, "this is not one of your servants, but the Palatine Prince of Hungary who stands before you and has come in the the name of the king to bring justice to these accursed walls!" Meanwhile the count's companions, Barons Zrinyi and Drugeth, along with Imre Megyery, had crowded into the tower room and bore witness to the terrible scene. They began rounding up Elizabeth's cohorts there, the three women—Helena, Jo, Dorothea Szentes, and Katharina Beneczky—as well as the young manservant Ficzko. Elizabeth herself was dispatched to her rooms. Further immediate investigation led to the discovery of a mass grave of murdered girls lower down in the tower.

The above account of the capture of the Blood Countess has been repeated with some incidental variation in several novels written about the Elizabeth Bathory case. Unfortunately for those interested in the sensational, although his companions were the same, the facts were different: The count and his party (the two sons-in-law and Megyery) had set out from Bratislava, the temporary capital of Hungary after the fall of Budapest, sometime around December 27, 1610. The trip from Bratislava to Cachtice took at least two days of continuous driving in those days. By the early evening of December 29, 1610, the party reached Novoe Mesto on the Vah River.

There was no midnight raid on Elizabeth's castle, because there was no need for any. Over the years there had been abundant evidence built up aginst the countess. When the raiding party arrived at Elizabeth's manorhouse in Cachtice, they found the beaten body of Doricza before the door. Elizabeth and her cohorts had not yet bothered to bury the body. Inside the house the nobles found two other female victims.

Another legend, still repeated by the local peasants, is that the actions of a young male peasant were at the root of the raid. One day he supposedly saw his beloved, a girl who lived in the Cachtice market area, go to the castle in order to get drinking water and bring it home in the usual two buckets. She never returned. After waiting for two days, the young lad became worried. He asked around and found out that the girl had been detained at the castle of evil reputation. He knew what that meant, so he hastened to Bratislava to the prince Palatine George Thurzo with the demand that Countess Elizabeth Bathory be brought to justice. But it is unreasonable to assume that Count Thurzo would have listened to a complaint from a peasant against one of his own aristocratic relatives.

The Calvinist preacher Elias Laszlo, who generally kept a very detailed diary, wrote only a laconic note in this regard: "1610. 29 December. Elizabeth Bathory was put in the tower behind four walls, because in her rage she killed some of her female servants."

A lot has been written about what caused the December raid on Elizabeth Bathory, and what really led to her downfall. Some have suggested that because she had committed such terrible atrocities she was bound to be found out, and that the wheels of justice simply finally caught up with her. Others (of a somewhat Freudian persuasion) have claimed that she actually brought it all in upon herself, because she unconsciously wanted to get caught—hence her lack of proper caution. Still others have written that it was *solely* because she began to pick on aristocratic girls, instead of confining her interests to peasants, that she ran into deep trouble. (There is some truth to that last analysis, as the reader will see, but it is not the whole story.) The most honest appraisal came from the pen of the authoritative biography by R. von Elsberg, who stated simply that the real reasons behind her capture and trial remain "unknown." Today, thanks to the newly found documentation at the Bytca archives, especially some private letters written by Count George Thurzo, we have much fuller information as to how and why action was finally taken.

First of all, Elizabeth's trial was totally planned before it took place. It was similar to the "show trials" in Moscow during the 1930s. The entire affair was based upon economic and political considerations, in which the question of what Elizabeth actually did or did not do played no role. She was merely a pawn in a vast economic and political power play. Gabor Bathory, Prince of Transylvania and cousin to Elizabeth Bathory, reigning at the time of Elizabeth's capture and subsequent trial, had unfortunately for her, already made his move against the power of the Hapsburg monarchy. He wanted to topple King Matthias II and expand Transylvania in order to absorb some of the Hapsburg land. As a member of the Bathory clan, Elizabeth was automatically a part of this conflict, got caught in the political crossfire and suffered the consequences. Her family feared that they would lose their property rights if she were to be found guilty of crimes warranting confiscation of her properties and cancellation of the debts owed to her by the crown, so her relatives became active accomplices in her capture and subsequent trial—to protect their own position.

Elizabeth's son Paul and his tutor at Sarvar, Imre Megyery, had been looking for a way to put a stop to this Hapsburg threat to the inheritance. The Hungarian king wanted to put Elizabeth on trial on capital charges leading to the expropriation of her estates. This had to be stopped at any cost. As we showed at the end of the previous chapter, Count Thurzo was enticed reluctantly into the whole affair, and only informed Elizabeth's immediate family about what was going on. Baron Drugeth in Vienna protected Elizabeth's son Paul from any direct involvement in the affair. The Hungarian king Matthias II was kept deliberately in the dark. Thurzo called together a small group of the Bathory family and made a backstairs political deal. He would control the judicial proceedings and see to it that the Bathory family properties could not be confiscated. In return, they would all pay him back at a later date.

The role of Count George Thurzo was so central in all these secret negotiations that it requires some clarification. His first wife, Sophia Forgacs, had died in 1590. Thurzo's second wife was Elizabeth Czobor; through that marriage he became related to Elizabeth Bathory. Rumors also circulated that Thurzo had even had a short-lived sexual affair with Elizabeth, so that his motives were probably far from pure.

Thurzo's letters to his wife after the famous raid on Elizabeth's mansion indicated that, as soon as he had the "damned woman" transferred from her manorhouse to the fortress at Cachtice, he was in a hurry to get to Bytca and set up the trial. He paused only long enough to spend New Year's Day with his wife. The count was intent upon arranging a very speedy "legal" process in his town of Bytca. If he could get things wrapped up while the Hungarian Parliament was not in session, he could present them with a *fait accompli*. His letters to his wife show that he had already decided that the subsequent verdict should be "in perpetuis carceribus" (life imprisonment) for the countess. Anything else he would not tolerate, especially any suggestions of having her property confiscated so that her heirs could not get it.

The otherwise reliable biographer of Elizabeth Bathory, R. von Elsberg, is at a loss to explain why Count Thurzo did not stay a while at Cachtice in order to take the time to ascertain all the facts and details in the case. But Thurzo knew all he wanted to already. Facts were not going to change his idea of what had to be done.

After his raid on Elizabeth's castle Count Thurzo wrote to his wife: "I took the Nadasdy woman into custody; she was immediately taken to her fortress . . . She will be well watched and held in strict imprisonment until God and the law decide about her . . . As we directly came then upon certain men and female servants in the manorhouse, we found a dead girl at the house, a second one was also dead due to many wounds and torture. I await only until the accursed woman has been deposited in the fortress and a suitable room found for her. Tomorrow I ride further . . ." Count Thurzo was obviously intent upon moving the juridical process as fast as he possibly could.

Painting by the nineteenth-century Hungarian
artist Istvan Csok: an artistic recreation of a typical
torture scene showing the naked female servants
of Countess Elizabeth Bathory being dragged before her in the snow and having water poured on
them by one of the woman servants. The original
is in the deposit of the Hungarian State Archives:

Portrait of Elizabeth Bathory: an idealized picture of the Countess, probably based on the original realistic painting (across), now located in the deposit of the Hungarian State Museum in Budapest.

Portrait of Elizabeth Bathory: the original, evidently realistic portrait of the Countess, who is referred to by a caption on the painting as "the tigress of Csejthe." Found by Dr. Raymond T. McNally at the Cachtice town museum, now in Czechoslovakia.

Gravure print of Count George Thurzo, Lord Palantine of the Holy Roman Emperor Matthias II and Elizabeth Bathory's principal antagonist. The count was responsible for convening the court trials of January 2 and January 7, 1611, at his family seat in Bytca.

BATTHYÁNY, a.

BATTHYÁNY, b.

The Bathory family crest: the official family seal of the Bathorys, depicting three wolf's teeth in the center, from the Vienna State Archives.

# NÁDASDY, I.

The Nadasdy family crest: the official seal of the Nadasdys, which Countess Elizabeth Bathory used after her marriage to Count Ferenc Nadasdy in the year 1575, found in the Vienna State Archives.

An illustration from a sixteenth-century Hungarian almanac showing the punishment of the leader of the peasant revolt in 1541, György Dozsa. Dozsa has had a metal crown heated red-hot put on his head by his aristocratic persecutors; an impaled peasant lies at his feet.

A seventeenth-century reproduction of an Iron Maiden, similar to Elizabeth Bathory's infamous sixteenth-century device.

(TOP). Town of Bytca: the main edifice of the town where court trials of Elizabeth and her accomplices were held on January 2 and 7, 1611, now located in Czechoslovakia, north from the city of Bratislava on highway E-16.

(BOTTOM). Ecsed Castle: a woodcut depicting the early castle in present-day eastern Hungary, the Bathory family seat, where Countess Elizabeth Bathory was born in 1560. Now called Nagyecsed (Great Ecsed), the town is located along the border between Romania and Hungary.

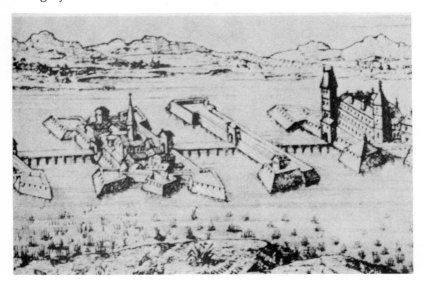

Varanno Castle: a woodcut depicting the castle where Countess Elizabeth Bathory and Count Ferenc Nadasdy were married in the year 1575.

Beckov Castle (ABOVE). A woodcut showing how Beckov, the scene of many of Elizabeth Bathory's atrocities, looked in the Countess's day.

Beckov Castle (ABOVE) is located in present-day Czechoslovakia on the eastern side of the Vah River, north of Bratislava.

Sarvar Castle: the main Nadasdy family seat, located today in western Hungary, where numerous torture sessions were ordered by Elizabeth Bathory.

Keresztur: woodcut depicting this town in western Hungary, referred to in documents of the court trial of January 2, 1611.

Gravure print showing Lobkowitz Square in Vienna. To the right of center was once located the Bathory-Nadasdy house, where Countess Elizabeth murdered a number of girls. The Augustinian church and monastery are to the left of the house (*Vienna State Archives*).

Cachtice Tower: the central castle tower where Countess Bathory had her main torture chamber (*photograph by Raymond T McNally*).

Cachtice Castle: the castle most often associated with the Blood Countess, located in Czechoslovakia (*photograph by Raymond T. McNally*).

Eastern Europe ca. 1500.

# 6

## *The Great Hungarian Show Trials of 1611*

ON January 2, 1611, a mere two or three days
after the arrest, Count Thurzo ordered the court to be convened in Bytca, where he had his main residence. Bytca was
a quiet, provincial market town on the Vah River—a rather
typical Slovak settlement, white-painted houses with tiny windows. The only important personage for miles around was the
Palatine Lord, Count George Thurzo.

Not much of historical importance had ever happened in the
sleepy town. Towards the end of the sixteenth century there
had been a slight flutter when the local Protestant minister
named Peter Berger came out strongly against the veneration
of holy pictures. Although Count Thurzo was a Protestant, he
considered that Pastor Berger was going too far. The pastor
was stubborn and would not back down from his purist position. Thurzo finally had him called up before the Trencsin high
church administration and in 1592 Pastor Berger found himself
without a post. Thurzo's will had prevailed.

Within Bytca there was a fairly famous Protestant school which
Thurzo had supported financially. His munificence brought
Thurzo local renown as a generous patron of the arts and lit-
erature. In 1605 a band of robbers had appeared in front of
Thurzo's castle in Bytca. Unable to penetrate into the castle
itself they contented themselves by burning down some houses

in the marketplace, and general plundering. Count Thurzo eventually suffered damages to his properties—he owned much of the town—reaching some 80,000 guldens, an extremely high sum in those days. Other aristocrats would have gone bankrupt from such a loss, but Thurzo had the houses rebuilt. By 1607 the town was again in fairly good condition. We know, therefore, that Count Thurzo was extraordinarily wealthy: the forests which he owned in the Arva-Varalja district were alone worth hundreds of thousands of gulden. With his money and influence, he usually decided what was right and wrong in his district.

In the past historians have treated that first trial of January 2, 1611, together with the second trial on January 7 of that same year. Though the two are obviously related closely in time, they must be analyzed separately. To that first trial Count Thurzo had convened only local officials who owed their positions to him. In that way he was certain that he would encounter no opposition to his grand plan, which had been arranged behind the scenes with the complicity of Elizabeth's close relatives. But he still tried to make the entire affair look very proper and legal. Under his orders two knights from Bytca, Daniel Eördeögh and Kaspar Nagy-Najaky, took part, as well as a public notary, Kaspar Kardos. This first trial was conducted entirely in Hungarian and was duly recorded by a court stenographer. Seventeen people testified; thirteen were witnesses and four were the close servants of the Countess: Helena Jo, Dorothea Szentes (Dorka), Katharina Beneczky (Kata), and Janos Ujvary (Ficzko). The witnesses generally knew only about events which took place near Castle Cachtice, whereas the accomplices who had accompanied Elizabeth on her many journeys told about occurrences beyond the area.

Such a "short trial" was not wholly unknown under Hungarian law at the time, but for a case of that importance the process seemed to run unusually fast. The main potential criminal, Elizabeth Bathory, accused of "an unbelievable number of murders," was not even present in the court room at Bytca castle. She was not allowed to confront her accusers but was instead forced to sit under house arrest at the Cachtice fortress.

In accord with Count Thurzo's plans, only Elizabeth's four accomplices were brought up for trial. Eleven questions in exactly the same form were put to each of them. They had, of course, been properly tortured before the trial—the usual practice in most of Europe at the time. There was no real attempt to specify the precise circumstances or the dates when the crimes took place. After the reading of their confessions, the defendants admitted to their crimes but pleaded that they had done them all under orders from the countess. Not even Elizabeth's own ladies-in-waiting were questioned about the allegations, much less the countess herself.

Some obviously confusing data turned up: For example, in answer to the question "How many persons had the countess killed?" Ficzko, in a rather clever demonstration that he was trying to be as accurate as possible, stated that he knew of no women killed, but some thirty-seven girls were murdered. Helena Jo put the number at fifty-one or more. Dorothea Szentes confessed that thirty-six servant girls, both maids and seamstresses, had been killed. Katharina Beneczky guessed at the number of around fifty for all those killed. So there was an obvious discrepancy in numbers.

Ficzko stated that Dorothea Szentes had done the pricking and slashing. Helena Jo had heated the goffering irons for the torturing. Helena Jo confirmed Ficzko's testimony stating that both the Countess and her women had burned the girls on their lips with the flat iron used to goffer Elizabeth's ruffs, and also on the nose and the insides of their mouths. Dorothea Szentes added that the countess herself took active part in torturing: "Her Ladyship stuck needles into the girls fingers and then said to them: 'If it hurts, you old whores, then simply pull them out'; but, if the girls dared to draw the needles out, then she (the countess) beat them immediately and cut off their fingers." Here was direct testimony linking the countess herself to the torturings, but she, of course, was not there to reply or defend herself.

Katarina Beneczky also claimed that the countess was a kind of cleanliness fetishist; even in the midst of her bloody deeds she ordered that the walls of the torture chamber be washed down periodically to get rid of any telltale signs of blood. But here again the countess was not able to respond to this statement.

At the end of the first trial Count Thurzo's coterie of so-called judges had found enough evidence to convict Helena Jo, Dorka and Ficzko. There was reportedly not enough evidence to sentence Katharina Beneczky to the death penalty, so she was to be held in prison pending further evidence and testimony. But, as Fessler pointed out in his *History*, "the only possible juridical connection between the deliberations and decisions of these lawyers and judges rested with their personal legal training, or with their own lack of scruples, or with their general sense of legality, self-interest or simple capriciousness" (Vol. 8, p. 176).

Count Thurzo went a step further and convened a solemn trial process on January 7, 1611, again in his town of Bytca. Some twenty judges and sworn jurors sat in ceremonial splendor in order to hear testimony from thirteen witnesses, both men and women. The process was recorded this time largely in Latin. State's attorney was George Zawodsky. The trial began with the readings of the confessions already made by the accused accomplices of Elizabeth Bathory. There was reference made to the blood-thirsty, blood-sucking, godless woman, caught in the act at Csejthe [Cachtice]. (The reader is cautioned not to take such statements literally.)

The record of that second trial of January 7, 1611 cites Count George Thurzo, Miklos Zrinyi, George Drugeth, and Imre Megyery as eye-witnesses to the atrocities of Elizabeth Bathory, having found the virgin Doricza "ex flagris et torturis miserabiliter extinctam" and two other girls in similar condition in Elizabeth's manorhouse. Depositions by the thirteen witnesses were then heard; the accomplices of Elizabeth Bathory did not testify at this trial.

The judges and jurors then met under the chairmanship of Supreme Court Judge Theodaz Szimmia of Szulo from the King's Court itself. Church authorities, in sharp contrast to a long-standing tradition, waived their right to question or try the accused, even though there were suggestions of sorcery, vampirism, werewolfism, and black magic. The king Matthias' representative tried several times to bring Elizabeth herself before the tribunal. But the secret deal made among the Bathory relatives and Count Thurzo was to prevail. The Lord Palatine declared: "As long as I am Lord Palatine in Hungary, this will not come to pass. The families which have won such high honors on the battlefield, shall not be disgraced in the eyes of the nation by the murky shadow of this bestial female . . . In the interest of future generations of Nadasdys everything is to be done in secret. For if a court were to try her, the whole of Hungary would learn of her murders, and it would seem to contravene our laws to spare her life. However, having seen her crimes with my own eyes, I have had to abandon my plan to place her in convent for the rest of her life." It turned into a battle between the Lord Palatine and the Hapsburg king's representative.

Among the witnesses a George Kubanovich stated that he himself had seen at Castle Cachtice an "existens cadaver puellae" and others, such as Janos Krapmann and Andreas Butora, supported his testimony. But the most surprising testimony came from a witness identified only as "the maiden Zusanna," no last name being mentioned. After describing the tortures by Helena, Dorothea, and Ficzko, as well as those by the dead Anna Darvulia, and after making a plea for mercy in the case of Katharina Beneczky, Zusanna then revealed the single most shocking piece of evidence in this trial, that Jacob Szilvassy of Cachtice Castle had found a list or register in the Countess's chest of drawers, which put the number of girls killed at 650 and that was in her Ladyship's own handwriting.

This incredibly large number of victims has caused some concern among experts on the subject, because it stands in such sharp contrast to the relatively low figures given by the four accused at the first trial and by most other witnesses at the second trial. For example, R. von Elsberg is at a loss to explain this. Did the culprits deliberately underestimate the number in order to soften the blow? Not at all! The reason is simple: most previous experts assumed that Elizabeth began torturing and killing servant girls only after the year 1604 when she became a widow. This would have meant one hundred deaths per year—certainly a rather high number, even in those days of badly treated servants. But from the evidence available today it is clear that Elizabeth was torturing and killing servant girls from her adolescence onward, and continued unhampered until stopped by Count Thurzo, late in her life.

The witness Zusanna also stated that she could assert that during the four years that she was in the service of the Countess, over eighty girls were murdered in the women's section of the house, and that she confirmed this number with the knight from Sarvar named Bicsierdy. Of course, like all the witnesses at this final trial, Zusanna could ultimately only talk about what she had seen herself. This Zusanna appears to have been in intimate contact with the castle people at Sarvar, which may explain the curious fact that she was able to go unmolested for four years at Cachtice. But I suspect that Zusanna's connections runs deeper than that. She was probably put up to her testimony by the secret conspiracy that had been formed among Imre Megyery at Sarvar, Bathory relatives, and Count Thurzo.

Elizabeth petitioned several times during the trial for the right to appear in court herself and defend herself against these charges. She persisted in maintaining her innocence. Her requests were not granted. She was denied any contact with the outside world. As the trial went on, Elizabeth decided to try to escape. If she could only reach her cousin Prince Gabor Bathory, prince of Transylvania, she would be safe. But Count Thurzo, a traditional enemy of that branch of the Bathory family, was not about to let that happen. The countess in turn denounced her cousin the Lord Palatine for not "defending her honor."

Elizabeth specifically blamed Pastor Ponikenusz for a good deal of the trouble. And it certainly appears true that the pastor was not Elizabeth's friend. He had written to his diocesan superior: "We have heard from the very mouths of the girls who survived the torture process that some of the boys were forced to eat the girls' flesh roasted on a fire. The flesh of the other girls was chopped up fine like mushrooms, cooked and spiced, and given to young lads who did not know what they were eating."

After hearing the witnesses, the judges delivered their final verdict on January 7, 1611, at Bytca. "Whereas" the sentence reads, "his Highness Count György (George) Thurzo of Bethlenfalva, etc. was unanimously elected to the Office of Lord Palatine by the Estates of the Realm, in order to protect all good persons and punish the evil without fear or favor, after God and his King, His Highness, not wishing to close his eyes and turn a deaf ear to the satanic terror against Christian blood and the horrifying cruelties unheard of among the female sex since the world began, which Elizabeth Bathory, widow of the much esteemed and highly considered Ferenc Nadasdy, perpetrated upon her serving maids, other women and innocent souls, whom she extirpated from this world in almost unbelievable numbers, had ordered a complete investigation of the accusations leveled against Countess Nadasdy . . ." In this lofty statement the court condemned Elizabeth without having even heard her side of the story. And yet, as absurd as it may seem to the modern reader, their actual punishment was carried out not on Elizabeth herself but on her accomplices.

The verdict then referred to the "voluntary confessions" of her main helpers and "the ones made under torture" (an acceptable legal method in those days), and the fact that they did not deny what the witnesses said that they had done. So, first of all, Helena Jo and secondly Dorothea Szentes, the so-called foremost perpetrators of such great crime, were sentenced to having all their fingers on their hands, which they had used as instruments in so much torture and butcherings and which they had dipped in the blood of Christians, torn out by the public executioner with a pair of red-hot pincers; and after that their bodies should be thrown alive on the fire. Because of his youthful age and complicity in fewer crimes, Ficzko was only to be decapitated. After that his body, drained of blood, was to be reunited with his two fellow accomplices and burned. Sixteen judges signed their names to that final decision. Only Katarina Beneczky escaped the death sentence. Later on January 24, 1611 another of Elizabeth's accomplices, Erzsi Majorova, widow of a tenant farmer from the town of Miava, was also found guilty and executed. The inexorable wheels of "justice" were thus thrown another bone; a kind of *hors d'oeuvre* strategy was already in operation, so that people would not go for "the main course," Elizabeth herself.

Elizabeth appears to have been unaware of the understanding which had been reached by her relatives behind closed doors. She thought that she could ride out these difficulties as she had so often in the past. What could the death of some peasant girls and a few minor aristocrats matter? Hungarian masters had been disciplining Slovak peasants for years. Perhaps she had been a bit more severe and demanding than some others, but this was hardly reason for the official retaliatory actions.

During the weeks after the trial, members of the powerful Bathory family launched a huge letter-writing campaign to pervert the course of justice and prevent any trial in which Elizabeth might appear in the future. On the basis of the new documentation it is known that the Hungarian king, Matthias II, was angry about what had happened during the two trials of 1611; he wanted to set up another trial in which Elizabeth would be forced to stand on charges meriting the death warrant. If found guilty of being a criminal, heretic, and witch, her extensive Bathory properties could be confiscated legally and his debts to her abolished. But Matthias did not accurately calculate the power of the Bathory family and the duplicity of Count George Thurzo.

The reader must have noticed that there was no evidence presented at either trial that Elizabeth might have bathed in maidens' blood, in order to try to maintain her beauty. Gabriel Ronay in his book *The Truth about Dracula* states: "The confessions and testimonies avoided, however, the Countess's acts of vampirism and bloodbaths" (p. 138), and that "her acts of vampirism and ritual murder were kept out of the trial records" (p. 139). But what Ronay failed to realize is that such "accusations" about blood-drinking or blood-bathing could not be supported by any evidence.

When the Reverend Ponikenusz came to the Cachtice fortress with other ministers in order to bring Christian consolation to the countess after the trials, she reproached him for being essentially responsible for her incarceration, and she told the other clergymen "without a doubt, the pastor of Cachtice, who castigated me in every one of his sermons" was to blame for her predicament.

Pastor Ponikenusz, who was mindful of the threat that could come from Elizabeth's powerful Bathory family, tried to excuse himself by stating, "I only spread the word of God, and if your own conscience pricked you, Your Ladyship, I am not to blame for that, because I never named you by name" (Pastor Ponikenusz's letter to the Very Reverend Elias Lanyi, dated Cachtice, January 11, 1611). But the countess showed that she was remarkably well informed about the political intrigues of her day and said: "For this you must die first, then Squire Megyery. For the pair of you are the cause of my bitter captivity. Don't you realize that there will be trouble because of this? There is already an uprising taking place east of the Tisza River, and soon the Prince of Transylvania will arrive here with his troops to avenge the injustice suffered by me." Elizabeth was not joking. She was referring to a real series of events, though apparently her utterances went largely unheeded. Her cousin Gabor Bathory had begun a full-scale revolt against the Hapsburgs already during 1607–08; there had been a successful rebellion led by three popular captains, Gergely Nemethy, Demeter Kovacs, and Andras Nagy; and in 1610 Gabor Bathory had sent these captains to stir up rebellion against Matthias II. The Reverend Ponikenusz was obviously frightened by these warnings and pleaded with his superior to intercede with the Lord Palatine on his behalf. As he put it: "I have many enemies [so the Lord Palatine] should not neglect to protect me, should my fate take a turn for the worse." There is indeed some evidence that Elizabeth was working on starting a rebellion in her own lands against the Hapsburg king, Matthias II.

Elizabeth also warned the Lord Palatine of "the dire consequences of his illegal action" and ordered that he release her from house arrest at once. All to no avail. During the course of a confrontation when Elizabeth was trying to escape to her cousin, Gabor Bathory, prince of Transylvania, the Lord Palatine openly denounced her in the presence of some of her powerful relatives: "You, Elizabeth, are like a wild animal," he told her, "you are in the last months of your life. You do not deserve to breathe the air on earth, nor to see the light of the Lord. You shall disappear from this world and shall never reappear in it again. The shadows will envelop you and you will find time to repent your bestial life. I condemn you, Lady of (Csejthe) Cachtice, to lifelong imprisonment in your own castle."

In Vienna, Matthias II remained outraged that, as he wrote to the Palatine Lord on January 14, 1611, "the guilty woman responsible for the death of three hundred girls [*sic*] and women, born into noble and peasant families," had escaped death by decapitation, the usual punishment for the murder of well-born victims. So Count Thurzo had some explaining to do. In his letters to Matthias he began to treat the case as a relatively mild one and actually came out more in favor of Elizabeth than against her. The king was not so easily fooled but realized that he did not have the power to override that of Count Thurzo in his own part of the world. Thurzo was too rich, too strong, and too clever for him.

Count Miklos Zrinyi, a famous war hero and son-in-law to Countess Elizabeth Bathory, wrote in support of Count Thurzo's solution and against the proposals of the king to put his mother-in-law on trial: ". . . I have received and understood your Highness's letter, as well as the copies of His Majesty's letter to your Highness and your reply to it. And although I am suffering with a hardened heart about the bitter and miserable condition in which my mother [in-law] Countess Nadasdy finds herself at present, nevertheless, by comparing her terrible, hair-raising and frightful acts to the present punishment meted out by your Highness, I want to choose this lesser of two evils." Zrinyi thanked Count Thurzo for his kindness and "kinsmanlike" good will. He urged the Lord Palatine to deter the king from having Elizabeth put on trial, "for your Highness can, without a doubt, envisage the extent of the disgrace and the magnitude of the harm that would befall all of us."

Elizabeth's only son Paul also wrote to the Lord Palatine and asked him, on the basis of their kinship, to do his utmost to prevent King Matthias from having his mother punished "in accord with the law." He argued that such a new trial would only serve to bring "eternal disgrace" upon the family. More to the real point, he cleverly demonstrated that the king could not profit very much from such a trial, since the crown would not be able to seize all of Elizabeth's many properties, as was usual in such cases, because the countess had already parceled out her lands, castles, and villages among her children years before her arrest. That fine legal point, along with some others, was to prove important in the negotiations with the king.

Under pressure from the lobby of Catholic nobles, the Hungarian Parliament officially informed King Matthias of its displeasure over the leniency shown by the Protestant Lord Palatine toward Countess Elizabeth Bathory. The reasons behind their "displeasure" were not concerns for justice or morality but were rather based on religious and economic motives. Reunification of the western Catholic Hungarian lands with the northern and eastern Protestant lands under the Catholic monarch Matthias II had given new impetus to the suppression of Protestants. The Catholic Hapsburgs had stepped up their anti-Protestant campaign. Lutherans like Elizabeth were being deprived of their properties. In upper Austria Protestant uprisings were ruthlessly put down. In fact, all over Europe a huge, intense struggle between Catholics and Protestants was looming, a prelude to the severe blood-letting of the Thirty Years War (1618–48) which would turn Germany into a wasteland.

But the Bathory clan still had sufficient power to influence the majority of the Royal Hungarian "camera of the king," and that body came out in favor of the way that George Thurzo had resolved the Bathory case. Judges Tamas Vizketely and Ferenc Lorant composed a letter dated March 31, 1611 that was signed by the learned secretaries of the royal house and council to the king. In it these legal experts gave the monarch their considered advisory opinion: no one could gain by any future trial of Elizabeth Bathory. The document hinted at the legal pitfalls. First of all, one would be obliged to prove beyond a shadow of a doubt that Elizabeth herself had engineered the murder of "well-born girls." Secondly, even if the charge could be proved, the crown could not hope for more than one-third of the estate of a person condemned to decapitation. Furthermore, "in the case of simple murder, i.e., of persons of lowly birth, a punishable offence, as well as in the case of murder of noble persons, a capital offence punishable by Your Majesty's Court by decapitation, it is not the duty of the state prosecuter to bring suit but that of the interested parties." They knew full well that under the circumstances no private person, "of lowly birth," would dare to come forward and confront such a powerful figure as the countess. There was one justice for the very noble and a different justice for the not noble. Elizabeth was, in effect, seemingly "home free."

The learned lawyers of the Royal Curia summarized their findings: "It is left to Your Majesty's pleasure," they added, "whether further proceedings should be instituted against the above named Lady with a view towards decapitation, or the present sentence of life imprisonment be left standing and be confirmed, the latter being recommended by the useful and faithful service of her Ladyship's deceased husband, and their daughters' service to Your Majesty, one of whom is married to Miklos Zrinyi, the other to György Homonnay [George Drugeth], both Barons of the Realm and faithful and useful servants of Your Majesty." According to newly found evidence, the report dated July 26, 1611 in the State Archives, Budapest (filed under Thurzo f. 28, 2.19), King Matthias persisted in his attempts to reopen the trial. He arranged for 224 witnesses to appear at Bratislava and testify to the extent and enormity of Elizabeth Bathory's crimes. The witnesses come from all over the areas under the Countess's administrative control, not only from Cachtice but from Kostolany, Vrobve, and Beckov. The chief notary, Andrei of Keresztur, wrote down the testimonies of these 224 witnesses in a long document dated July 26, 1611. Matthias also saw to it that twelve witnesses from the other

Bathory transdanubian estates such as Sarvar, Keresztur, and Leka (Lockenhaus) testified and were duly recorded on December 17, 1611. (Both of these documents are in the State Archives, Budapest, Thurzo section, folio 28, no. 19). The evidence implicated Elizabeth's dead husband, the beloved hero Ferenc Nadasky, who had done nothing to curb his wife's murdering instincts. It thus tarnished the reputation of a great Hungarian military leader, a valiant warrior against the Turks. Furthermore, personnel of Sarvar Castle were accused of aiding the countess in massive killing, but Elizabeth's son Paul and his tutor Imre Megyery lobbied fiercely to prevent any action against their servants at Sarvar.

Thus, after much reluctance—he really did want those properties and a legal release from his debt—King Matthias II gave in. He decided to support the Lord Palatine's position: Elizabeth Bathory would not be brought to trial. Workmen were called in to wall up the windows and doors of the small room which the countess now occupied in the Cachtice fortress. Only a very small food hatch and some ventilation slits linked Elizabeth with the outside world. How difficult it must have been for the lady who so loved to travel to be shut up in solitary confinement for the rest of her days! Four gibbets were built at the four corners of the castle in order to demonstrate to the peasants that "justice" had been done.

From her icy prison cell the countess continued to try to play the role of *grande dame*. She never stopped proclaiming her innocence in her letters to the outside. She suffered the deprivation of some of her lands. Sarvar fell to her son Paul, other parts of her estate to the administrative control of her sons-in-law—she was incapable of running her vast estates from her isolated prison cell. By 1612 Elizabeth's archenemy King Matthias II was crowned Holy Roman Emperor at the age of fifty-five.

Meanwhile Elizabeth tried to have the last word about her properties. On July 31, 1614 she wrote her last will and testament in the presence of two cathedral priests from the Esztergom bishopric, Andreas Kerpelich and Imre Agriensy. They stood outside her walled-in room, and her jailer served as intermediary. In that document the countess commanded that her remaining properties be divided up equally among her children, including those under the administrative control of her sons-in-law. Elizabeth's favorite daughter, Katharine, was to receive the castle at Keresztur, but her son Paul and his descendants were the basic inheritors.

Late in August of the year 1614 one of the countess's jailers wanted to get a good look at her, since she was still reputedly one of the most beautiful women in Hungary. Peeking through the small aperture in her walled-up cell, he saw her lying face down on the floor. Countess Elizabeth Bathory was dead at the age of fifty-four.

The Hungarian chronicler Istvan Krapinski reported: "Elizabeth Bathory, widow of Count Nadasdy, His Majesty's Chief Master of Horse, who was notorious for her murders, died imprisoned in Cachtice Castle on August 14, 1614, suddenly and without crucifix and without light." Actually she died one week later than the date given by Krapinski, on August 21, 1614. Count Thurzo, who was at Bytca at the time, was informed about Elizabeth's death by Stanislav Thurzo in a letter giving the exact time. (State Archives at Bytca, "Letter of Stanislav Thurzo to George Thurzo," Thurzo Correspondence, Fund II-T/22.)

Elizabeth's body was evidently quickly interred in Cachtice in a crypt beneath the main church in town. That church had had a rather checkered history: traditionally Catholic, it had become Hussite and eventually Lutheran. When Elizabeth died in 1614 the church was still Protestant in orientation, so it was a logical place to have her buried. However, many of the local inhabitants grumbled at the idea of having the "infamous Lady" from Cachtice finding eternal rest in hallowed ground under their parish church. So, as Elizabeth was in fact one of the last descendants of the Ecsed line of the Bathory family, the Bathorys had her body removed to the original Bathory family seat in the town of Ecsed in northeastern Hungary.

But the direct influence of Elizabeth Bathory and what she is assumed to have done persisted after her death. At the end of the first decade of the seventeenth century one of the main leaders of the Catholic Reformation, Cardinal Forgach, tried to topple that "heretical" Lord Palatine on the basis of his mild treatment of Elizabeth Bathory. The Cardinal's attempt did not succeed, but it made Count Thurzo's role as protector of his fellow Protestants very precarious.

A kind of tragic destiny seemed to pursue many of Elizabeth's relatives in the Bathory family. One of her cousins, Anna Bathory (sister of Gabor Bathory, prince of Transylvania), was formally accused and tried on charges of being a witch and a "perpetrator of foul deeds." Her trials, held in 1618 and again in 1629, resembled those of Elizabeth. She too was not called to appear at her own trial and was eventually hounded out of her properties. The motive behind these charges was, once again, desire for property.

A young man named Gabor Bethlen in the entourage of the Bathory prince of Transylvania had been marked for death by that prince around 1613. Instead, Bethlen managed to escape; he received Turkish support, and threw Gabor Bathory out in order to rule himself from 1613 to 1629. But Gabor Bathory was still alive abroad when Bethlen took over in Transylvania. When Bethlen received word that Bathory had been assassinated in broad daylight on October 23, 1613, he must have breathed a sigh of relief. But he should not have rejoiced so obviously, since rumor quickly spread that Bethlen had been guilty of arranging for Bathory's death, and this factor hindered Bethlen in his attempts to secure aristocratic support for his rule.

Bethlen was a relatively poor person compared to previous princes of Transylvania. Most of whatever land he had, had come from donations to him by Prince Gabor Bathory. Bethlen had been elected prince because of orders from the Turkish sultan; and the fact that he had gained power with the aid of Turkish troops did not endear him to the native Transylvanian populace. (In the early period of Bethlen's reign he even had Turkish bodyguards, an additional affront to the local population.) So, though he had the critical Turkish support he needed, he lacked a broad, fiscally sound material base for his rule. Thus the prospect of confiscating the lands of wealthy women by having them found guilty of witchcraft was very appealing to him.

In addition, the trials of Elizabeth Bathory, with their attendant suggestions of sorcery and witchcraft, had created an atmosphere conducive to witch trials. In March 1614 the local parliament in Transylvania issued a strongly worded law directed against the prosecution of "soothsayers," "clairvoyants," and others who practiced "the Satanic sciences."

Most previous books on the subject have stated that Bethlen brought these trials about, because he, like so many of his contemporaries, actually believed in witches. He attributed the death of his first wife Zsuzsanna Karolyi to the work of the witch Anna Bathory and other witches like her. But shortly before the death of his wife, his assumed fear of "the witch" Anna Bathory had not prevented him from attempting to divorce his wife and marry this same Anna. It is certainly true that most people believed in witches in Europe well into the eighteenth century, when a virtual epidemic of witch trials took place all over Europe. Bethlen may in fact have sincerely believed in witches, but his reasons for staging his witch hunts were primarily economic: he wanted their land.

Anna Bathory had been born in 1594, when her cousin Elizabeth Bathory was thirty-four. Anna's mother, Zsuzsanna Bebek, had died shortly after Anna's birth, and her father, Istvan Bathory of Somlyo, nephew of the Polish king, died in 1601. Anna and her brother Gabor were then taken in by their uncle—also named Istvan Bathory—from the Ecsed branch of the Bathory family.

Anna lived at the family estate of Ecsed until the autumn of 1605. Three years later, when she was fourteen, she was married off in a lavish wedding celebration held at Kolozsvar (Cluj in Romanian, Klausenburg in German) to a much older "Reformed Hungarian noble" named Denes Banffy, who died soon after. Anna then married Zsigmond Josika.

The first big witch trial began in February 1614 with accusations brought against the wealthy Mrs. Kata Török, who was condemned to death and her properties confiscated in March of that year. Anna was actually tried twice, once on 1618 and again in 1621. She was accused of witchcraft and also "shameful, unnatural conduct." One witness testified that Anna Bathory had had sexual relations with her own brother. (Gabor had been dead for five years by this time, and was unable to say anything in her defense.) The accusations appear to have been groundless.

Anna Bathory's trials were "show trials" somewhat similar to Elizabeth's. Not many Hungarian contemporaries seriously believed many of the specific accusations made against Anna Bathory. They were staged by Prince Gabor Bethlen. In this sense, Anna Bathory's trials were similar to most other witch trials in Transylvania during the seventeenth century and to those in Europe during the eighteenth century.

This trial of Anna Bathory should be seen against the historical background of an extensive witch craze throughout Europe between 1580 and 1640—a factor acknowledged by almost all historians. By the fourteenth century the accusations that witches had sold their souls to the devil had already became part of the standard attribution of witchcraft. The University of Paris added to witchcraft the accusation of heresy in 1398, and in 1484 the papacy confirmed this. Witch trials usually took place in areas where one of the warring Christian factions was emerging victorious (in the case of the Hungarian principalities, Catholicism had only recently turned back the Protestant tide). The fact that some 75 percent of all accused witches were women lends one to suspect severe male discrimination against women as one of the general motives.

But the Bathory family was to suffer even further ignominy and tragedy a few decades later. Elizabeth Bathory's grandchildren were implicated in a conspiracy against the Hapsburgs. On April 30, 1671, two of their famous uncles, Ferenc Nadasdy and Peter Zrinyi, were found guilty of treason to the crown and beheaded.

After reading about all these conspiracies against the truth, some readers might find it hard to believe that Countess Elizabeth Bathory herself really did any of the things that she was accused of having done. Could she not have been the victim of a conspiracy similar to that of her cousin Anna Bathory? It is, of course, true that the various testimonies made at her trials on January 2 and on January 7, 1611, were made under extreme duress; after all, the accused accomplices of Elizabeth Bathory were on trial for their lives; they had been tortured— one can presume they would have admitted to almost anything in order to satisfy the judges.

If one had only those trials to depend on for evidence, the case could be questionable, but one cannot explain away so easily the hundreds of witnesses who testified at the investigations before and after the formal trial. Specifically, there were substantial testimonies that she bit human flesh, a fact which was simply later confirmed at the formal trials. To doubt all this evidence one would be obliged to assume that the hundreds of witnesses were part of a vast conspiracy to entrap Countess Bathory; but such a huge plot, involving so many people, is not a likely prospect given the conditions of those times. There exists, nonetheless, the extreme possibility that Elizabeth Bathory was caught up in some general mass hysteria about witchcraft. The "conspiracy" evidence, however, consists of agreement only among members of her family and Count Thurzo, and that is all. Attempts to whitewash Elizabeth's reputation have been made recently by Hungarian writers, anxious to clear the Bathory name, but such appeals are nationalistic in tone and idiosyncratic in argumentation. Though she was obviously a victim of a family conspiracy to save the property, there can be no doubt that she was a real sexual sadist. We leave to the psychohistorians and analytic theoreticians the debate as to whether or not she was insane.

# 7

## *Bloodlust and Bloodlore: The Count Dracula Connection*

"HIS right hand gripped her by the back of the neck, forcing her face down on his bosom. Her white nightdress was smeared with blood, and a thin stream trickled down the man's bare breast which was shown by his torn-open dress. The attitude of the two had a terrible resemblance to a child forcing a kitten's nose into a saucer of milk to compel it to drink." So occurs that crucial scene in Bram Stoker's novel *Dracula*, in which Count Dracula rips open his shirt, cuts into a vein with his sharp fingernail and forces Mina, his beloved, to drink his blood. What one is witnessing is a form of oral sex.

Dracula has drunk her blood—now she must learn how to drink his. It is, as Leslie Fiedler wrote in his provocative book *Freaks*, "an adulterous union more intimate than mere copulation."

"At long last the secret is out," Leslie Fiedler adds. "The analogue always implicit in vampirism becomes manifest as Mina Harker wipes from her chin the vital fluids she has sucked . . ." (p. 344). Subsequent events in *Dracula* confirm this, since throughout the novel the count conducts the affair as if he were sexually paralyzed from the waist down. Mr. Fiedler suggests that the powerful appeal of the Dracula novel today is due to the current fascination with oral sex: "it is not merely that fellatio and cunnilingus are permitted these days but—in an age which has chosen orality over full genitality on all fronts—they have come to occupy the center of lovemaking, or so at least contemporary erotic literature would seem to indicate."

The ordinary businessman Jonathan Harker, who has had to go to Castle Dracula in Transylvania not out of choice but because of the prospects of a property sale, has a very close encounter with Dracula's women. He also feels the essential oral eroticism of it all. His diary reads: "The girl went on her knees, and bent over me, simply gloating. There was a deliberate voluptuousness which was both thrilling and repulsive and as she arched her neck she actually licked her lips like an animal—I closed my eyes in a languorous ecstasy and waited—waited with beating heart." During the Victorian era and even today, any girl who "went on her knees" was not likely to be one whom a man would bring home to introduce to mother. Jonathan Harker lets himself be "taken" orally and is overwhelmed by the experience. Next morning, again in control of himself, Harker feels guilty about what went on the night before. He loved those deadly women at night, but during the daylight he finds the very thought of it all repulsive.

It is significant that Count Dracula demonstrates a definite preference for girls who are either engaged or newly wed, as if he were trying to prove himself to be a more exciting sexual partner than their lovers or new husbands. And he does. His oral method of lovemaking turns rather sedate Victorian girls into sexual juggernauts.

For example, early in the novel, Lucy, who has received three proposals of marriage in one day, asks, "Why can't they let a girl marry three men, or as many as want her, and save all this trouble? But this is heresy, and I must not say it." (Letter from Lucy Westerna to Mina Murray dated 24 May). After her close sexual encounters with Count Dracula, Lucy becomes very sexually active. She moves from "purity to voluptuous wantonness" (Dr. Seward's Diary, 29 Steptember continued). Even Mina, who does not give in as readily as

Lucy, eventually also succumbs to the practice, and her latent sexuality is aroused.

However, as Mina finds herself falling slowly under Dracula's power she recognizes that her strange sexual practice with him has made her "unclean." She feels so guilty about oral sex that she asks her husband and his "noble band of men" to kill her: "Think, dear," Mina says, "that there have been times when brave men have killed their wives and their womenkind, to keep them from falling into the hands of the enemy. Their hands did not falter any the more because those they loved implored them to slay them. It is men's duty towards those whom they love, in such time of sore trial" (Dr. Seward's Diary, 11 October).

People today feel free to admit oral sex openly. To some this all must appear as a weakening of traditional sexual morality, because heterosexual men and women seem to be committing acts traditionally attributed to homosexuals and lesbians. But to others, particularly some among the women's and men's liberation movement, it signifies a healthy development towards equal, mutual sexual satisfaction, in which both partners play leading roles. The hardened Bogart male has been replaced by the androgynous male.

But to still others, oral sex represents "arrested sexual development," a reversion to infantilism, since young children get their thrills primarily through their mouths. Infantile and adult oral symbolism seem to have been intertwined in Stoker's own mind, as we see in his anthology of children's stories, *Under the Sunset*. In one tale, "The Wondrous Child," a brother and sister decide that they want a child. Scarlet milk—the color of blood—is poured into the girl's mouth!

The vampire stinks, literally; and, as Ernest Jones points out: "Bearing in mind the anal-erotic origin of necrophilia . . . we are not surprised to observe what stress many writers on the subject lay on the horrible stink that invests the Vampire." Count Dracula has fetid breath. Van Helsing's emphasis on the "child mind" and "child-brain" of Count Dracula confirms one's suspicions that the vampire is fixated at the infantile erotic level.

The human sucking instinct, of course, goes back to developments within the human fetus, and in this light can be seen as a kind of desire to return to the womb and infancy. Blood is, after all, the human's first nourishment, transforming the fetus into a human being in the mother's womb. The vampire sucks blood much as a baby sucks the life-giving milk from the mother's breast. In Stoker's novel Dr. Van Helsing describes Dracula as having basically child-like instincts.

The vampire rests in his coffin like an unborn baby in the damp darkness of his mother's womb. And like that baby, he has not made the break from the warmth and security of the womb. He cannot sleep just anywhere. He is still attached as by an umbilical cord, to the "womb-tomb" to which he must return or perish. He is not only undead; he is unfree. The vampire is constantly doomed to dependency upon surrogate mothers—like Renfield in the novel—who will guard his coffin. As lesser beings, such surrogate mothers are by nature weak and undependable; in the end Renfield betrays him. Dracula kills Renfield and comes to experience the trauma of being alone, thrust out into the world like a newborn babe. He has not yet succeeded in completely transforming Mina into his new surrogate mother lover, so his first instinct is to try to return to his old safe, dark environment, to hurry back to his Transylvanian home. (Perhaps his failure is all the proof, if alas proof be needed, that one cannot ever really go back into the womb.)

It is now evident from Stoker's notes that the author at first wanted to situate his story in Styria, now eastern Austria, and that the main character was to be called simply "Count Vampyr," not Dracula. The inspiration for that had come from the work of another Irish author, Sheridan Le Fanu (1814–73), who in 1871 had published a famous short vampire novel *Carmilla* with definite suggestions of lesbianism. According to one expert, Sheridan Le Fanu knew about the Elizabeth Bathory story.

In any case, Stoker became fascinated with Le Fanu's vampire tale and decided to try to write one himself. Le Fanu had set his story in faraway Styria, and Stoker initially thought of doing the same. The vampire in Le Fanu's story was a woman, an old countess who unexpectedly turns up at a Styrian castle where a young Austrian girl resides. The countess, the obviously anagrammed Carmilla also known as Millarca and as Mircalla, falls in love with the young girl Laura and begins speaking to her about "cruel love." Laura confesses: "Sometimes after an hour of apathy, my strange and beautiful companion would take my hand and hold it with a fond pressure, renewed again and again . . . her hot lips traveled along my cheek in kisses; and she would whisper, almost in sobs, 'You are mine, you *shall* be mine, and you and I are one forever.' " The countess appears only at night. In the end of the novel it is discovered that this countess is actually a vampire, the dead Countess Mircalla Karnstein of an illustrious old Styrian family. A raid on the Karnstein chapel is staged, and her body is found in a chapel coffin. The requisite stake is plunged into the heart of the corpse, in order to keep it from moving about any more. Nonetheless, the young Austrian heroine Laura still continues to imagine that she sometimes hears the "light step of Carmilla at the drawing-room door."

The creator of Count Dracula, Bram Stoker (1847–1912), had not only read about Elizabeth Bathory in Sabine-Gould's *The Book of Werewolves* (containing the first full account in English of the Elizabeth Bathory case), he had taken copious notes from that book, some of which he incorporated directly into his novel. (These notes are among the unpublished Stoker papers located today in the archives of the private Rosenbach Foundation in Philadelphia, Pennsylvania.)

For example, in his depiction of Count Dracula's physical appearance Stoker drew heavily upon Sabine-Gould's description of the human addicted to werewolfism as having "squat hands" and "long pointed nails with hair growing in the palms of his hands." So, the often close physical connection between the vampire and the werewolf in folklore was put in the Dracula novel by its author.

Furthermore, in the original manuscript of Stoker's novel there was an entire section subsequently deleted from the text published in 1897. In that original portion of the novel, Jonathan Harker goes on an excursion from Munich to a deserted village where he has a close encounter with a female vampire, a certain Countess Dolingen from Styria.

What then caused Stoker to shift the locale of his novel from Styria to Transylvania? His reading of the Bathory legend from Transylvania was part of the reason, but there were others as well. In the book *An Account of the Principalities of Wallachia and Moldavia* by the English writer William Wilkinson, Stoker read some details about an historical character named Dracula from Transylvania who had been infamous because of his cunning and cruelty. A book by Emily Gerard entitled The *Land Beyond the Forest* (1888) also evidently impressed Stoker, especially the chapter "Transylvanian Superstitions," from which Stoker plagiarized entire sections which he included in his novel.

The author of the Dracula novel also met and talked with the famed Hungarian orientalist Professor Arminius Vambery from Budapest University at the Beefsteak Room in London. Professor Vambery must have told Stoker something about the history of his native Hungary, though there is no definitive evidence as to exactly what they discussed together.

In the novel Count Dracula is presented not as a Romanian as the historical fifteenth-century Vlad Dracula was, but as a Hungarian of Szekely origin. In the novel Count Dracula asks, "Is it strange that when Arpad and his legions swept through the Hungarian fatherland he found us here when he reached the frontier; that the Honfoglalas [the Hungarian invasion during the ninth century, the millenial anniversary of which was widely celebrated during 1896 while Stoker was completing his novel] was completed there and that when the Hungarian flood swept eastwards the Szekelys were claimed as kindred by the victorious Magyars, and to us for centuries they entrusted the guarding of the frontier of Turkeyland?"

The exact origins of the Szekely is still a matter of some dispute among scholars. During the nineteenth century it was thought that they came to Transylvania during the fifth century with Attila's Huns, about five hundred years before the Magyars (Hungarians) arrived. But today most scholars assume that the Szekely may be simple descendants of warrior Hungarian frontier guards stationed in eastern Transylvania by King Lazlo during the twelfth century. However, no scholar disputes the fact that these Szekely were of Hungarian, not Romanian, stock.

One of the main virtues of Stoker's novel is precisely the emphasis on reality rather than fantasy. Almost all of the facts cited in the novel are correct; the railroad timetables given are impeccably accurate; the descriptions of the landscape from Budapest to Bistritza are based upon actual descriptions extracted from travel books. The entire initial section of the novel has nothing unbelievable in it at all. The geographical locations are exact in minute detail. Stoker obviously wanted to create an atmosphere of reality. After mounting verifiable facts one after the other Stoker carefully and unobtrusively slips in the impossible: Jonathan Harker sees Count Dracula climbing headfirst down the slippery castle walls at night.

Count Dracula claims that he has the title "Count of Bistritza" ("Beszterce" in Hungarian), which was the title of the famous fighter against the Turks, John Hunyadi, who was strongly linked to the Hungarian cause. Count Dracula, like Elizabeth Bathory, was very proud of his Hungarian heritage.

The reader should be aware that a literary figure is almost never an exact copy of any historical personality. Usually a literary personage is a combination of various people whom the author knew or read about. So it is in the case of Count Dracula. No claim is being made in this book that the real Elizabeth Bathory was the *sole* basis for the character of Count Dracula. But her legend certainly played a major role in the creation of the character of Count Dracula in the mind of the author Bram Stoker in a very specific way:

One of the central themes in the novel *Dracula* is that after drinking blood, the count begins to look younger. This idea did not come to the novelist from any known vampire folklore but from the legendary blood-bathing of Countess Bathory to keep her skin looking young and healthy. When Count Dracula first appears in the famous novel he is old and white-haired, unlike the character film actors have generally portrayed. However, later on in the novel, after feasting on fresh blood, the count appears "as if his youth had been half-renewed," because his white hair "changed to dark iron-grey, the cheeks were fuller and the white skin seemed ruby-red underneath."

Still later in the novel, when Jonathan Harker sees Count Dracula walking down Piccadilly in London during broad daylight, the count has seemingly grown even younger, because of all the fresh, healthy blood he has sucked. The vampire count, made healthy and vigorous by blood, is thus able to walk during the daylight, like the legendary "vampire countess" and unlike the vampire of folklore who is generally obliged to rest in his coffin during the daylight hours. Like Countess Elizabeth Bathory, Dracula is an aristocrat who disdains the common folk around him, the way Countess Elizabeth Bathory looked down upon her peasants. He is the ultimate authority figure in his world, much in the way that Elizabeth was a commanding figure in hers. Like Elizabeth, Count Dracula keeps a storehouse of various women in his Transylvanian castle. There are at least three vampiric women whom he considers his own in his mini-harem. Just as Elizabeth was uncontrite, so Count Dracula is unrepentant. Above all else, Count Dracula, like Elizabeth, demands absolute obedience from his underlings, such as his pitiful minion Renfield.

There is certainly a great deal of sexual confusion in the novel. The female vampires in Dracula's little harem in Transylvania are referred to as "sisters." Since two of them resemble Count Dracula it appears that they may be either his daughters or his own sisters. One of them taunts Dracula: "You yourself never loved; you never love!" To which he replies, "Yes, I too can love; you yourself can tell it from the past. Is it not so?" (implying that Dracula had had a kind of incestuous relationship with them in the past).

Most readers of the Dracula novel have concentrated upon Count Dracula's blood-drinking and paid too little attention to the werewolfism of Renfield. As Stephen King puts it, "that most engaging of maniacs, Mr. Renfield also symbolizes the root source of vampirism—cannibalism" (*Dance Macabre*, p. 73). In Stoker's novel the character of Renfield embodies a good deal of Elizabeth Bathory. Renfield is a zoophagus, i.e., one who devours living things. He begins with flies and moves on to higher forms of life, such as spiders, birds, and cats. Finally in a fit Renfield attacks his physician, Dr. Seward, cuts the doctor's left wrist with a knife and laps the blood up while repeating the Biblical phrase: "The blood is the life! The blood is the life!" (Deut. 12:23) which he repeats during a subsequent incident.

Renfield, while in a quiet state of mind, claims: "I used to fancy that life was a positive and perpetual entity, and that by consuming a multitude of live things, no matter how low in the scale of creation, one might indefinitely prolong life. At times I held the belief so strongly that I actually tried to take human life. The doctor here will bear me out that on one occasion I tried to kill him for the purpose of strengthening my vital powers by the assimilation with my own body of his life through the medium of his blood—relying, of course, upon the Scriptural phrase, 'For the blood is the life.' " It is, naturally, *physical* immortality which Renfield seeks, not any promised Christian immortality beyond the grave. In this sense, he is a kindred spirit to the Elizabeth Bathory of legend, who sought to conquer the aging process. He believes that by eating other living creatures he can gain more and better life for himself. Like Elizabeth, Renfield is subject to fits similar to a certain form of epilepsy. He alternates between moments of apparent madness and times of extreme rational lucidity. Elizabeth was known to fluctuate in that way too.

In the novel there is a deliberate attempt to show how the lines between madness and sanity become blurred. Normal and abnormal activities become confused. For example, in the early stages of the novel Renfield is treated as the insane patient, whereas he actually speaks the truth which the others are incapable of admitting as true. However, as the novel progresses the others come to realize that the insane talk of Renfield has some truth behind it.

Another important female source at the root of the Dracula story is the story of Elizabeth Siddall, wife of the famous English pre-Raphaelite poet Dante Gabriel Rossetti. When she committed suicide on February 11, 1861, but two years after their marriage by taking an overdose of laudanum, Dante Gabriel Rossetti was inconsolable. For three days following her death her appearance was so lifelike that the poet refused to believe that she was really dead. He insisted upon having a last opinion before placing her body in Highgate Cemetery in London. There is a touching story of how Rossetti placed a small red-edged book of poems addressed to his dead beloved in the coffin near her face. On October 5, 1869, some eight years after her death, a small group of his friends who felt sorry about Rossetti's state of mind went to Highgate Cemetery at night to dig up her corpse and recover the book of poetry. They built a bonfire to ward off infection and proceeded in their ghoulish work. Bram Stoker's dearest friend, fellow Irish author Hall Caine, was a member of that select, macabre crew of grave diggers. When they opened the grave, Caine felt that the woman still looked more lovely than in life. Hall Caine wrote that "the body was apparently quite perfect on coming to the light of the fire on the surface, and when the book was lifted, there came away some of the beautiful golden hair in which Rossetti had intwined it." Another eyewitness, Charles August Howell, also described how "her shining red hair had grown to such an extent that it filled the coffin and she looked more alive—more beautiful in death than she ever had in life."

Actually, despite the romantic Victorian notions, neither hair nor nails grow after death. Both grow from cells fed by nutrients in the bloodstream. When the heart stops beating, blood no longer circulates through the body and hair and nails can generally no longer grow—except for the brief period of time during which they can still get some nutrients from the stagnant blood stream. So how does one explain the Elizabeth Siddall case? First of all, Elizabeth Siddall's hair had been luxuriant before her death. She went to the grave with it. Secondly, the human corpse tends to shrink after death, accounting for the superficial impression that Elizabeth's hair seemed to have grown in the grave.

During the late 1890s when Stoker was working on ideas for *Dracula*, Hall Caine met with him often, not only in London but also in New York City. While Bram Stoker was managing one of the Irving tours, Caine must have told his close friend about the unearthing of Elizabeth Siddall. In the novel, the disinterment of Lucy Westerna is remarkably similar. Stoker owed such a literary debt to Hall Caine that he dedicated his entire novel *Dracula* to him. The dedication reads "To Hommy Beg," which means "Little Tommy" in the Gaelic tongue of the Manx island where Hall Thomas Caine was born. Caine's grandmother affectionately used to call him "Hommy Beg," as did his close friends.

It is not by chance that many writers of fantasy were influenced by the Irish cultural heritage. Dubliner Jonathan Swift, creator of *Gulliver's Travels*; Edgar Allan Poe, whose father was of Irish descent; Emily Brontë, whose father Patrick Prunty had come from County Down; William Blake, whose parents were Irish; to say nothing of Oscar Wilde, James Joyce, Samuel Beckett, Flann O'Brien, Charles Robert Maturin, Joseph Sheridan Le Fanu, Fitz-James O'Brien, and Lord Dunsany.

Elements of sexual and sadistic hostility, such as one can see in Elizabeth Bathory's treatment of her servant girls, are evident throughout the Dracula novel. It is this oral aggression on the part of Count Dracula, namely, his desire to bite others, that generates much of the excitement in Stoker's *Dracula*.

Freudian psycholanalyst Ernest Jones, in his monograph *On the Nightmare*, found that the vampire belief embodied in the character of Count Dracula "yields plain indications of most kinds of sexual perversions." Yet, there is no evidence in Stoker's writings that he was conscious of writing a pornographic-type book, and he probably would have been shocked by any such suggestion.

Stoker, like most respectable late-Victorian authors of his day, largely avoided any depiction of direct genital sexual encounter. In fact, to a Freudian it would seem that the "perverted forms" of sex that appear throughout the novel are a direct outgrowth of Stoker's extreme reluctance to deal with "normal" sexuality, which he obviously suppressed.

The regular humans in the novel in their struggles with the

vampires adopt hostile behavior as well. After Lucy Westerna, fiancée of Arthur Holmwood, has become a vampire, Arthur drives a stake into her heart "deeper and deeper . . . whilst the blood from the pierced heart welled and spurted around it." That is a strange culmination of Arthur's Victorian courtship. He draws blood. He bangs the stake into Lucy's body, creating a look of pleasure and peace on her face, the final release from sexual turmoil and torment—real death. The spread of the vampire cult poses such a threat to the bourgeois normalcy of the community that the humans start acting as aggressively and violently as the vampires.

Bram Stoker's wife Florence was a beautiful woman. Her granddaughter Ann asserted that "she was cursed with her great beauty and the need to maintain it. In my knowledge now, she was very anti-sex. After having my father in her early twenties, I think she was quite put-off." It is indeed highly probable that Florence refused to have any sex with Bram after their only child Noel was born in 1879. He therefore went to prostitutes like so many other Victorians such as Charles Dickens and Wilkie Collins. As a result, Stoker may have died of tertiary syphilis, as his grandson claims.

Many books in Stoker's private library testify that Stoker read a great deal about the anthropology of blood lore and the magic of blood, which he incorporated into his novel. Stoker knew that people have usually treated blood with great awe. They generally have prized or feared it as the mysterious forbidden source of life itself. Some people cringe at the very sight of blood, whereas others find it exciting to the senses and the imagination. Generally even today few of us are neutral when it comes to blood.

Primitive man often smeared himself with blood to give himself more life. He must have noticed that when he got cut and his blood flowed out, he became weak. So why not take blood in to give oneself vitality? Ruddiness or the presence of blood is usually a sign of health. The use of rouge and lipstick to give that appearance is but a modern application of the old ritual.

The ancient Gauls, Carthaginians, and Sioux Indians drank

the blood of their dead enemies. In Rome on the "Day of Blood" (March 24th), the novice priests of Cybele and other of her worshipers used to castrate themselves with their own hands in order to honor the god Attis as a visible sign of public mourning for his death.

In Stoker's novel he has Renfield twice refer to the words from the Bible "The blood is the life!" But, whereas Renfield is extolling his own attraction to blood-drinking, the Biblical texts are generally admonitions *against* blood-drinking. The Pentateuch, for example, explains a reason for the taboo against blood-drinking: "For *it is* the life of all flesh, the blood *is* the life thereof; therefore I said unto the children of Israel, Ye shall not eat the blood of any manner of flesh, for the life of all *is* the blood thereof; whosoever eateth it shall be cut off." (Lev. 17:14).

Royden Keith Yerkes, in his book *Sacrifices in Greek and Roman Religion and Early Judaism*, gives an example of an old pagan blood ritual known as "taurobolium," which apparently originated in Persia. The neophyte was put beneath a specially built wooden platform which had been punctured with holes. On the platform above the initiate a bull was slain. As the fresh bull's blood dripped through the holes, the neophyte bathed in it, rubbing it over his face, head, and body. It was against ancient pagan practices such as this that such Biblical phrases obviously waged war.

If the blood is indeed the Life Principle, then one had to take special precautions not to let it simply fall on the ground. In Colobraro, Calabria, women still keep some of their menstrual blood in a bottle by their bedside in case they have need of it.

In a clan relationship blood is vital because the members are bound together by blood ties. If the blood of one member is shed, this is a loss for the whole community, whence blood feuds and vendettas. Among a tribe in West Africa if a man sees his blood falling to the ground he must immediately cover the blood with soil and stamp on it until all traces are gone. If his blood falls on a tree, he must cut off that piece of the wood and destroy it. In Israel and in Australia when a youth was circumcised, the operation had to be carried out on the very bridge of the skin, so that most of the blood could be easily gathered up; the rest had to be sucked from the wound.

The blood of a young victim was considered essential in order to secure the foundation of important buildings in the past. The founding of the temple of Shiva was consecrated with the blood of an adolescent; the first stone laid in the construction of the city of Jericho was blessed with the blood of the two sons of the king of Canaan. Master Manole, who constructed a church at Curtea-de-Arges in Romania, walled up a young girl in the foundation. Trying to win the favor of Louis XIV of France, the abbot Guibourg poured the blood of young boys on a living altar, dedicated to the god Astaroth, constituted at times by the naked stomachs of Madame de Montespan, Madame d'Argenson, and Madame de Saint-Pont.

The practice of making offerings of human blood to the dead is also very old. Australian aborigines and the Huns lacerated their faces in order to have their own blood mingle with their tears falling upon the corpse. The ancient Hebrews were so given to self-laceration at the grave that the Old Testament had to condemn it specifically: "Ye shall not make any cuttings in your flesh for the dead." Some peoples in the past painted their dead with red ochre in what we believe was a *symbolic* blood offering to them.

In that classic of Western civilization, *The Odyssey*, the magical, curative properties of blood are shown in connection with the returning dead. When Odysseus wants to summon up the "shade" of the dead seer Tiresias, he digs a pit and pours sheep's blood into it. The spirits of the dead then throng around, eager to drink the blood, which can communicate some of the faculties of life itself. But Odysseus holds them off with his sword, because he only wishes Tiresias to drink his fill. The more that Tiresias is able to drink of the blood, the more his is able to adopt characteristics of living people, and, in this case, speak.

Christianity added the idea that certain blood is especially beneficial. In the Gospel of John are some statements that could be read easily as encouragements to both werewolfism and vampirism. It is written that "Jesus said unto them verily, verily I say unto you, unless you eat the flesh of the Son of Man and drink his blood, you shall have no life in you. Whosoever eats of my flesh and drinks of my blood will live forever, and I will raise him up on the Last Day" (John 6:53-57). This is still a shocking statement, as it must have been in Christ's day, even if his listeners are assumed to have known that he was speaking not literally but poetically and metaphorically.

Men everywhere have traditionally killed their gods in order to absorb their powers by eating them after the god's "death." It was usually thought important to kill the god when he was at the height of his powers, and so the human victim chosen to represent the god always had to be in the prime of youth. Afterward the god was invariably resurrected.

Aztec priests killed the corn goddess Chicomecohuath and then resuscitated the goddess. On the day of the autumn equinox the bloody marriage of Nature to Chicomecohuath (represented by a Virgin) took place. The virgin was dressed up like a bride, golden corncobs hung from her neck and wrists, and on her head was placed a headdress with a large feather, waving like an ear of corn in the wind. Though weakened by a seven-day fast, the girl danced all night in the temple. At dawn the faithful went down on their knees before her to offer some blood which they made spurt from their ears. The music suddenly stopped. The Aztec priest threw himself on the virgin and severed her head from her body. Her blood was gathered up in vessels and taken away to fertilize the earth. Then the priest carried out the traditional rite of resurrection. He peeled the skin from the dead virgin, put her bleeding skin on himself, and began to dance the same ritual dance that the dead virgin had danced before the rejoicing crowd (Sir James Frazer, *The Golden Bough*).

In the Catholic and orthodox Christian liturgy, it is assumed that a basic magic takes place each time the liturgy is performed. The bread *becomes* the body of Christ and the wine *becomes* the blood of Christ. After the miracle, the faithful are encouraged to eat the flesh of Jesus Christ and to drink his blood. So, it was but a short step from the regenerative power of Christ's blood to the notion that the Virgin Mary's blood should also be curative, and, short of that, the blood of virgins. Virgin blood, supposedly so favored by Elizabeth Bathory and others, was historically considered special, since it was assumed to be "innocent" blood.

The belief in the curative power of virgin blood was particularly widespread in the Middle Ages. Physicians from Montpelier and Salerna, the two famous seats of medical learning in medieval Europe, favored it in the treatment of those diseases for which there existed no known cure. Hartman von Aue, a twelfth-century German poet, described in great detail how the doctors of Salerna used fresh virgin blood. If a knight was sick with leprosy, the good doctor first quizzed the virgin girl to make certain that her desire to sacrifice herself was genuine. She was told that if she was doing it because of threats from her parents or from the knight in question, her sacrifice would be useless. After assuring himself that the girl's sacrifice was authentic, he undressed her in order to give her a lesson in humility before death:

> *"I will undress you," the physician tells her, "so*
> *that you will stand naked*
> *And your shame and hardship will be great*
> *Which you will suffer because*
> *You stand naked before me,*
> *I shall then bind up your arms and legs*
> *And if you do not feel pity for your life and*
> *body, think of this pain:*
> *I shall cut into your heart and tear it*
> *out live from your breast."*

If the girl persisted in her desire to sacrifice herself after all those doctorly warnings and admonitions, she was led to a high table. There she was tied securely and the physician "took a sharp knife to her as he was accustomed to do on such occasions. Its blade was long and wide . . . because he felt sorry for her and wanted her to die quickly."

Behind this lay the idea that illness was in reality punishment for sin. It could be washed away by "pure" blood. So the blood of virgins became a highly prized commodity. The blood of young male virgins was used by a Jewish doctor to bring temporary relief to Pope Innocent VIII, but it cost the lives of three youths. Some ladies of the Renaissance, not having ready access to human blood, would rub their faces each morning with the blood of doves in order to hold off the arrival of wrinkles. These and other similar notions about the supposedly rejuvenating power of virgin blood must have formed part of the background for the ready acceptance of the legendary use of virgin blood by Countess Elizabeth Bathory in her day.

Sir Thomas Malory, a fifteenth-century English poet who had spent lonely years as a prisoner in France in the castle of the duke of Nemours, described the case of the lady of the castle whose life depended upon drinking virgin blood by the dishful. In Book XVII of his *Morte d'Arthur* Malory has Sir Percival, his sister, and Sir Galahad come across this lady's castle in France, where they were accosted by knights who demanded that Sir Percival's sister yield to the custom of giving a dish of blood from her right arm. Sir Percival and Sir Galahad fought them off, but Sir Percival's sister decided in the spirit of true Christian charity to give in to the custom. Whereupon Sir Percival's sister "bled so much that the dish was fulle."

Even during the late nineteenth century members of high Parisian society used to go to the Porte de la Villete to drink the blood of recently slaughtered animals after a night of carousing. (*Le Monde Illustré*, June, 1874). If one became sick, it was generally a sign that one had "bad blood." The solution was obviously to get rid of that bad blood and acquire good blood. Hence the origin of blood transfusions. But sometimes mistakes were made, such as the transfusion of sheep's blood into human blood, from which death occurred. So simple bloodletting was used. Even George Washington underwent this blood-letting technique. If leeches were available, all well and good, but if not, then one used "cups" to suck out the bad blood from the afflicted. In fact, doctors were often known as "leechers" in old England.

Milk, also one of the early sources of nourishment for the human child, has often been associated with blood. In East

Africa the Masai tribe nourish themselves on a mixture of milk and blood. That nomadic people travel with their cattle, which they tap periodically for blood. After cauterizing the wound in the cattle's neck, they mix the milk with blood. This curdled food is drunk, and apparently these people do very well on their high-protein diet. In some tribes mothers rub their breasts with blood before feeding milk to their babies.

During the old German ritual of *Bruderschaft* the participants used to slash their wrists causing blood to flow and then link wrists together, so that their mutual blood could mix together, making them literally "blood brothers." In our day, beer or wine is substituted for real blood, but the arms are still linked together in a way similar to the one which allowed real blood to flow and intermingle. Children still do it, as do some American Indians.

There is a not surprising connection often made between sexual pleasure and digestive human functions. One is often substituted for the other. A Breton husband begins his honeymoon by cutting his wife's breast slightly and then sucking the blood from it. There is also the notion that a person in love may lose his or her appetite for ordinary food and drink. This attitude was especially prevalent during the Renaissance, when there was concern that many a lover might waste away and die for want of proper nourishment.

This notion is linked with the idea that semen and female secretion are, like blood, excellent forms of nourishment. In the Spanish language, male semen is called *leche*, "milk," and the word *papa* (from *papar*: "to eat creamy food") is used for the female sexual organ. It is known that in Africa the young Nandi tribesmen consider female secretions as nourishment. Before puberty, when they masturbate, they repeat the ritualistic formula: "Grow, grow, and I will give you something to eat" (Suren, suren, ce kwamon peka metet, see Boris de Rachewitz, *Eros Nero*).

During the year 1959 police in New York arrested a Puerto Rican youth for alledgedly committing assaults and murder at night. During his nocturnal escapades, the youth dressed in a black cloak and referred to himself as "Count Dracula." The boy was eventually tried and convicted on murder charges. This case brings up an interesting psychological point:

Most mentally unbalanced people usually tend to think of themselves as important historical personalities such as Napoleon, Julius Caesar, etc. Such sick people do not generally adopt a literary character as a model. However, Count Dracula is a revealing exception. The Count is one of the few fictional figures whom these unfortunates see as their ideal—perhaps because of his special powerfulness and lack of scruples.

Blood flow is especially mysterious when there is no evident cause, such as an arrow, lance or sword wound. Nosebleeds were thus particularly frightening. But a menstruating woman was treated as one of nature's true horrors. Many uninformed girls can testify to the shock as they discovered blood coming out of their vaginas. To some men it seemed that the blood was coming from their "natural wound." There are countless stories in the folklore of many nations, especially Jewish and Russian, about the evils of a menstruating woman. The Roman historian Pliny claimed that a menstruating woman could destroy the harvest, turn wine into vinegar, rust iron and copper, and, when the moon was also on the wane, cause bees to die.

According to the Talmud, a menstruating woman who passes between two men will cause the sudden death of one of them; among Russians even the shadow of a menstruating woman was considered lethal. Among the Bri-bri tribe of Costa Rica anyone who eats from the plate or drinks from the glass of such a woman will die; within the Ila tribe such carelessness can make a male impotent. If the menstruating wife of an Australian aborigine should try to lie down beside her husband, he is obliged to commit suicide rather than give in to an act of sexual intercourse.

At the time of a girl's first menstrual period, the Hudson Bay and Chippewa Indians put the girls in cabins far from the village and force them to wear hats with leather fringes that cover their eyes. In Bolivia the Chiriguani Indians send them to live in a hammock slung from the roof for at least three months.

Among Sudanese Arabs and some African tribes who have come under Semitic influence, the labia majora of the little girls' vagina are sewn up with a metal needle when they are about three years old. Only the future husband has the right to open it again; if he prefers not to tear it open by intromission, he has the option to use a knife. There is, of course, a very close connection between masculine pride and the cult of blood. For example, there is the blood-stained sheet which is proudly displayed the morning after the wedding night—a custom still in practice in southern Europe.

Under the rules of vendetta requiring bloodshedding from the family of given assassins, a revealing substitute exists, i.e., a marriage can be arranged between a relative of the assassin and a relative of the victim. The blood shed by the virgin on her wedding night is considered as compensation for the blood of the victim. In this context, as Mademoiselle de Lespinasse has suggested, woman is simply man's monster.

A sensually aroused woman was and is often treated as a frightening thing, something not to be spoken or written about except in monstrous terms. The development of this male notion of woman, projected as a sensual vampire, and the various types of "living vampires" are the subjects of the next chapter.

# 8

## *The Sensual Vampire: Unusual Encounters of the Third Kind*

ONE of the earliest representations of a vampire is found on a prehistoric Assyrian bowl which depicts a man copulating with a female vampire whose head has been cut off. (Montague Summers, *The Vampire*, p. 226.) The earliest mythologies about the vampire linked the creature with the destructive side of the feminine, not only in the Orient but also in ancient Greece, that foundation of western civilization. E. Neuman in his work *The Great Mother* gives numerous examples of the positive and the negative sides of the feminine as portrayed in many ancient religious cults: Kali in India, Isis and Hator in Egypt, Hecate in Greece, and especially Artemis Orthia, goddess of ancient Sparta. An ancient ivory plaque from the eighth century shows that goddess strangling two large birds by the neck. Animals from which "a member was cut off" were sacrifices to her (p. 274). According to Neuman the crucial moments in the life of the female involve blood sacrifice—menstruation, defloration, and childbirth. Her negative side demands the reciprocal bloody sacrifice of castration from the male.

Sex with its mysteries and extreme pleasures must have always appeared somewhat magical. Seasonal rites related to plowing, sowing, reaping, and harvesting were connected with sexual magic. Mother Earth was fertilized by the Father God in the form of rain. Plowing the field was the ceremony open-ing and preparing the earth to receive the seed that was going to be planted within the furrows of the earth's womb, where male and female united.

Philosophers have always sought to explain the attraction between male and female. According to Plato in his *Symposium*, in the beginning male and female were two halves of a pri-mordial androgyne (man-woman) which had existed in united form and had been later divided. The idea of splitting underlies the Greek word *sex*, which means "division." These halves thus naturally seek to become whole to become complete through sexual union.

In Chinese belief the masculine principle of the universe is the *yang*, which corresponds to the sky and to male semen. The female principle, the *yin*, corresponds to the Earth and to female secretion. When the *yang* and the *yin* are reunited, they achieve the harmony of the universe. Human immortality be-comes possible if one can insert oneself into that harmony. The Chinese compared the sex act to the union of sky and earth made possible through rain.

The vampire is portrayed as male *or* female, and often even looks suspiciously like some real person who once was human. Vampires, like female succubi and male incubi, have been very convenient monsters. Not only could one frighten bad children with the threat of their coming, but one could especially use their supposed nocturnal visits as alibis for illicit pregnancies. How could one deny the existence of incubi when virtuous unmarried girls became pregnant? Like the incubus and suc-cubus the vampire's sole preoccupation is, after all, with sexual encounters at night.

The church fathers spent many sleepless nights trying to figure out the true nature of the incubus and the succubus. Saint Augustine sparked the controversy by proclaiming that the demons had "corporeal immortality and passions like human beings." He declared that the incubi could not produce semen by themselves but gathered it from the bodies of men and injected it into the women, causing pregnancy.

Saint Clemens, in the homilies attributed to him, gave the

Christian world the reasons behind the attacks of these demons: "Since these spirits want to partake of food and drink
and feel the desire to do so but cannot, because they are spirits
and have no organs, they turn to humans to make use of their
organs. Once in control of suitable organs, they can get whatever they want and take it through the mouth of possessed
humans."

So, the notion of demons who yearn to act like humans lies
behind diabolical "possession." If real humans showed a tendency to want to eat human flesh and drink human blood—
both acts officially taboo—it was assumed that they had become possessed, had been taken over by demons.

On December 9, 1484, Pope Innocent VIII issued a papal bull
warning against sexual encounters with demons: "It has come
to our ears," the bull reads, "that numbers of both sexes do
not shun having casual intercourse with infernal fiends and
that by their sorceries they afflict both man and beast . . ." The
Spanish Benedictine monk Juan Caramuel coined the word
"demonality" in order to define "copulation of a human with
a corpse which has no feeling and movement and which only
moves due to the artifice of the demon." The fifteenth-century
theologian De Spina then advanced the novel notion that incubi and succubi were "formed from the odor and sperm of
men and women in intercourse."

The Italian Franciscan Ludovico Maria Sinistrari d'Ameno
(1622–1701), advisor to the Tribunal of the Holy Inquisition in
Rome and later personal theologian to the archbishop of Milan,
sensationally declared that "in his commerce with a woman,
the incubus demon generates the human foetus with his own
personal semen" (*De delictis et de poenis*) [On Crime and Pun-
ishment]. So, Sinistrari disagreed with Saint Augustine's views
on the sexual capabilities of the incubus. In asserting that the
incubus generated his own semen, he concluded that the incubus could not be a demon, especially as prayers, holy relics,
etc. had no effect on him. Only noxious fumes and herbs, he
added, seemed to ward off the sexual attacker.

Father Sinistrari reported the special case of a lady named
Hieronyma from his own city of Pavia. At night a demon kissed

her cheeks softly, while her husband snored on. She resisted and crossed herself. He came back night after night. She told her confessor about it; exorcism was performed on her, house, bedroom, and bed—but all to no avail. He appeared in the form of a fair-haired Spanish noble with sea-green eyes. But the faithful woman still spurned him. He got angry and beat her. While attending mass one day in her own church as she crossed the threshold, her clothes all fell to the ground leaving her embarrassingly naked. Fortunately two gentlemen, who happened to be standing by, gallantly covered her nudity with their cloaks. Finally the incubus on his own simply got tired of pushing his rejected advances and left her alone.

A Venetian priest named Brognoli traced the story of a twenty-two-year-old man from Bergamo who upon retiring at night heard the sound of a soft footfall near his bed. He was amazed to see his fiancée Teresa there. She said that her parents had thrown her out and she came to him for refuge. She got into bed with him, her lust was boundless and insatiable. In the morning she told him that she was a succubus. She visited him again and again until he became exhausted. Staggering to the confessional, he begged Father Brognoli for deliverance. Brognoli did his best and wrote: "This monstrous commerce lasted for several months; but God finally delivered him through my pleas, and he did suitable penance for his sins."

During the late sixteenth century the Protestant scholar Louis Lavater wrote *De spectris, Lemwibus et magnis atque insolilis Fragoribus* (Of ghosts and spirits walking by night)—a most extensive study of vampires and other demons, which he believed to have a real existence. He concluded that these demons were not the spirits of dead men from purgatory but angels. So, despite slight differences in emphasis, the Protestant explanation did not go much further than the traditional Catholic one. Both ended up with some kinds of strange spirits at the root of the "unnatural" practices. Father Gabriel Rzaczynski, a learned Polish Jesuit, wrote about several cases involving *vampiers*, "dead men who, while already in their graves, are lustful, and similar ghosts who kill living beings" G. Rzaczynski, *His-*

*toria naturalis curiosa regni Polonia et magn. Ducat Lithuanise annexarumque Provinciar* [The Curious Natural History of the Polish Kingdom and the Annexed Provinces of the Grand Duchy of Warsaw].

During the 1720s, a high point in the so-called Enlightenment, when a vampire craze spread particularly across Hungary and the neighboring states of the Hapsburg empire, an abbé of Senores in Lorraine, Dom Augustin Calmet, took up his pen to try to explain the vampire pestilence in "rational" terms. As a result of his research, he eventually published a learned treatise entitled *Dissertations sur les apparitions des anges, des démons et des esprits.* [Dissertations on Angels, Demons and Spirits.] In his work Calmet raised the issue of whether or not this rise in the number of vampire cases had something to do with the increasing number of persons excommunicated from the church and buried in unhallowed ground. But he failed to notice that most of the reported cases of vampires came from border areas where Catholic and Protestant Hungarians mixed with Orthodox Serbs and Romanians. The alleged vampires invariably had Slavic names, indicating their probable adherence to Greek Orthodox rituals. Since most of the reports of vampirism were written by the official Roman Catholic authorities of the Hapsburg empire, one cannot help but suspect a certain anti-Orthodox and anti-Slav bias in many of them.

One scientific explanation for the appearance of actual life beyond the grave is premature burial. It has always been difficult for doctors to ascertain exactly when death occurs. In the past, premature burials happened rather frequently. At the beginning of the century, it was estimated that at least one case of premature burial took place each week. As recently as 1974, a group of doctors in a British hospital who were dissecting a corpse for a kidney transplant discovered to their horror that the body was still breathing. Recently, in a southern state of the United States, the sight of a policeman knocking at her door so frightened an unwed mother-to-be that she collapsed and was certified as dead. A week after the burial, her mother demanded to see her daughter's body. When the grave was opened, they found that the baby had been born and the mother's fingers worn down in efforts to try to claw her way out of the dark coffin.

In another case, a young woman from Indianapolis was attested to as dead by several doctors and was about to be buried. Her brother clung to her body and noticed her lips were quivering: "What do you want?" the boy cried. "Water," whispered the woman, who recovered and lived to an old age.

But vampires are not merely spiritual or imaginary manifestations; they are also real people who drink human blood.

Contemporary medical doctors distinguish two types of living vampires: 1) those with a chemical or physical need for healthy human blood, since their own is deficient in some way (as in severe anemia); and 2) those with a psychopathological need for human blood. Many words have been used to categorize living vampires of the pathological variety such as hematomania, hemothymea, hematophilia, hematodipsia, hemosexuality, oral-sanguinary sadism, and sometimes simply blood fetishism or blood mania.

Dr. Magnus Hirschfield, an important contributor to the field of sexology, maintained in *Anomalies et perversions sexuelles* that society in fact owed its preservation to the ordinary human mechanism of "displacement." He cites a pertinent example of "F.N.," a male patient under the care of a Doctor Stekel, who had uncontrollable urges to stab and see flowing blood. The man was unable to approach any woman unless a second woman were present, and if the second was not a robust woman, then yet a third had to be there. No orgy ensued from all this, so Doctor Stekel concluded that the man wanted to provide himself with a bodyguard capable of thwarting him from murdering his girlfriend. F.N. tried to pursue a career in surgery, where he would be allowed to indulge in his aggressive instincts; in a socially approved fashion, he could cut up human beings. However, upon witnessing the sight of blood in the anatomical theater, F.N. reacted with such violent thrills that he had to give up that ambition. The outbreak of World War I provided him with an opportunity to become a soldier rather than a surgeon. In war he was able to exercise his dubious aggressive instincts, for which he was eventually awarded the Medal of Honor! Less fortunate people who prove incapable of channeling their killer instincts in socially acceptable ways are branded murderers and hunted down like dangerous, wild beasts.

Dr. Lawrence Kayton has explained vampirism as an adolescent yearning for love and affection redirected into extreme oral needs. In an article entitled "The Relationship of the Vampire Legend to Schizophrenia," Kayton describes both the vampire and the schizophrenic as totally attached to need-satisfying impulses. The schizophrenic has "enormous needs to be given to, to be fed, and to be mothered," and the vampire "is possessed by enormous oral needs which rule his life." Dr. Richard L. Vanden Bergh and Dr. John F. Kelly, in "Vampirism: A Review with New Observations," attributed the practice simply to oral sadism.

A male ego not strong enough or developed enough to resist the forces of an overpowering female becomes repressed. The price for such repression is that the male often turns to masturbation, self-castration, or to violence.

Psychiatrists have assembled extensive materials on past famous cases of actual living vampires: the Italian Vincenz Verzeni in 1872; the Frenchman Leger in 1827 (detailed by Krafft-Ebing in *Psychopathia Sexualis*), and the German Fritz Haarman known popularly as "the Hanover Vampire," executed in 1925 for killing about twenty-four adolescent males. But, as Ernest Jones pointed out in *On the Nightmare*, several of these popularized figures termed "vampires" in the annals of sexual criminology were actually necrophiles (pp. 98–103).

Karl Abraham divided the oral phase of the infant into the sucking and the biting stages. In the first stage the nursing infant is a relatively passive recipient of whatever food is put in his mouth. With the development of teeth, the infant finds himself provided with weapons for aggression, which he can use if his needs are frustrated. If the conflict between the good, need-satisfying object and feelings of aggression is not resolved, depression and eventual schizophrenia may result. ("The

Influence of Oral Eroticism on Character Formation," *Selected Papers on Psychoanalysis*, pp. 396–400.)

Cyril Marystone in his book *The Shepherds Are Lost* describes the case of Veronica Leuken who has been termed the "Seer" of Bayside, New York, because she supposedly was having visions of Mary, Mother of Christ. This "seer" has a group of followers who call themselves the "Faithful and True Believers"; they believe that the UFOs, appearances of Bigfoot, and the recent cattle mutilations in the western United States have all been caused by the devil. One of Veronica Leuken's "visions" on September 13, 1977, led her to claim that a Satanic creature called "The Vampire" is busy organizing covens throughout the United States to supply himself with the blood he needs for sustenance. A retired Anglican priest, the Reverend Donald Omand, has stated that he personally exorcised demons who had been forcing victims to become obsessed with drinking human blood. (*National Enquirer*, February 20, 1979, p. 2.)

On October 23, 1981, a defense attorney, John T. Spinale, told a jury in Brockton, Massachusetts that his client James P. Riva II had "shot his grandmother twice and sucked the blood out of the bullet holes because he believed a vampire told him that was what he had to do." Spinale claimed that his client "felt he needed human and animal blood." The assistant district attorney Henry A. Cashman objected to the introduction of vampirism as a defense plea, but Judge Peter F. Brady allowed the defense attorney to pursue his pleadings. The defendant's mother, Janet Jones, had already testified at a probable cause hearing held in 1980 that her son believed he himself had been a vampire for four years and needed blood for sustenance. During the trial Dr. Robert Moore testified that James Riva had killed a cat in 1978 and had drunk its blood. He had also hit a horse on the head with a fence post and then had drunk its blood mixed with crackers. The jury found the defendant guilty of murder. In earlier centuries, as we have seen, the charge of vampirism has been used by the prosecution. The 1981 Brockton, Massachusetts case may be one of the first in which "vampirism" was used as a defense! (Of course, the contemporary assumption is that if one acts like a vampire, one must be clinically insane.)

Though some contemporary judges allow vampirism as a defense pleading, the courts up to now have resisted any pleadings based upon "diabolical possession," one of the common rumors about Elizabeth Bathory and others. The work done by Dr. Robert S. McCully at the University of South Carolina provides information that puts this Riva case in some historical perspective. In *Rorschack Theory and Symbolism*, Dr. McCully reported on his study of another youth who had killed his mother and sister, and in "The Laugh of Satan; A Study of Familial Murder," he looked at the case of a teenage murderer who killed his mother, tiny half-brother and his stepfather. This latter subject was an eighteen-year-old single white male. His parents divorced when he was one year old. After the divorce the boy and his mother lived with his maternal grandmother. When he was eight years old, his mother married again. The boy recalled that his stepfather, who was subject to sleepwalking, one night came into his stepson's room, apparently mistaking it for the bathroom, and then got into bed with his stepson. His mother divorced this man when the boy was twelve. About a year later his mother married his second stepfather. After the boy began skipping school, he was sent off to live with his grandmother in another city. When the subject was fifteen, his mother bore a son by her third husband. The boy then got interested in Nazi ideology and bought some Nazi guns. While living with his grandmother, he tyrannized her.

A month before the actual murders, he felt the urge to kill his mother and stepfather, and their new child. A few days later he had plastic surgery done on his ears, which, he felt, protruded too much. He may have done this to make himself less identifiable by police in the future. (George McMillan states in his biography of James Earl Ray that Ray had his nose changed shortly before his assasination of Martin Luther King to avoid easy police identification.)

On the evening before Thanksgiving the boy went from his grandmother's house to his mother's place in another town.

His stepfather, half-brother and mother were all at home. As his stepfather sat with his son on his lap, watching television, the boy shot them both and then killed his mother as she came out of the bathroom. After that, he said, he heard "the laugh of Satan" ringing in his ears. In the past, as in the case of Elizabeth Bathory, excessive evil was generally credited to satanic influence.

In the modern judicial world there are limits. During a much-publicized murder trial held in Danbury, Connecticut, the defendant's attorney on October 28, 1981, tried to plead that his client was "possessed by the devil" when he fatally stabbed his landlord, Alan Bono. Defense attorney Martin J. Minelli sought to demonstrate that "there is such a thing as demonic possession." Unfortunately, before the trial he had boasted to reporters that "the devil, in fact, is going to be on trial in this particular case." Judge Robert Callahan refused to allow such a plea on the basis that one could not actually prove demonic possession. In Elizabeth Bathory's day vampirism, werewolfism, and demonic possession were believed in and were acceptable accusations. Not so today. One cannot plead in court, as many might wish, that "the devil made me do it."

The devil is blamed, because he is the first rebel against authority, Lucifer, who was "like unto God" but defied God and became the arch criminal. It is not the angelic part, but the human, defiant aspect of Satan that interests us. This is because most of us are like Stevenson's Dr. Jekyll and Mr. Hyde where goodness and evil are but two aspects of the same person. It is this basic recognition of an evil tendency within each of us that is truly frightening. The monster is often but a distorted image of elements buried within each of us, which we hope will never come to light. That is one reason why many people are sometimes literally frightened by their own faces. The German philosopher Nietzsche wrote in his *Also Sprach Zarathustra* (the inspiration for the movie *2001*): "But then I looked in a mirror, I gave a cry and my heart shook, for it was not myself I saw but the grimacing face of a demon." It is the devil *within* who is most feared. Heinrich Heine pointed out in his *Harzreise*: "Nothing can frighten us more than chancing to see our face in the mirror by moonlight."

Many primitive peoples have a fear of mirror images. It seems to some as if there is a mysterious life in the mirror which imitates human life. One risks getting caught up and lost in the mirror life. In Transylvanian homes and in those of certain Orthodox Jews throughout the world, when a person dies, the mirrors are covered with cloth. Since it is assumed that the human soul remains around for a time after formal death, the soul could get trapped in the mirror life and never find eternal rest. Following in a similar line of thought, it is believed that a vampire casts no reflection in a mirror, because the vampire is an "undead" without a real human soul.

This primitive fear of the "double" is not dead in modern society. For example, a recent TV commercial in the United States showed a man looking in a mirror in which the image opposite him comes alive, saying "Hi, guy," as the human eventually screams for his wife in order to establish normality. This fear is connected with that of the alter ego, the double or *doppelgänger*, a person like oneself, but usually representing an aspect of the self which is either hidden, ignored, repressed, or denied. Science has made it a technical possibility grafted from one's self through the popular new alchemy, genetic engineering. Gene therapy may be able to correct birth defects resulting from such things as hereditary blood diseases, but many people question whether we really wish to replace the random workings of nature with the purposeful interests of the human will. Too many recall how the eugenics of the late 1920s and 1930s in Germany led to the macabre Nazi experiments in concentration camps during the 1940s.

Edgar Allen Poe in "William Wilson" described the fate of a man who had been tormented since childhood by the presence of his double who had intimate knowledge of the seamy aspects of his own life. In fact, this double tries to prevent the participation in any further vices by William Wilson. In the end Wilson, unable to endure the strain, destroys his double and kills himself.

Allied with this fear of the double is the frightening notion that certain night creatures, such as vampires and demons, are capable of sex and hence of procreation. In the historical records there are even questions concerning the rights of the children coming from such liaisons. An example from the Eastern European Jewish heritage is instructive in this regard. In the city of Posen in 1681 demons possessed an old stone house. The local Jesuits proved unable to drive out the demons, so Rabbi Joel of Zamosz, a noted miracle worker, was called in by the local populace. Rabbi Joel was also unable to dislodge the demons, but at least he got them to admit who they were and what they wanted. The demons claimed a legal right to the property in question and wanted to defend their right in a court of law. Rabbi Joel agreed to arrange for a formal law trial. In court, the demon lawyer, who could be heard but not seen, argued that the former owner of the house had engaged in an illicit affair with a demon who had borne him children who then lived in the cellar of the house, granted to them by the home owner who had subsequently died. The demon lawyer concluded that, since the home owner and his human descendants had all died, the demon descendants were the rightful surviving heirs to the property. The lawyer of the new human owners of the property countered that the mother of the demons had forced herself upon the former owner against his will. Besides, he argued, demons were not entitled to the same legal rights as humans in such property matters. Having seriously weighed all the arguments, the court duly decided against the demons and issued a formal statement that the lawful abode of demons was certainly not in the property of humans but in deserts and wastelands.

During the Russian Revolution in Russia a blood-drinking Russian baron, Roman von Sternberg-Ungem, believed himself to be the reincarnation of Genghis Khan and proceeded to engage in drinking human blood. The Bolsheviks eventually caught up with him, and he was tried and executed in 1920.

On April 18, 1959, the Associated Press carried the story that a girl named Angela Papas was burned at the stake for vampirism in a small Greek fishing village. Angela claimed that an "undead" had attacked her and that she had acquired a blood lust after that. She infected young Angelo Gregor with this affliction, so that he in turn sought out victims of his own. Angelo was caught in a young wife's bedroom by her husband. The villagers, enraged that Angela Papas had brought the vampire plague to their village, seized her and had her tied to the stake and set on fire.

Dr. Robert McCully from the department of psychology and the medical school at the University of South Carolina has reported in an article in *The Journal of Nervous and Mental Diseases* entitled "Vampirism: Historical Perspective and Underlying Process in Relation to a Case of Auto-Vampirism," the following bizarre case:

The patient was a young adult, white, male, and unmarried. Masturbation began at age eleven and "became associated with drawing his own blood and a compulsion to see it." He achieved this by puncturing his neck veins, and by performing the Valsalva maneuver, he could make his blood pour rapidly while watching it in a mirror. In time he learned to get arterial blood from his neck by using a broken razor to puncture first a small artery and later the common carotid artery. He discovered that if he lay down on his back, he could catch the spray of blood easily in his mouth and drink it. Sometimes he had to gather the liquid in a cup. Later on, he found out how to puncture a vein in his arm and suck the blood from it directly. Masturbation began after having started the bloodletting and resulted in ejaculation. This effect he accomplished by fantasies of taking blood from some "young, smooth, hairless boy with prominent neck arteries" (p. 141).

*The London Times* of July 31, 1969, reported that an elderly barber from Medan, North Sumatra, was charged with having behaved like a vampire. In court it was alleged that he had sucked the blood of two babies. A very recent case of a living vampire is the following: A girl in North America who called herself simply "Lillith" (a reference to the old legend that Adam had had another wife before Eve) met a young man in a cemetery who tried to kiss her. (What she was doing in the cemetery in the first place was not made clear.) She plunged her teeth into the neck of this young man with such an "unnatural surge of strength" that she tasted blood and became a blood addict. She stated that "I never considered myself a Dracula, but only someone who liked the taste of blood." In another contemporary case involving a living vampire, a young man crept into his sister's bedroom while she was asleep, gently pricked her on the leg and sucked her blood. He found that he liked the taste and "could feel himself getting stronger as he drained her."

Among the Bathory family, like many aristocratic families especially in Eastern and Central Europe during the Middle Ages and Early Modern Times, constant intermarriage led to a plethora of similar genetic disorders, which are documented. These nobles, afflicted with various genetic illnesses, were often specifically ordered by their doctors to drink healthy human blood in order to replace what they had lost. The nobles took the blood from their servants and peasants. This medical treatment fed into all sorts of rumors about aristocrats sucking the blood from the lower class people, like vampires. Having looked at some of the ancient and relatively modern religious concepts of vampirism, and having examined some case histories of "living vampires," let us turn to the werewolf.

Carol Borland as Luna, the "vampire girl," in Tod
Browning's movie *Mark of the Vampire* (*MGM, 1935*),
a remake of the silent movie *London After Midnight*
(1927).

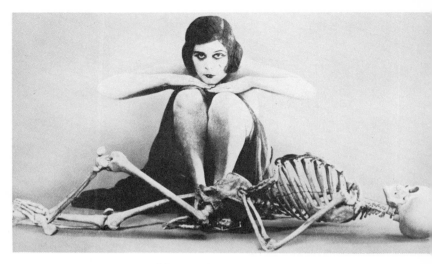

A publicity photograph of Theda Bara, the first screen vamp, hunching over a male skeleton. She was not a bloodsucking vampire, but devoured her male victims figuratively—a movie version of the voluptuous *femme fatale.*

Christopher Lee as Count Dracula being impaled upon the spokes of a carriage wheel in the British movie *Dracula A.D. 1972,* also titled *Dracula Today,* directed by Alan Gibson (*Hammer Productions, England, 1971*).

Christopher Lee in DRACULA A.D. (1972)

A victim of a vampire's attack from the British Hammer Productions film *The Vampire Lovers* (1970), directed by Roy Ward Baker.

The three female vampires in Count Dracula's harem lean over the fallen body of Jonathan Harker, eager to bite him, in Tod Browning's famous *Dracula* (*Universal, United States, 1931*).

The dead, decaying daughter of Dr. Van Helsing reaches out to beg for a kiss from her father in John Badham's movie *Dracula* (*Universal, USA, 1979*), starring Frank Langella as Count Dracula and Sir Laurence Olivier as Dr. Van Helsing.

A female vampire on the attack in the British Hammer Production *The Vampire Lovers*, (1970), directed by Roy Ward Baker.

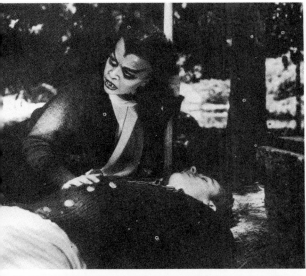

Actress Sandra Harrison as a teenage vampire on campus. Under the influence of her college science instructor, Harrison sprouts fangs and assumes a devil-like face. From American International Pictures *Blood of Dracula* (1957), also entitled *Blood Is My Heritage*, directed by Herbert L. Strock.

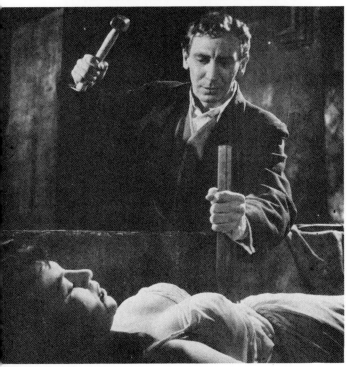

Actor John Van Eyssen, portraying Jonathan Harker, the vampire-killer, raises his mallet to drive a stake through the heart of a young, buxom vampire, played by Valerie Gaunt in the British movie *Horror of Dracula* (*Hammer Productions, England, 1958*), directed by the late Terence Fisher.

British actress Ingrid Pitt portraying Countess Elizabeth Bathory being admired by one of her elder female servants in the British Hammer Productions movie *Countess Dracula* (1972), directed by Peter Sasdy.

Ingrid Pitt as Countess Bathory, blocking the door to prevent her lover from leaving, in *Countess Dracula*.

A still from Hammer's *Countess Dracula*, showing the procurement of girls for Countess Bathory (1972).

An aged Elizabeth Bathory clutching a knife and readying herself for the kill in *Countess Dracula*.

The veiled, old Countess Bathory with her male cohort and female accomplices as depicted in *Countess Dracula*.

Two vampire girls equipped with the requisite fangs watch the struggle between Baron Meinster, the vampire, and Dr. Van Helsing in Hammer Productions' *The Brides of Dracula* (1960).

A female vampire, held fast by churchmen, struggles to be free in the British Hammer Productions movie *Dracula, Prince of Darkness* (1965), also titled *Blood for Dracula*, directed by the late Terence Fisher.

Illustrations from a sixteenth-century pamphlet entitled *The Life and Death of Peter Stubb* depicting the stages of Stubb's life, from werewolf to horrible torture and execution. Peter Stubb claimed that he possessed a magic belt that changed him into a wolf. (The belt was never found.)

The German sixteenth-century artist Lucas Cranach depicted this lycanthrope biting a baby, surrounded by the dismembered parts of human corpses. This werewolf has not assumed the physical attributes of a wolf, but only the creature's predatory be-

ABOVE LEFT: A man with a medical ailment, known as hirsutism, in which excessive quantities of hair grow on the face and body. ABOVE RIGHT: Movie make-up producing a similar effect on Michael Landon in American International Pictures *I Was a Teenage Werewolf* (1957).

The gradual application of make-up by master cosmetician Jack Pierce to actor Henry Hull, transforming him from human into werewolf for the Universal movie *The Werewolf of London* (1935).

 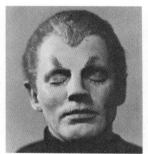 

# 9

# *The Werewolf: Mirror, Mirror on the Wall . . .*

DURING the first official trial of Elizabeth Bathory on January 2, 1611, her young manservant Ficzko declared on the stand that the Countess kept by her side "a mirror enclosed in a pretzel-shaped frame" and that "supporting her head with her arms, she would gaze into the mirror for over two hours at a stretch." The Countess also reputedly made incantations to the mirror. The reader who recalls fairy tales from childhood will at once recognize the similarity between Elizabeth's practices and those of the Wicked Queen in the famous story of Snow White, who addressed the spirit in the mirror with the incantation: "Mirror, mirror on the wall! Who is the Fairest One of All?"

*Snow White* is one of the most popular fairy tales; it exists in hundreds of versions in many countries. As in the case of Elizabeth Bathory the myth is as important as the shadowy reflections of history. Everyone remembers that the Wicked Queen, jealous of Snow White's beauty, hated her so much that she tried to have Snow White killed. But how many readers recall that the queen wanted Snow White dead so that she could eat Snow White's insides and *thereby assimilate* her beauty?

The queen, who is fixated on a level of primitive self-adoration, and is also arrested at the "oral stage of sexuality," cannot tolerate seeing young girls develop into lovely women. She orders the hunter not only to murder Snow White, but to return with her lungs and liver. When the hunter brings back the lungs and liver of an animal to "prove" that he had executed the queen's command, "The cook had to cook them in salt," according to the unexpurgated version in the Grimm Brothers Collection, "and the evil woman ate them and thought thereby that she had eaten Snow White's lungs and liver." The queen was trying to incorporate Snow White's beauty and attractiveness; afterward the queen turns to her mirror with the same question, hoping that she will be the fairest one of all—only to discover that Snow White is still alive.

The notion that a human being would kill and eat the remains of another is a difficult one for most of us to deal with. But it is not merely a "notion": some adults today do it, actually or symbolically. As Bruno Bettleheim puts it in his provocative chapter "The Jealous Queen in Snow White" in *The Uses of Enchantment*: "We do not know why the queen in *Snow White* cannot age gracefully and gain satisfaction from vicariously enjoying her daughter's blooming into a lovely girl, but something must have happened in her past to make her vulnerable, so that she hates the child she should love" (p. 195). He offers a likely clue: some women show love for their children as long as they are young and dependent, because the children are a part or extension of the parent. But when the child begins to grow up and reach for mature independence, then such a parent feels threatened; it is a sign that the parent, like the Wicked Queen, is aging. I postulate that this fear of aging is in large measure the underlying psychodynamic of Elizabeth Bathory's treatment of the women in her service.

The hatred of the queen is so strong and deep that even after failing to kill Snow White several times, she reaches out again and again in the story to eliminate the younger woman. Temporary reversals only serve to heighten her fervor. After two temptations by the disguised queen, Snow White succumbs to eating the apple. The queen cuts the apple in half and gives the red, "poisonous" part to Snow White. Snow White eats it and sinks into a passive, languid state. She is not really dead;

her body does not decay. Lying in her transparent glass coffin above ground she only appears to be dead. As her Prince Charming is carrying her coffin off, she coughs up the poisonous apple and returns to life. The Wicked Queen is forced to wear red-hot shoes in which she must dance until she dies. The reader applauds the "happy ending." Unfortunately in real life such sexual jealousy of older women and mothers towards younger girls and even children often ends in ruinous destruction for the girls, as the Bathory case demonstrates. According to the court testimony, Elizabeth Bathory bit parts of the girls' bodies whom she was having killed. Thus, Elizabeth became popularly known in her lifetime as a werewolf, not just a vampire. The notion of an ordinary person being so in the thrall of oral desire as to rend flesh could not be tolerated by the common people. She had to be seen as another other-than-human phenomenon, the werewolf.

According to the available evidence, Elizabeth Bathory presumably received some of her sexual gratification by biting her female servants. The act of biting usually has erotic significance. Some people like to bite their sexual partners while making love, and provided that one does not bite too deeply, this is not considered to be terribly pathological. In fact, bite marks are often displayed with pride by teenagers as evidence of the passion from the night before. In his classic study of sexual psychopatholgy Krafft-Ebing recorded the case of a man treated for severe bites in his pectoral muscles, inflicted by a woman in a state of extreme sexual excitement during copulation.

The kiss and the love bite are mild expressions of the unconscious urge to devour the beloved. Think carefully about the common terms of affection; most of them are about things considered good to eat—"Honey," "Sweetie," "Sugar," etc. When fussing over children, adults often exclaim "Oh, you're so sweet, I could just eat you up!" Such remarks bring to light things which most people feel had better remain hidden. The folkloric concept of the werewolf allows humans to deal with taboos, such as the biting of other human beings.

In many parts of southeastern Europe it is believed that any person who bit and ate human flesh in life would become a vampire upon death. The two concepts are linked together often in folklore. The werewolf bites human flesh, and the vampire drinks human blood. Both are predators. Both acts are condemned by most world religions as taboo. The deep, social reasons for such condemnations are relatively clear: both practices are considered basically to be antisocial. If one were to allow such activities to go on, then obviously some person's flesh would have to be eaten and someone's blood drunk. Who would choose which human was to be sacrificed for the rest? Yet, it is still a truism that in nature, life feeds on life.

It appears that human beings have no instinctual aversion to chewing human flesh. It is a learned taboo which has become so widespread that most contemporary people shudder at the very thought. One need only think of those South American Catholic athletes wrecked in an airplane accident high in the inaccessible Andes Mountains who had such terrible pangs of conscience when, forced by circumstances, they chewed on the flesh of their dead comrades. Human flesh can be as tasty and nourishing as animal flesh (although reports from some cannibal tribes indicate that they prefer not to eat the flesh of twentieth-century man, evidently because all that junk food which modern men eat has ruined the taste).

Some years ago a missionary living with an African tribe had an unfamiliar dish set before him. Not wishing to appear impolite he began eating the meat which reminded him a little of pork, a little on the tough side but otherwise tasty. After a length of time which he considered proper, he casually asked his hosts what the meat was. He was calmly informed: "Roast young man."

The word "werewolf" (alternate spelling "werwolf") evidently came into English via Germanic Anglo-Saxon roots. The term *wer* meant "man" (like the Latin *vir*), linked with "wolf," hence the literal meaning, "manwolf" translated into English as "wolfman." The notion of changing from human to animal form is very old and is found in many cultures. (In fact, it may indicate that primitive man may have had a vague notion of evolution long before Darwin. Since humans came from animals, why not a possible reversion to beastlike behavior?)

According to legend, a person can inadvertently become a werewolf by being bitten or scratched by another werewolf, or even by eating the flesh of an animal previously killed by a werewolf. However, if one chooses to become a werewolf, one can do so by removing one's clothing and putting on the skin of a wolf. One of the main ideas behind many of such tales is that one becomes what one ingests—man is what he eats.

One of the reasons why people connected eating human flesh with a reversion to animal form was probably based upon man's fascination with animals themselves. Tribes or clans revered their totemic animals: in ceremonies they dressed up like their totemic animals and for a time "became" that animal. Ancient Egyptians, worshipped crocodiles in order to placate them, as they did many other terrifying animals, some of them halfway between human and animal. Lionesses were connected with savage heat and desert winds, the symbols of plagues and pestilences, so the Egyptians associated them with Sekmet, the patron god of doctors. The jackal which scavenged graves and devoured corpses was especially feared by the Egyptians who above all wanted their bodies to remain intact after death (only thus could one attain immortality). So, Anubis, protector of the dead, had the head of the jackal.

In ancient Greece and Rome, a belief in a number of werewolflike creatures was prevalent. Pliny, Herodotus, and Virgil were all familiar with these phenomena. Horace in his *Ars Poetica* asserted that night creatures (called *lamiae* by the Greeks and *striges* or *mormos* by the Romans) ate children alive and drank their blood (Neu pransae lamiae vivum puerum extrabat alvo). Ovid wrote that *striges* often took the form of huge birds "which fly about at night, suck the blood of children and devour their bodies."

Herodotus wrote in volume 1 of his *History* about the Massagetes, who considered only the eldest members of their family and oldest friends worth eating: "They do not lay down any term for human life, but when the Massagete is very old, all his relatives get together and immolate him, and after cooking his flesh, they eat it. This form of death is considered the happiest; if, however, someone dies of illness, they do not eat his flesh but bury it, since they consider anyone unfortunate who has not lived long enough to reach the age of immolation" (p. 216).

Today the name Arcadia or Arcady summons up pleasing visions of the bucolic life—rolling green pastures with roaming flocks of gentle sheep. But in the times of ancient Greece, Arcadia was a place where wolves ravaged sheep and violent human sacrifices were made to the gods; the Greeks considered these Arcadians to be cannibals as well.

According to the Roman poet Ovid, Zeus, king of the gods, heard rumors about the evil being done in Arcadia, especially by its king Lycaon. Zeus went to earth to investigate and found the rumors to be true. He went to Lycaon's palace and let it be known that he was a god. Lycaon decided to see if it were true. Lycaon served up human flesh to Zeus, who flew into a rage and changed Lycaon into a wolf, except for his eyes which stayed human. After that a cult developed among the Arcadians: every nine years, a festival was held, at which a certain family had to choose one of their members to be a "wolf" until the next festival.

Saint Patrick reputedly changed the king of Wales, Veretricius, into a wolf by divine power, and Saint Thomas Aquinas claimed that "all good and bad angels have the ability to transform our bodies by some natural virtues" (Omnes angeli, boni et mali, ex virtute naturalis habent potestam transmutandi corpora nostra).

Transformation of man into beast and back again is very common in folklore and fairy tales. The prince who had been transformed into a frog turns back into human form; the wolf in *Little Red Riding Hood* speaks and acts like a human. Among the American Indians it was known as "shape-shifting."

It was thought that the effects from the light of the full moon served to turn a person into a wolflike creature. The wolfbane plant itself was rumored to bloom only during the full moon and to be the only cure for werewolfism and lycanthropy. Actually there are two plants known commonly as wolfbane. The more familiar is *Aconitum napellus*, sometimes also called monkshood, a very poisonous plant which grows in mountainous regions of Europe and Asia. Its main ingredient, aconite, severely lowers blood pressure and blood circulation. Painful death occurs in a few hours. The second wolfbane refers to plants of the genus *Arnica*, from whose flowering parts a drug causing violent intestinal pains is produced. Hence its use is primarily external, as a salve for wounds, though it can also cause blistering and inflammation.

Holy Roman Emperor Sigismund (1368–1437), who became king of Hungary and Bohemia in 1433, was so concerned about the presence of werewolfism in his lands that he ordered it to be studied by a council of learned theologians. After lengthy debate and discussion, these theologians unanimously decreed that anyone who dared to deny the fact that a human being could transform himself into a wolf should be found guilty of heresy, a sentence carrying the maximum penalty, death at the stake.

There is an important difference between the legendary werewolf and the lycanthrope. Lycanthropy refers specifically to a disease whereby a person *thinks* that he or she has become wolflike. A physician called Marcellus of Sida who lived from about 117 to 161 A.D. was one of the first to analyze the illness which he termed "lycanthropy." He described in detail how such afflicted patients frequented the tombs of Athens at night, and how they had a yellow complexion, hollow eyes and a dry tongue. The physician to Emperor Julian, Oribas, added the notion that their legs were covered with sores. Gradually there emerged a picture of a man, woman, or child with very pale, green- or yellow-tinted skin, and numerous skin lesions, a red mouth, and unsteady eyes. Occasionally all this was also accompanied by hirsutism (the excessive growth of body hair).

Even today the Toradja natives of the Celebes in the Dutch East Indies describe their lycanthropes as having unsteady eyes with dark green shadows around them. They do not sleep soundly. Their teeth remain reddish in spite of chewing betel nuts.

Avicenna, the eminent medieval philosopher and physician,

wrote about the lycanthropy syndrome, in which afflicted persons would run howling into graveyards at night and could not be persuaded that they were really not wolves. The illustrious commentator on the texts of Aristotle also noted that this illness was very prevalent in Hungary and Bohemia.

In most of Europe the most ferocious animal around was generally the wolf. In Russia as late as the winter of 1815 some 160 people were attacked by starving wolves. So it is easy to see why a human who ate human flesh was thought to have changed into a wolf (though in southern parts of the world one hears of were-tigers, and among the Gabons of Africa were-leopards, and in northern Europe were-bears and were-reindeers).

During the ninth century Viking invaders often dressed up in bearskins or bear shirts. This gave birth to the term "berserker," meaning someone who acted like a wild beast. These Vikings evidently believed that in donning bear skin they would acquire the strength of the bear. Reputedly they fought with the crazed courage of a wounded animal. There is now some evidence that the Norsemen ate a substance which made them hallucinate, a derivative of ergot, a rye mold related to LSD. This would certainly have made it easy to believe oneself a bear, a wolf, or some other animal. According to the legends women and men alike could become lycanthropes. Armenian and Ethiopian stories describe women who were so afflicted. In one Ethiopian tale a woman went into a trance, her fingers clenched, her eyes glazed, and nostrils distended. When she came to she laughed hideously and began to run around on all fours. So she was thought to be a werewolf and the local exorcist was called in to cure her. He held garlic up to her nose and tried to question the evil spirits who, he presumed, were within her.

Giraldus Cambrensis in his twelfth-century chronicle *Topographica Hibernica* writes about a case of lycanthropy in Ireland. During the sixth century in the ancient kingdom of Ossory the local abbot Natalis, who was later proclaimed a saint, condemned the people there because of their wicked behavior. According to the abbot's curse, two persons of the region had to become wolves every seven years. If they survived, they would be permitted to resume normal human lives—but two others from the region then had to carry on the tradition. Giraldus Cambrensis concludes his narrative with the following perceptive comment:

> We hold then with Saint Augustine that neither demons nor sorcerers can create or essentially change their natures, but those whom God created are able with His permission to change themselves so far as mere outward appearance is concerned, so that they appear to be really what they are not, and human senses of beholding them are fascinated and deceived by their glamour, so that things are not seen as they exist, but the human vision is deluded and masked by some phantom power or magic spell, since it rests upon unreal and fictitious forms.

The most famous German lycanthrope was Peter Stubb or Stump who was tried and found guilty in Cologne in 1589. Under torture he claimed that a magic belt enabled him to become a wolf. The judges ordered that "his body be laid on a wheel, and with red-hot burning pincers in ten separate places the flesh be torn from the bones, after that, his legs and arms to be broken with a wooden axe or hatchet; afterwards to have his head struck from his body; then to have his carcass burned to ashes."

In 1558 in the Auvergne section of France a hunter in the forest met a neighboring noble who asked him to bring him some game. A savage wolf later attacked this hunter; he drove the beast off by severing one of its paws. He put the paw in his knapsack as a souvenir of the fight. On his way home the hunter stopped off at the noble's chauteau and told about his encounter. But when he reached into his pouch he found not a wolf's paw but a delicate female hand. The noble recognized the gold ring on one of the fingers. Dashing upstairs he surprised his wife bandaging the bleeding stump of her wrist. She confessed to being a werewolf and was burned at the stake.

On September 13, 1573, after several children had been found killed or partially eaten, local authorities in the French town of Dole organized a werewolf hunt. A stooping, bushy-browed hermit named Gilles Garnier confessed to werewolfism. He was burned alive on January 18, 1574.

In 1598 an entire family of werewolves was recorded in western France. Two sisters, their brother, and their son were known as "the Werewolves of St. Claude." One of the girls named Peronette suffered from lycanthropic hysteria and ran about on all fours. The entire family was burned to death.

In France, the *loup-garou*, the French name for a lycanthrope, flourished as early as the sixth century and was later brought to the New World by French emigrants. Sixteenth-century Judge Boguet recounts the story of a farmer's wife who thought she had changed into a wolf and attacked a neighbor. During the ensuing struggle the "wolf" lost a paw, and when she changed back into a woman, one of her hands was missing. This sixteenth century account is virtually identical to the 1558 Auvergne story which I cited earlier in this book—except that one is a noble and the other a farmer. They are no doubt the same story; and the first one is probably a folkloric distortion of the original tale cited here. Boguet also describes lycanthropes as having a pale skin; one such creature, he writes, was so disfigured as to be scarcely recognizable as a human being.

The most popular story concerning human flesh-eaters is that of *Sweeney Todd*, the subject of a long-running Broadway musical. The nineteenth-century novelist of numerous "penny dreadfuls," Thomas Preskett Prest, wrote his popular original novel based on an actual historical case. In 1843 John Nicolson of Kircudbright, Scotland, had detailed the horrific circumstances in his book *Historical and Traditional Tales Connected with the South of Scotland.*

It seems that a man named Sawney Beane, born in East Lothian not far from Edinburgh, grew up to be a lazy, vicious youth and ran away with "an idle and profligate woman." Together in a cave by the North Sea in Galloway, along with fourteen children and thirty-two nieces and nephews, they eventually formed the infamous "Bean Clan" who captured travelers and survived on eating their flesh. Finally the community was aroused and a raiding party was sent out. When the Bean Clan was finally smoked out of their lair, not only were piles of bones found in their cave but also a huge store of parts of human bodies. Some parts were pickled in brine, others dried out and hung up like beef. The Bean Clan were taken prisoner and transported to Edinburgh, where they were all executed in the year 1435. In Thomas Preskett Prest's novel the hero, Sweeney Todd, after killing his victims, cut up their bodies and sold the meat to a Mrs. Lovett, the owner of a local meat-pie shop. The quintessential irony: one day when they ran out of human meat and had to use real mutton for a change, all of Mrs. Lovett's customers complained that the meat pies were less tasty than usual.

Jonathan Swift's satirical *Modest Proposal* in 1729 "for preventing the children of poor people in Ireland from being a burden to their parents or country, and for making them beneficial to the public" asserted that "I have been assured by a very knowing American of my acquaintance in London, that a young healthy child well nursed is a most delicious, nourishing and wholesome food, either stewed, roasted, baked or boiled; and I make no doubt that it will equally serve in a fricasse or a ragout."

Around 1850 a beggar named Swiatek appeared regularly in a small village in Austria. Children mysteriously disappeared from the village. One day a local innkeeper noticed that some of his ducks were missing. He suspected the beggar Swiatek and went his to cottage. There the innkeeper smelled meat cooking. But when Swiatek saw him, he hid something under his clothes. The innkeeper, thinking that it was one of his ducks, grabbed Swiatek and wrestled with him until the hidden object rolled out onto the ground. It was not a duck but the head of a young girl. Swiatek was taken prisoner and confessed that he had killed and eaten six people. He explained that he had acquired the taste for human flesh when, after a tavern had burned down with people inside, he had eaten the partly roasted flesh. After that he craved human meat above all else. Swiatek hanged himself in his jail cell before his trial could take place.

A French wine grower named Antoine Leger, twenty-four years of age, met a little girl in the forest (shades of Little Red Riding Hood), grabbed her, raped her, tore out her heart, which was dripping with blood, and ate it. During his subsequent trial at Versailles he was asked by the judge, "What did you want to do with this little girl?"; his straightforward reply was "Eat her, Your Honor." The judge then asked, "And why did you drink her blood?", to which Antoine Leger replied: "I was thirsty, Your Honor."

In the work *Observations Medicales* (vol. 4), a physician named Dr. Schenk describes the case of a woman who upon seeing a baker carrying loaves on his shoulder was seized with the urge to bite his shoulders. Her husband persuaded the baker with a large sum of money to allow his wife to bite him. She proceeded to dig her teeth into his flesh twice until he could not stand it any more.

The railroad man Joseph Vacher killed and mutilated eleven victims of both sexes and chewed especially their sexual organs. His short but terrible career began when he was twenty-five and lasted until he was captured three years later; he was tried and executed at Bourg on July 31, 1898.

The tall, hefty, red-bearded John "Liver-Eating" Johnson, an American trapper and Civil War veteran, liked to hunt alone. In 1847 he married a Flathead Indian woman. After seeing her well provided for, he left on a trapping expedition. He did not know that she was pregnant. When he returned in the spring he found the clean-picked bones of his wife and the skull of his newborn infant. A feather laying nearby told him that the killers had been Crow Indians. He declared a private war that would lead to the deaths of some three hundred Crow braves. Whenever he killed a Crow Indian he would slash the dead Indian's chest open with his Bowie knife, take out the still warm liver and eat it raw. "Liver-Eating" Johnson was apparently not averse to eating other parts of the human body. In 1861 the Blackfeet captured him with the intention of selling him to the Crows. He escaped, and amputating the left leg of one of his Blackfoot captors, he took the leg along for food. Ultimately he made his peace with the Crows. (In December 1899 he entered veterans hospital in Los Angeles, California, and the seasoned Liver-Eater died of old age in 1900.)

At full moon one summer night in Rome in 1949 police heard

wolflike howls from a clump of bushes. The police discovered a man digging furiously in the mud like an animal. When taken to the hospital the man explained that for years when the moon was full, he felt these uncontrollable yearnings.

Some people are able to sublimate their oral aggression into a socially acceptable form. For example, a Japanese dentist named Masayuki Sebata wrote his doctoral thesis in 1961 on the subject of the "bite." Dr. Sebata specifically selected certain women from among a hundred patients between twenty-one and thirty-six years of age, whom he himself then bit on the shoulders, necks, and arms each morning for an entire year. The good doctor scrupulously recorded his bites and photographed them—all in the cause of science, of course.

Eating human flesh is not a thing of the past. As recently as 1961 in Detroit, Michigan, one cold January night a twenty-one-year-old man accosted a girl, beat her, strangled her to death, raped her dead body—and then took out his cigarette lighter and calmly roasted parts of her body which he then tore, bit, gnawed, and ate.

The Austrian psychoanalyst Karl Abraham traced such lycanthropy back to a basic cannibalistic wish-fantasy in all humans. To illustrate his theory he turned to mythology where he found tales of anthropomorphic gods devouring their children. He felt that these stories represented the unconscious desires of the people who created them. In Greek mythology Titans ruled the earth before the Olympian gods. The ruler of the Titans, Kronos (Saturn in the Roman version), heard a prophecy that he would be dethroned by one of his children. So he made it a practice to eat each of his offspring as soon as they were born. (Goya has immortalized the powerful myth in his famous painting "Kronos Devouring his Children.")

In fact, in some societies cannibalism was not relegated to the gods but was part of religious ritual: Among the Khond (a Dravidian tribe then living in what is now Bengal), during their periodic fertility ceremony, the body of the sacrificial victim was tied to the trunk of a revolving wooden elephant. As the elephant turned, each member of the tribe dutifully helped himself to a slice of human meat.

Raw meat, whether human or animal, is not regarded with indifference by most humans. Either you like it or you abhor it. Some like their meat as rare as steak tartare. Others make supreme efforts to cook out any red or pink traces of the meat they eat. They want it well-done. Few of them can eat it bloody. The meat is chopped and filleted, so that it is unrecognizable and disguised; so that there is little hint that it was once part of a living, breathing organic creature.

Out of all the literature on lycanthropes there emerges a general composite picture. All the sources agree that they prefer to move at night rather than during the daylight hours. There is also common agreement that their skin has a strange yellowish, pinkish, greenish, or very pale tint to it with many scars and abrasions. Occasionally they are also depicted as very hairy.

When a belief is as widespread as this one, and especially when the stories seem to have similar features, one searches for some underlying reality-based explanation. One particular theory suggests that "werewolfism" has a medical underpinning. A disease now diagnosed as erythropoietic (congenital) porphyria can produce the symptoms universally attributed to werewolves. This porphyria is a relatively rare disease, caused by a recessive gene, in which the patient produces too much porphyrin in the bone marrow, a substance basic to red blood cells.

Such afflicted people shun sunlight because exposure can sometimes cause skin lesions. Their eyes are extremely photosensitive, and they cannot endure being in the light, especially during the summer or in mountainous regions. Over the years the skin lesions can develop into mutilated areas, especially the nose, ears, eyelids, hands, and fingers. The teeth become reddish or reddish brown because of the deposit of porphyrins.

The earliest symptom of this disease is often what is described as a burning sensation in their skin. Itching and swelling of the skin results. Some patients find that they can endure only a few minutes in the sun; others can tolerate up to several hours.

Nervous disorders ranging from mild hysteria to manic-depressive psychosis to delirium and to epilepsy sometimes accompany the disease. In former times healthy, ordinary people probably reacted so negatively to such afflicted patients that they increased the incidence of severe mental disorders among such patients.

In today's world, such patients tend to choose indoor occupations or night work. When they do go outside, they wear sunglasses and heavy clothing in order to protect them from the light.

One can fairly easily imagine that someone afflicted with porphyria, half-crazed by the accompanying nervous disorders made worse by other people's reactions, would seek the relative safety and tranquility of a nice dark cave deep in the woods. On occasion, starved by lack of small game, he might even kill an unwary child or peasant. Certainly the disappearance of any local villagers would be attributed to such a person. This could be some of the "reality" behind the werewolf legends of folklore.

# 10

## The Sleeping Beauty Syndrome and The Necrophile

THE fact that Elizabeth Bathory sometimes kept the bodies of the girls she had killed around for a good while after their deaths led to the legend that, in addition to being a vampire and a werewolf, she was also what would be termed a necrophile today, i.e., someone with an abnormal attachment to dead bodies. The idea that anyone could get some enjoyment out of a dead body must strike the average reader as wholly unintelligible. Here the fairy tale Sleeping Beauty may be of some help.

In the Grimm Brothers' version of Sleeping Beauty, the last witch prophesies that at age fifteen the princess will prick her finger on the distaff of a spinning wheel and fall into a hundred-year sleep. Her father, the king, is unable to destroy all the spinning wheels in the realm. The princess enters the locked door to a forbidden chamber and sees an old woman spinning. The fifteen-year-old girl asks about the distaff: "What kind of thing is this that jumps about in such a funny way?" As soon as she touches the distaff on the spinning wheel, it pricks her and she falls into a deep sleep. In some interpretations this signifies that the girl had reached sexual maturation and the event had so overwhelmed her that she fell into a deathlike coma.

Beauty sleeps for a hundred years in a forlorn castle where

all the servants are also "asleep." The castle lies in the middle of an overgrown, inaccessible forest, believed inhabited by a man-eating ogre. (The description fits that of a cemetery—an area of perpetual sleep which living humans fear and avoid. The man-eating ogre in the story could be Death itself.) The fearless prince finds his princess, but only "at night and unknown to all." (That is a highly suspicious phrase for those who know about the behavior of necrophiles.) After intercourse many people are exhausted and assume the pose of the dead. Like Sleeping Beauty they "appear" to be dead. Of course, for most people the pose is temporary. But Sleeping Beauty's trauma must have been very severe. After one hundred years of deathlike sleep she maintains her youth and physical beauty (like a vampire).

Some people are intrigued by the exotic, the strange, the unusual in order to achieve sexual excitement. What stranger, more exotic creature than the dead? The dead belong to a different race, completely independent of ordinary human life; they have their own laws, custom, and rhythms.

Hungarian gypsies are so afraid of the power of the dead that they will not sleep in any bed in which a relative has died; so, for economy's sake their dead are thus generally put out to die on the ground. (Sir James George Frazer, *The Fear of the Dead*.) Certain gypsy tribes are so convinced that the human heart does not die at the same time as the body that they habitually plunge hatpins into the chests of their dead. In England an Act of Parliament was passed as late as the year 1824 in an attempt to terminate the old English practice of transfixing suspicious-looking bodies with nails.

Among the Moslem gypsies of Yugoslavia who settled in the Balkans at the end of the Middle Ages is the belief that a corpse is capable of impregnating a woman. So sometimes a male peasant courting a widow there would dress up at night like a corpse in a winding-sheet or white cloak. The widow would be expected to act as if she believed it to be her dead husband returned to life and would not dare to reject his advances.

In the ancient tombs of Egypt, Mesopotamia, and places along the eastern Mediterranean shore so-called "stone concubines" have been found with their sex organs portrayed in exaggerated form. These were apparently meant to aid the dead men to return to normal sexual activity, which had been temporarily interrupted by the death experience. Among the Hindus and other peoples it was the custom for wives to hurl themselves on their husband's funeral pyre; some of them apparently believed that they had to do that so that their husband could continue a normal married life after death.

Among some nomadic tribes in Sweden, a female companion was placed in the grave alongside the corpse; in other cases a straw doll was buried with the dead man as a substitute. Ancient Egyptians were so aware that the living are sexually attracted to the dead that they never trusted strangers to "guard" a dead body, especially if the body were that of a young man or woman. According to the Greek historian Herodotus, embalmers in the House of the Dead had to wait patiently for several days after a death before they could begin their work on the corpse.

The story of Philinnion, recorded by Phlegon during the second century A.D. and cited in *Fragmenta Historicorum Graecorum* is a revealing case of love of the dead for the living. Although dead for almost six months, Philinnion has such love that she comes back from Hades and visits a young man named Machates at night and sleeps with him. Once discovered in bed with him, her body is burned, and Machates—out of love for his dead beloved—kills himself in despair.

The first-century A.D. Roman writer Philostratus wrote about a young, well-endowed youth named Menippus who fell in love with a strange-looking foreign woman. His friend Appolonius of Tyana warned him to be wary of the woman whom he detected as an undead, a vampire, but to no avail. Under pressure the woman finally admitted that she was merely "fattening up Menippus with pleasures before devouring his body, for it was her habit to feed upon young and beautiful bodies."

Polycrites of Thermon, governor of Aetolia, was thought to have returned from the grave "pale and horrible to see, clothed in a black robe blotched and spattered with blood, just as his wife and young infant were being put to death by a mob. Upon seeing that the mob was intent upon burning his wife and child at the stake, he suddenly seized the child and tore it to bits with his teeth." Polycrites swallowed the child's flesh until only the child's head remained. The head proceeded to foretell (correctly) the coming defeat of the Aetolian army.

Apuleius, born around 125 A.D. in Madura, a town in northern Africa, recorded the case of a young student named Thelyphrion who volunteered for the task of guarding a dead body but fell asleep on the job. Vampires entered the death chamber and "cut off Thelyphrion's nose and then his two ears" replacing them with wax replicas "in order to hide their horrid deed." When Thelyphrion discovered what had happened to him, he fled to a distant country where he supposedly managed to live out his life but, of course, with no evident ears and no nose. The sexual symbolism is very strong in this story— the nose has long been a substitute for the penis. (The nineteenth-century Russian writer Nikolai Gogol later exploited this theme of a man's missing nose in his superb story "The Nose," one of the most bizarre creations in all of literature.)

The tyrant Periandes lived with the dead body of his beloved Melissa for a year. Herod slept for seven years next to the corpse of his dead wife Marianna, whom he obviously loved more in death than in life, since he himself had arranged for her murder. Charlemagne could not bear to part with the body of his dead Saxon mistress.

Christianity added the new element—the transfigured, resurrected body. Most bodies, must, of course, die and putrefy; but one's soul remains immortal until the Last Judgment when all the bodies of the dead will somehow rise up nonetheless transfigured out of their coffins. But there were differences of opinion among the early followers of Christ. Had Jesus Christ not summoned Lazarus directly from the dead? And had Lazarus not come forth like a human? In a strange way by affirming the immortality of the soul and denying it to the body, Christianity inadvertently encouraged some people to believe in the immediate possibility of a resurrected body before the Last Judgment like that of Lazarus, a walking dead.

Early Christian chroniclers recorded many cases of excommunicated persons leaving their graves because they could not find rest. The ancient notion of the returning dead was tied up with vague ideas about purgatory. Hence the Christian pronouncement "May he rest in peace!" which raisès the question "Why *shouldn't* he rest in peace?" Why is one obliged to pray that he will not go wandering around—unless one feared that many unfortunately do not sleep the sleep of death in their graves? Troubled souls will not remain in their graves as they should. So, one must pray for them that they be released from the torments of purgatory and go to the land of eternal bliss. Otherwise there could be trouble for the living; the unfortunate dead might return to plague the living.

The historian Gregory of Tours (*Historia Francorum*, Vol. 1, p. 47) records the following case which demonstrates how death even facilitated sex denied in life: In the French town of Clermont-Ferrant, a senator named Injurieux decided to marry a highly pious lady called Scholastica in the year 390 A.D. Unfortunately for him, his chaste wife died within a year of their marriage. At her funeral the senator felt compelled to deliver a public eulogy to her and to give God thanks for having given him such a "treasure of purity," which he had returned to God "as intact as he had received her." The meaning was clear to those in public attendance. The man had not had sexual relations with his wife before her untimely death. But, according to Gregory of Tours, just as the husband uttered those words, the dead body of his wife rose from her coffin and exclaimed with an enigmatic smile, "Why, my husband, do you raise matters in public which concern only ourselves?" After saying that, she promptly lay down again and allowed herself to be buried.

Shortly after the burial of his wife, the senator himself died and was buried in a tomb separate from that of his virginal wife. However, his tomb was found to be empty on the next morning, and his body was discovered entwined in the arms of the body of Scholastica in her tomb. Death had evidently enabled the two of them to achieve the embrace which they had not been able to accomplish in life. Even today the visitor is informed that Scholastica's grave is known as "the bed of the two lovers."

Queen Juana of Castile kept the corpse of her husband, Philip the Handsome, at her side for three years, from 1506 until 1509. She even arranged for his body to travel with her entourage and set up bodyguards to prevent any woman from approaching his body. Philip was a well-known philanderer in real life, so that in her own strange way Queen Juana was merely protecting her dead husband from any possible extramarital affairs.

In 1730 an imperial officer in the Austrian army, the count of Cabreras, wrote down the following case for the scrutiny of a Freiburg University professor at Brisgau: A man who had been dead over thirty years returned to his home at mealtime and on his first visit "fastened upon the neck of his own brother and sucked his blood." During his second visit, the walking corpse "treated one of his children in the same way and during the third visit, he assaulted one of the family servants." The count issued orders to disinter the body and found the man's blood "in a fluid state as if alive, so a great nail was driven through his temple, and he was re-buried." A special deputation was sent to Emperor Charles I awaiting further instructions.

Horace P. Walpole related how, when Lord Holland was close to death, his close friend George Selwyn insisted on seeing him. After Selwyn had gone away, Lord Holland told his majordomo: "If Lord Selwyn returns, let him in by all means. If I am still alive I shall be pleased to see him; if not, he shall be pleased to see me." George Selwyn was well known in his time as a devotee of the death penalty. He made a special trip to Paris in 1756 just to witness the execution of Damiens, the attempted assassin of Louis XV.

As art historians are well aware, many painters consider corpses to be ideal subjects: one does not have to worry about any fidgeting by the model. According to the famous Italian art historian of the Renaissance, Vasari, the painter Luca Signorelli's immediate reaction upon witnessing the death of a youth he liked was to remove the clothes from the dead boy and begin to paint a picture of it.

Around the year 1900 a Russian provincial governor of about sixty years of age had forced a young girl to marry him but had died shortly after. However, before his death, he had made her swear never to marry again and had threatened that if she did, "he would return from the grave and kill her." Despite the warning, she did remarry; on the night of her betrothal feast, "her body was found to be black and blue in places, as from the effects of pinches, and from a slight puncture on the her neck, drops of blood were oozing." Upon recovering from this, she stated that her deceased husband had entered her room "appearing exactly as in life" and had tormented her in the same way as during his lifetime.

Two psychiatrists, Franklin S. Klaf and William Brown, in the journal *Psychiatric Quarterly* (October, 1958) published a paper entitled "Necrophilia, Brief Review and Case Report" and referred to the three categories of necrophilia established by Wulffen: 1) *lust murder,* in which murder precedes the sexual act with the corpse; 2) *necrostuprum,* in which the corpse is stolen; and 3) *necrophagy,* in which the corpse is mutilated and parts eaten. Next the authors analyzed the more modern cases of necrophilia. The first type, called inhibited necrophilia, is an overextension of the part love plays in any excessive mourning for the dead. The second type includes "all overt necrophilic gratifications such as the sex act, biting, tearing or devouring"; it is a reversion to infantile sadism. The third contemporary category is termed pseudonecrophilia, in effect, a "substitute for the sex act in the mentally ill," consisting of "erotic fantasies or masturbation but no actual sexual contact with the corpse."

In a block of apartments along the rue Chaudron in Paris, the wife of a collar starcher suddenly died, and his neighbor kindly offered to keep watch over her dead body. The husband was pleased by this neighborly gesture and concurred. But, when the husband returned home in the dead of night, he caught his helpful neighbor literally red-handed in the act of posthumous adultery.

The reader may find it difficult to comprehend how Elizabeth

Bathory seemed to like to see her girls so tortured as to be tottering on the brink of death. It must seem strange that she had them pricked and cut with knives, so that their life's blood gradually ebbed away. But other people, like the American writer Edgar Allan Poe, have also found something beautiful in seeing the signs of life and health fade slowly from the cheeks of women close to death. Poe invariably fell in love with women who were wasting away and dying from incurable diseases. The fact that Poe lost his mother when he was only three may explain his preoccupation with women on the brink of death.

Poe's first platonic love, Jane Stanard, died when he was fifteen; at twenty he lost Elmira Royster. At age twenty-six he married his thirteen-year-old cousin Virginia Clemm. Before Virginia died, he fell in love with Frances Osgood, who died of tuberculosis four years later. Virginia Clemm then died too, and Poe attached himself to Helen Whitman, who suffered from fainting spells—a pseudodeath, if you will.

One of Poe's most erotic stories, "Bernice," deals with mutilation of the dead beloved. It traces the obsession of the hero Egaeus with his beloved Bernice's teeth. To him Bernice is the epitome of adorable beauty—except for her "long, narrow and excessively white teeth." The hero becomes morbidly obsessed with that horrid part of her anatomy. Bernice wastes away and dies. Egaeus goes into a trance, and when awakened, his servant finds his master's shoes dirty with earth. Egaeus reaches in his own pocket and finds Bernice's teeth! In his trance he had dug up her body and cut the teeth out of her corpse; at last she was perfectly lovely—in death if not in life!

Another of Poe's stories relevant in this context is the one entitled "The Oblong Box" (1844) about an English collector named Cornelius Wyatt who embarks alone on a trip on the day after his marriage. He takes with him a pine chest, the most valuable part of his collection. Each night in the seclusion of his cabin Mr. Wyatt opened the chest "in order to feast his eyes on the treasure enclosed in it." A shipwreck takes place, but Mr. Wyatt refuses to leave the oblong box with its very precious collector's item in it, and he drowns. In the chest was discovered the beautiful corpse of Mrs. Wyatt, who had died prematurely on their wedding night.

In 1909 Dr. Franz Hartmann published an erotic account demonstrating that the dead retain their sexual attractiveness for some living people. He and several friends were visiting a castle, situated in a wild and desolate section of the Carpathian Mountains. The local people had tried to burn it down, because they suspected that a vampire or undead inhabited it. At the castle one of Dr. Hartmann's friends sees the portrait of a dead countess named Elga. That night in his room he heard the rustling of silk and upon opening his eyes he saw Countess Elga entering his room "looking more youthful and seductive than in her portrait." As he put it, "her looks and gestures left no doubt as to her desires and intentions," but he does not tell the reader what he did about it.

Some sexual encounters with the dead can be dangerous and hence exciting to some people. It is "forbidden fruit." In British Columbia widows and widowers from the Shuswap tribe sleep on a bed of thorns in order to discourage their evidently lustful dead spouses from returning to have intercourse with them. Widowers in the Mekeo district of British New Guinea must always carry a hand ax to defend themselves against their dead wives who may come back to seek them out.

The Etruscan Locumon kept their dead buried in holes within their palace walls, so as to be able to keep an eye on them. Medes, Parthians, Persians, and Iberians fed their dead to wild beasts. Scythians and Bretons ate theirs. Even today, New Guinea's Fore tribesmen regularly eat selected portions of their dead relatives, though the current government is trying to eliminate this custom. (The practice appears implicated as the cause of a nerve disease which begins in giggles and ends in death.)

Bushmen, who have the praying mantis as their totem, consider that once a girl attains puberty, she becomes identified with the mantis, and her look must be avoided, since it is thought to have become lethal. The actual actions of the praying mantis provide clues to this curious notion of sexual excitement with the dead.

During intercourse, the female praying mantis holds the male in a tight grasp with her teeth and proceeds to eat him. The male, concentrating upon his sexual function, continues to hold onto the female, even as she nibbles away his head, neck, and thorax. In fact, his body remains closely pressed to hers as she, with her head resting on his shoulders, goes on gnawing up the remains of her gentle lover. Deprived of his head, the male seems to be a more efficient lover; perhaps conditioned reflex is no longer inhibited by cerebral functions. So, at last, for this insect anyway, there is sex after death.

Some cultures have embodied strict warnings about the real dangers to the living from taboo contacts with the undead. For example, the female Eskimo undead devours her victims with her vagina, like the Irish Sheila na gigh, represented with a huge vagina threatening to swallow up the male like a vacuum cleaner. Among the Eskimo the returning dead female is unfortunately so very lovely that most men faint when they look at her. In one Eskimo tale the young male Nukapiartekak is so taken with her beauty that he goes to her igloo and kisses her. But "in the end, with a cry, he disappears completely inside her. When, in the morning she lights the stone lamp, Nukapiartekak is no more. The beautiful woman goes out of the igloo to pass a little water and with her water the skeleton of Nukapiartekak comes out from within her" (Roger Callois, *Le Mythe et l'homme* [Myth and Man]).

Some people apparently can lose their sexual inhibitions only with someone who appears cold and indifferent, particularly if such people are "abnormal" sexually. They are ashamed to do what they like with "normal" equal sexual partners so they choose inferior mates, but even these are sometimes shocked. The dead are never shocked by their living beloveds.

Sarah Bernhardt would agree to meet her lovers only in a coffin, according to the actress Marie Colombier. In many whorehouses there are death chambers for prospective lovers, complete with black satin curtains, pale candles, and, of course, a comfortable coffin. According to a report from a Parisian brothel, one male customer used to like to visit his favorite girlfriend in the death chamber, where she would lie all white, powdered up and immobile like a corpse, while an organ off stage played the old Catholic ritual for the dead, the Dies Irae and the De Profundis.

Adoration of the beloved dead is fostered in the Christian world, where one can find Saint Anthony, who died in the fifth century, under glass in full view; countless other saints are similarly on display throughout the world. One of the most famous is Saint Teresa of Avila. In 1583 the nuns from the convent of Alba smelled an unusual fragrance coming from the tomb of the future saint, Teresa of Avila, who had been buried one year earlier. Upon exhuming the body they found it to be in perfect shape. Father Graziano neatly cut off the saint's left hand on the pretext of taking it to Avila, which he did not do. Instead he hid the severed left hand in his own house in Lisbon. After another inspection in 1585 it was decided to transport the corpse to Avila, Teresa's home town. The priest in charge of the removal, Father Gregorio, cut off the left arm (without the hand, of course) to leave it as a souvenir for the Alba convent.

In December 1585 a commission of bishops and priests at Avila investigated the body. They stood it on its feet. When they pressed their fingers into the cheeks, the flesh there responded flexibly. Weeping with joy, the bishops saw that the remaining right arm and the legs were also flexible. Later the mother superior of another convent, Catalina di Sant' Angelo, cut out the heart for herself. Between 1604 and 1616 Teresa's body lost a rib, the right foot, and a number of pieces of flesh to the private collections of various members of the faithful.

Some painters, as well, sought out the hearts of the dead, since the human heart was assumedly the only source of a particularly marvelous shiny brown patina. After the French Revolution the artist Saint-Martin used fragments from the heart of Louis XIV in his paintings, with results that pleased him. He also secured Louis XIII's heart, which had been preserved in the reliquary of the Church of Saint Louis of the Jesuits in Paris. Unfortunately, he did not have the time to use it before the restoration of the French monarchy, at which time he was compelled to return Louis XIII's heart to the reliquary (he was given Louis' gold tobacco box as a kind of consolation prize).

In 1776 Pierre Gautier wrote a short work based on the question "Will a decapitated head preserve its ability to feel for several instants after decapitation?" Sixteen years later when the guillotine went into high-gear operation, it was found that the head could survive for a time after decapitation. For example, when François le Gros, the executioner's assistant, slapped the head of Charlotte Corday, who murdered Marat in the bathtub, the head turned red with anger. (Alister Kershaw, *A History of the Guillotine*.)

According to W. A. F. Browne's article "Necrophilism," which appeared in the *Journal of Mental Science* in 1875, in western India two women used to visit tombs together at night, if only to make makeshift beds in the graves. But: "The resting places of the bodies visited appeared to have been violated, the corpses exhumed and some of them kissed, caressed or embraced, and taken home by their ravishers, *despite the fact that they were strangers.*"

Some undertakers and surgeons are sometimes covert necrophiles and necrosadists in disguise. Society permits and even approves as these "professionals" go about cutting up human bodies, an otherwise criminal offense. Society generally admires such surgeons and undertakers assumedly because they, like witch doctors of old, can get away with doing what others would be prosecuted for.

Baudelaire's Mademoiselle Bisturi gave herself to the first suitor who appeared, provided that he would let himself be called "surgeon." Her fondest memories were those she spent in the clinic. "Certainly, certainly," she declared to one of her casual lovers, "I was very impressed by you when I saw you helping at the outset of the most delicate operations. Yes, yes, you are a real man, you like to cut, slice, work delicately . . ." In the end Mademoiselle Bisturi became engaged to a young doctor; as she put it, she hoped that one day he would come to her with his store of surgical instruments and his coat spattered with blood.

When doctors in Los Angeles went on strike in 1976 an 18 percent drop in the death rate occurred. During the same year, according to Dr. Robert Mendelson, when doctors in Bogota, Colombia, refused to provide any services except emergency care, the result was a 35 percent drop in the death rate. When Israeli doctors cut their daily patient service in 1973, the Jerusalem Burial Society recorded that the death rate dropped by 50 percent, and the only similar drop in the death rate had taken place twenty years before precisely at the time of the last doctors' strike. One is forced to conclude that doctors are sometimes not good for one's health.

M. Bertrand, a French gentleman of taste and education, while lounging in a village churchyard, witnessed a funeral and was seized with an overwhelming desire to dig up the corpse and tear it apart. For years he preyed upon the dead like a human hyena.

Alexis Epaulard, a student of sexual pathology, presented a doctoral thesis to the University of Lyons in 1901 with details on a subject which he called a "vampire" but would be termed a necrophile today. In his dissertation, *Vampirisme, necrophilie, necrosadisme, necrophagie,* he detailed the revealing case of Victor Ardisson, a grave digger's assistant. Epaulard claimed the distinction of having discovered the "Vampire of Muy," as he called him, in the madhouse of Pierrefeu in the Var district of France. Epaulard's observations were seconded by Doctor Belletrud, director of the asylum and by his deputy-assistant Doctor Mercier, so the case is supported by three expert eyewitnesses.

Victor Ardisson, though he came from an upper-class family in the Var district in the south of France, where people were known for their exuberance and expansiveness, was melancholy and reserved. He believed firmly in God, the Virgin Mary, and the Devil. He was a collector of antiquities. When visiting a cemetery he usually picked up a few pieces of terra-cotta to take home, where he kept these objects in a sock as "souvenirs." In this same spirit of collecting, Victor Ardisson took home the head of a thirteen-year-old girl named Gabrielle with whom he had been infatuated. He would take out the dead head and caress it but had no "sexual" relationship with it. He considered the head to be his fiancée. He respected her more than the body of his self-proclaimed mistress, a dead little girl Louise, aged three and a half, whom Victor had brought home one moonlit night while passing through the village cemetery of Muy. Each morning when he woke beside her in bed he asked her what she wanted to eat. She never answered him, so he thought that she was not hungry. According to Dr. Belletrud, director of the asylum of Pierrefeu, Ardisson thought that the dead were capable of speaking and if they did not, it was because of their "isolation and defective education." (Michel Belletrud and Edmond Mercier, *Contribution à la Nécrophilie. L'Affaire Ardisson*.)

Ardisson apparently knew that women were strange, erratic creatures who were sometimes subject to moods of bad temper. So, despite the exceedingly taciturn character of his mistress, he was very considerate towards her. During the daytime he would often interrupt his work in order to check that she was alright, and at night he looked forward to sleeping with her next to him, like a nice new toy.

Ardisson was strictly heterosexual, but within that group—female—he showed no marked preference. As Leporello said of Don Giovanni in Mozart's opera of the same name, "peasant girls, maids, countesses, baronesses and princesses" were all the same to him, just as long as they wore petticoats. He got in the habit of frequenting the Muy cemetery at night where he violated female corpses. Afterwards he could not remember any of them except a girl named Berthe who, he felt, had beautiful breasts.

The only corpse Ardisson rejected was one with a leg amputated (legs were high in his considerations). In the Muy village there was a girl who had what Ardisson considered to be the best calves in the neighborhood. By an extraordinary bit of luck for him, she died, and Ardisson was at the time assigned to assisting his father at grave digging. The night after the girl's burial Ardisson went out to the cemetery, dug up the earth covering her grave, jumped down to her coffin, opened it, took out the corpse which he propped up at the edge of the coffin and contemplated it lovingly, especially her beautiful calves.

Necrophilia, as the Freudian psychologist Marie Bonaparte confirms, is not just a search for dead women, but rather for the mother usually lost in infancy. (Victor Ardisson's mother had died when he was a child.) Ardisson usually slept in a large double bed next to his father and his father's latest mistress and one of these women introduced Victor to sex in his father's own bed. Apparently, this must have seemed like incest to him, as if he were sleeping with his father's wife, that is, his own mother. But Victor Ardisson not only had no evident compunction about such incest, but a positive attitude towards it: "I would willingly have gone to bed with my mother if she had wanted it," he said.

The necrophile is primarily interested in a passive sexual partner—and a corpse is certainly just that. One can do what one wants with a corpse, and there is no evidence that any of the dead have ever talked back.

John Haigh, the so-called "Vampire of London," was also like Ardisson really a necrophiliac. A nightmare came to him before he committed his bizarre crimes: "I saw a forest of crucifixes which gradually turned into trees. At first I seemed to see dew or rain running from the branches, but when I came nearer I knew it was blood. All of a sudden the whole forest began to twist about and the trees streamed with blood. Blood ran from the trunks. Blood ran from the branches, all red and shiny. I felt weak and seemed to faint. I saw a man going round the trees gathering blood. When the cup he was holding in his hand was full he came up to me and said 'drink.' But I was paralyzed. The dream vanished. But I still felt faint and stretched out with all my strength towards the cup." (John Haigh, *Confession*.)

Don Juan goes from one woman to another because he is not really pursuing the women but the image of his mother in them. Both the Don Juan and the necrophile express, albeit in different ways, a tendency not only toward imaginary incest but also a kind of masturbation, since neither is capable of love with another human being.

According to the Catholic and Orthodox Christian death rituals, the corpse must be uncovered and visible until buried. In particular, dead girls were dressed up in bridal costumes and carried through the streets of the city to a given church where they would be kissed by parents and friends. Alexis Epaulard commented that "such a custom seems expressly to have been made to encourage necrophilia." Epaulard also observed that "professions that diminish the chances of meeting women, like those which frequently bring the subject into contact with dead bodies, predispose the subject to necrophilia, all the more so as those carrying out these professions are necessarily less sensitive because of their social class."

Out of twenty-three cases of necrophilia which Alexis Epaulard studied there were four undertakers, two medical students, two priests, two aristocrats, two vagabonds, two idiots, one attendant in an anatomical dissection room, one gardener, one shopkeeper, one writer, one sergeant, one high French military commander, and three with unknown jobs or professions.

Dr. A. A. Brill probed a particularly frightening modern case of necrophilia in a paper entitled "The Sense of Smell in the Neuroses and Psychoses," which appeared in 1932 in *Psychoanalytic Quarterly*. A man had no desire for normal coitus or genital satisfaction. Instead he tried to satisfy his gustatory, olfactory, and tactile senses to the nth degree. Brill wrote: "His description of what a dead woman would offer him reads like a gourmet's idea of a Lucullan feast. He delighted in all delicacies of decayed flesh, how to cure it to bring out the odor, etc.; but as the smell of a human body would attract too much attention he finally decided to be satisfied with a dead horse."

In Moscow there is dead Lenin under glass. His beloved body lies in a special mausoleum on Red Square and it is, from the official government's own admission, "the most popular attraction in Moscow." Anyone who goes to Moscow cannot say that he has been there without viewing dead Lenin. (The author of the present book took part in that pilgrimage; the inside is as cold as in a refrigerator, and Lenin looks like a wax dummy, glistening in the light.)

It is true that Egyptologists have put pharaonic mummies on

display for years, although the Egyptian government recently closed down the mummy display section in the Cairo museum, because looking over dead bodies is in violation of Moslem tradition. But who besides Communists have ever put their *recent* dead on permanent display?

After Lenin's death in 1924 Soviet authorities preceded their mummification of Lenin with a public act in which they exposed natural mummies from the Russian past, called *mochtchi*, out in the open and succeeded in reducing them to dust in 1919, in order to demonstrate the victory of their scientific mummification procedures over those of the past. Lenin's body is a great political asset, even though the author of Communism, Karl Marx, had said, "I hate all gods." Mao Tse-Tung was also mummified and put on display in Peking. Affection for the beloved dead goes on even under modern scientific Communism.

Historians and archeologists do research and write about dead subjects. But they are not motivated merely by desires to escape into the past. It is true that they seek to "recapture the past" and by creative, artistic prose to try to make it live again— an essentially impossible task. But the historian and archeologist differ from the necrophile in so far as they do not fall in love with the past or with dead characters; they seek to liberate humans from the burdens of the past, imposed by their ancestors. As such, historians and archeologists represent the human desire to abolish time as a way of measurement and to break through the confines of one's own time.

Some historians and archeologists have an unconscious need to resuscitate their own past, as well as that of others. Often, they have suffered from the loss of a beloved person during their youth, sometimes their mothers. Freud analyzed the case of the archeologist Norbert Hanold, the main protagonist in a novel entitled *Gradiva, ein pompejanische Phantasiestuck* by W. F. Jensen, in his *Delirium and Dreams in the Gradiva of W. F. Jensen.*

In order to love any woman, Norbert Hanold had to believe that she was a dead woman brought back to life. In Jensen's novel the woman, Gradiva, is brought back to life in Pompeii, the dead city unearthed, where sudden death froze humans for all time in a fleeting moment of human activity. Hanold comes to understand that Gradiva was in reality a forgotten person from his infancy, and he is "liberated" by that awareness in the novel.

Having looked at necrophilia from the point of view of folklore, anthropology, history and psychology, we will now turn to the various ways in which the themes of vampire, werewolf, and necrophile have been treated in literature, movies, and theater.

# 11

## Vampire, Werewolf, and Necrophile in Literature, Theater, and Cinema

THIS study of the Elizabeth Bathory story and the related analyses of the historical, sociological, psychological, and anthropological significances of vampirism, werewolfism, and necrophilism would not be complete without a look at the *fictional* horror story—in literature, theater, and the movies. Although the connection between real and fictional horror has rarely been recognized, the two are strikingly similar. One reason why the link between historical and fictional horror has often been ignored is because of the restrictions imposed upon the writer of historical, as distinct from fictional, horror. The biographer of historical horror must adhere to the evidence; unlike the fiction writer, he cannot make up anything from his imagination. (In fact, I have not allowed myself to invent even the weather in narrating the Bathory story. A writer of fiction can throw in a terrifying storm whenever he wishes to "heighten the tension.") However, in the Bathory case (as in some others), the real story is as horrible as almost any fiction that one could have imagined. Truth in this case is even stranger than fiction, and historical horror takes its rightful place alongside fictional horror as a "good story."

The original legend referred, after all, simply to a woman who took blood baths for cosmetic purposes; however, evidence demonstrated, as we have seen, that she was "into" something much more horrible than mere blood baths—she was a sadistic torture-murderer who even bit human flesh. That, as they say, is an entirely different kettle of fish. Just as the fictional horror story thrives on surprise, so do the best tales of historical horror. Both the historian of horror and the fiction writer have a common challenge—both have to tell a good story, and a good horror story usually has a Hitchcockian twist or surprise. The fiction writer can make it up from his imagination; the historian of horror has to hope that his search may lead to some such startling discovery.

The unfolding of the fiction horror story or movie is also similar to that of the best historical horror. At first the existence of some sort of mysterious monster or aberration of nature becomes the focal point of interest; then the real nature of the threat to society is established through investigation by some researcher (the hero); it is not, however, acknowledged by the powers that be, and it becomes the job of the investigator to convince others of the exact nature and scope of the unbeliev- able horror, which the protagonist (and by identification, the audience) knows to be real. The investigator becomes a kind of psychoanalyst trying to get the patient (society) to come to recognize the terrible reality which the patient is afraid to un- cover.

In most horror stories and films there is a presentation of normality against which the author contrasts the monster. "Normality" is usually a heterosexual monogamous family re- lationship, duly fostered and supported by traditional social institutions such as community, church, and police. Into this scene of domestic tranquility the monster is thrust. Usually the presence of the monster exposes the underlying tensions within the family itself with which the spectator (having grown up with those tensions) is usually familiar.

Most books about horror fiction have been anthologies pre- senting many examples of the genre with little analysis of the common bases of horror stories; the historian of horror in search of some rationale behind the genre will find little help there.

The historical novel is a blend of both genres; a writer takes an historical setting and invents upon it, usually creating imaginary dialog in the manner of Sir Walter Scott, or following some preconceived formula for the neo-Gothic novel. This mishmash of history and fiction is very popular, but it does not lie within the scope of the present study.

There are few "scientific" standards by which to evaluate whether a fictional or historical horror story is a good one or not. Isolated attempts have been made to reduce the entire subject to a set of unscientific, orthodox Freudian or neo-Freudian explanations—but they have not proved convincing. The subject of horror has remained elusive for a long time. Most evaluations have been based upon subjective feelings about good and bad taste. Many critics have denounced the genre as "repellent," "indecent," "disgusting," and "foul" (I particularly like "foul"). Since the horror story often relies precisely upon the violation of contemporary standards of "good taste" the problem is compounded—it is specifically designed to jar, to disturb, to disorient.

On the one hand, specialists in literature have looked upon the horror genre from an aesthetic point of view, and tried to answer the question "is the story well constructed and well written?" according to the tenets of whichever contemporary school of literary criticism they belong to. Historians, on the other hand, have been interested mostly in whether the given horror story was based upon evidence, or whether it was widely read and remembered, and are not concerned with aesthetic judgment. The relationship of the story to historical events, or the popularity the story had in a given era (no matter that it was denounced as junk by established critics) are the features of interest to the historian. I trust that it is clear to the reader that my interest, my point of view, is historical, not literary.

There are two major theories about the nature of horror that have gained currency. One holds that shock scenes of violence frighten people the most. This theory puts the emphasis upon what is called today the "gross-out"—the vivid depiction of violence and destruction. The life of Elizabeth Bathory belongs in this category.

But another theory depends upon the ability of the human mind to conceive of horrors going beyond any material depiction by any author or artist. Stories following in this line thrive on suggestions and unseen horrors, rather than any graphic gross-outs. Although one method is obviously more subtle than the other, no one has been able to prove conclusively that suggestive horror is more frightening than the visual gross-out; or vice versa.

In most horror stories, whether real or fiction, a blend of both elements takes place. Really deep fear, as Edgar Allan Poe understood so well, comes ultimately from nothing. In *The Pit and the Pendulum* he wrote: "It was not that I feared to look upon things horrible, but that I grew aghast lest there be nothing else." Although the most profound fears usually arise from the wholly unknown or unseen, the continual threat of a total "gross-out" must lurk in the back of almost any horror story, historical or fictional, in order to achieve maximum effect.

Rules of socially appropriate behavior are generally overturned in the fictional horror story, as they are by Elizabeth Bathory. At least one character in the story must usually go beyond the limits of the conventionally acceptable, as does Elizabeth. This, it seems to be, is designed to teach a lesson: In the lives of most people things seem to be going along quite smoothly until almost invariably something startling and unsettling happens, and then all hell breaks loose.

Most people have difficulty handling unanticipated changes in life; but the outcomes are almost invariably better (less horrible, I should say) than what we feared would happen next. Reality is almost never as bad as anticipated. That is probably one reason why many horrors come from nightmares when our rational conscious guards are down. Nightmares are dreams in which one confronts repressed wishes that the conscious mind finds so terrible and loathsome that it has rejected them.

In the West a marked distinction is usually made between dreams and the "real" world. But for Freudians and in other cultures, such as among the East Africans and the Australian aborigines, the dream world is considered more revealing and more significant than the so-called "real" world. For example, in East Africa when the tribal head tells his subjects about a dream he had in which he went to Europe, his subjects have to welcome him officially back home, as if he had actually returned from a long trip. In that same culture if a man should happen to dream about the wife of a friend, he must make the appropriate apologies to her husband on the next day. In *On the Nightmare* hard line Freudian Ernest Jones contends that nightmares are always related to sex. This *may* be true of nightmares (although I doubt it), but it certainly is not true of the horror story: the genre deals quite specifically with antisocial feelings as well as sexual anxieties.

The horror story, historical or fictional, allows one to deal with personal feelings about the world one lives in—feelings that one might be afraid to show more directly. As Stephen King put it in *Danse Macabre*: "Much of the horror story's attraction for us is that it allows us to vicariously exercise those antisocial emotions and feelings which society demands we keep stoppered up under most circumstances, for society's good and our own" (p. 75). In short, the horror genre is society's release valve.

The aim of any horror story appears thus to be the Aristotelian catharsis, the purging of our emotions of fear and pity. If one lets the real and fictional monsters roam through the pages of literature and history or across the silver screen one is, in effect, feeding the monsters within, so that they will not have to burst forth hungry and ravenous into real life. As we all know, it is a wise man who keeps his animals fed.

To take the position, as some critics have done, that the horror artist or writer is a secret sadist and that the audience is an unconscious masochist—or worse yet, to adopt the fatuous word "sadomasochism"—does not go very far to explain the popularity of the genre for large numbers of "normal" artists and writers, on the one hand, nor for the audiences, on the other, made up of substantial numbers of quite ordinary people. Those who ascribe such confusing traits to artists and to audiences are usually the same ones who find the whole genre distressing and distasteful. Such "reasoning" is really an emotional way of trying to discredit the horror story as an art form and a psychologically therapeutic device which has been around for thousands of years.

Most of us are attracted to the horror story, because we are fully capable of psychological displacement. We make the transference of our aggressive instincts to some symbols and do not feel at all compelled to carry out such instincts. It is precisely the sexual criminal who finds himself unable to make the displacement or transference.

And yet, in the overall scheme of life, even the sexual criminal also serves a socially useful purpose, akin to that of the historical and the fictional horror story. As Marie Bonaparte wrote in her psychoanalytical study of Edgar Allan Poe, *Edgar Poe, sa Vie, son Oeuvre*: "We may say that we, unhappy civilized beings with inhibited instincts, are in some ways grateful to the great disinterested criminals who now and again offer us the spectacle of our most brutal and guilty desires being finally satisfied. . . ." Over the entrance to the School of Criminal Anthropology in Lyons, France, the following words are inscribed in stone: "Every society has the criminals it deserves." Historically it does appear that certain general types of social deviants are popularly referred to in specific eras, almost as if the designations give us some clues as to what the given historical societies feared most. For example, the witches and warlocks popular during the Middle Ages gave way to the werewolves of the sixteenth and seventeenth centuries. The werewolves were in turn replaced by the vampire craze of the eighteenth century. The eighteenth-century vampires were replaced by the sadists and necrophiles of the nineteenth century and by the psychopaths of the twentieth century. But the so-called vampires and werewolves of yesterday have by no means disappeared from society but are today merely referred to by modern terminologies.

In this section I deal only with those literary works and films which have advanced the horror genre of the vampire, werewolf, and necrophile. So the reader should be aware of the restrictive nature here; this is not a complete survey. My point of view is that almost anything worth being afraid of is also worth making fun of. Many readers or spectators sometimes laugh when being presented with something horrible. By laughing they are trying to regain a sense of proper order and

stability. The laugh helps them recall that what they are reading or watching is, after all, just make-believe.

Most audiences have a fondness for imaginary terrors, and
enjoy a kind of fabricated fright—under controllable conditions, of course. There are certain misguided critics who claim
that the horror story summons up memories of old ancestral
beliefs in ghosts and the supernatural. But the historical fact is
that the horror story really only came into its own *after* the
belief in the supernatural had almost died out, that is, during
the Age of Reason, the 18th century. As such, the modern
"horror story" is of fairly recent vintage and is often designed
as pure entertainment. Usually there is an exciting journey
through distant lands, a kind of "renaissance of wonder" with
ruined abbeys, haunted galleries. In many ways it represents
a revolt against the materialism, dullness, and drab actuality
of the postindustrial world rather than simply a reversion to
the past.

Several specific nightmares and "wet dreams" with sexual
connotations lie at the source of much modern horror literature. The word "nightmare" probably comes from the Old English *maere*, Old Irish *mar/mor* (demon) signifying "one who leaps
on, oppresses or crushes." In the folklore of the South Slavs
is the belief in the female demon *Mara* (Croation *mora*) who,
having tasted the blood of a man, falls in love with him and
returns for nightly visits with him.

The first modern horror story, *Castle of Otranto*, was inspired
by a frightening dream. Its author, Horace Walpole, wrote: "I
waked one morning, in the beginning of last June, from a dream,
of which all I could recover was, that I had thought myself in
an ancient castle (a very natural dream for a head like mine
filled with Gothic story) and that on the uppermost banister of
a great staircase I saw a gigantic hand in armour. In the evening
I sat down, and began to write without knowing in the least
what I intended to say or relate. The work grew on my hands,
and I grew so fond of it that one evening, I wrote from the
time I had drunk my tea, about six o'clock, till half an hour
after one in the morning, when my hands and fingers were so
weary that I could not hold the pen to finish the sentence."

The year was 1764. It was the Age of Reason, when "enlightened" minds were dismissing the idea of the supernatural as nonsense. Walpole discovered a large audience who, if they did not believe in ghosts, could still be frightened by them and find the fright enjoyable. To this author we owe "a revolution in public taste," as Montague Summers put it.

One of the main themes in Walpole's story has direct humorous sexual implications and is still one of the staples in most contemporary Gothic novels: the innocent woman pursued by a strange, handsome, powerful man who, she thinks, is intent upon either murdering her or forcing her into (what was then thought to be) a fate worse than death! In Walpole's *Otranto*, Marquess Frederic saunters along a castle corridor and, finding the door to the oratory open, he enters silently and comes upon a figure in long woolen garb, kneeling before the altar, its back to him. The figure very, very slowly turns around and Frederic sees to his horror that its face is of a corpse with the fleshless skull and empty sockets where eyes once were! (Shades of the final scene in Hitchcock's film *Psycho!*)

The horror story is often so bizarre as to elicit laughter since it borders on the ridiculous or grotesque. One finds it difficult to believe that people in the past acted and thought in the ways they actually did. They often seem to have been silly and even absurd.

From the outset the modern fictional horror story was often a kind of put-on, and the authors knew it. Walpole in a letter to Elie de Beaumont wrote about his *Castle of Otranto*, that first Gothic horror novel: "If I make you laugh, for I cannot flatter myself that I shall make you cry, I shall be content" (quoted by Robert Kiely in *The Romantic Novel in England*, p. 25). When someone slips on a banana peel through some quirk or misfortune, most of us laugh out of sentiments which Germans call *Schadenfreude*. We are happy to see someone worse off than ourselves. The ugly monster is pitiable, because he is generally more ugly than we, but he is also "funny."

This genre of humorous horror seems to me to have been developed most strongly by American writers, so that it can be considered a peculiarly, though certainly not exclusively, favorite American style. Edgar Allan Poe strongly blended horror and humor. His earliest stories, in *Tales of the Folio Club*, were satires and parodies of the serious horror story, especially his pair of stories "How to Write a Blackwood's Article" and "A Predicament." Poe's tale "A Predicament" is immediately recognizable as satire. The narrator, Suky Snobbs, having "heroinized" her name to Psyche Zenobia, longs to feel horrible sensations, so that she can imitate the style of *Blackwood Magazine* tales such as "The Dead Alive" and "The Man in the Bell." Listen to her: "On a sudden, there presented itself to view a church—a Gothic cathedral— vast, venerable, and with a tall steeple, which towered into the sky. What madness now possessed me? Why did I rush upon my fate? I was seized with an uncontrollable desire to ascend the giddy pinnacle." She gets her head caught in the clockworks of the ancient clock tower. Her emotions move from horror to amusement, as she gains release from that pain only to face another. "But now a new horror presented itself, and one indeed sufficient to startle the strongest nerves. My eyes, from the cruel pressure of the machine, were absolutely starting from their sockets. While I was thinking how I should possibly manage without them, one actually tumbled out of my head, and, rolling down the steep side of the steeple, lodged in the rain gutter which ran along the eaves of the main building." Zenobia's head is eventually cut off by the minute hand of the huge clock, but her head goes right on narrating the tale as it looks up at her body from the street below. In Poe's tale "Some Words with a Mummy," an ancient Egyptian mummy is brought back to life through the use of electric shock. The resurrected mummy turns out to be a decent, kindly fellow whose main critical remarks are directed at the absurdity of certain American political activities.

Ambrose Bierce (1842–1914), an American writer now largely forgotten, succeeded in making even murder humorous. In "A Watcher by the Dead" a man bets that he can stay the night locked in a house with a corpse. The corpse is actually a friend of one of his enemies playing a practical joke. The corpse, of course, seemingly comes back to life and his watcher dies of fright. But entrapped with the man he has frightened to death, the practical joker goes insane as well. Bierce's tale "An Imperfect Conflagration" begins with the lines "Early one June morning in 1771 I murdered my father—an act which made a deep impression on me at the time."

H. P. Lovecraft also had a flare for humorous horror. In his stories he liked to refer to nonexistent books such as the imaginary *Grimoire Necronomicon* of Abdul Alhazred; his reference to the *Cultes des Ghouls* supposedly written by Comte d'Erlette was in fact an in-joke, a tribute to his fellow American horror writer August Derleth. The awesome high priest Klarkash-Ton who is referred to in several Lovecraft tales was his California colleague Clark Ashton Smith. Smith, who was a recluse like Lovecraft himself, often lightened his horror tales with slices of humor.

In 1934 Robert Bloch, the famous author of *Psycho*, wrote "The Shambler from the Stars." The story is set in Lovecraft's home town Providence; in it, Lovecraft falls victim to one of his own demons. Not to be outdone, Lovecraft responded with "The Haunter of the Dark," in which the hero, a certain Robert Blake, encounters a horrible fate while investigating a purportedly haunted church. Not to be outdone in the continuing charade, Bloch in turn countered with "The Shadow from the Steeple."

Arch Obler, the first playwright to have a nationwide radio show "Lights Out!" during the 1940s, mixed horror and humor, especially in the memorable show "The Chicken That Ate the World." A scientist who by accident spilled some chemicals on a chicken heart that just kept growing and oozing its way across the entire earth, muses with his young protégé as they fly in a light plane 5,000 feet above the chicken heart, which has by now spread across the earth's surface: "The end of mankind . . . because of a chicken heart!" The airplane engines sputter; they are out of gas and plunge downward—a splat and slurping sound is what the listener hears.

Robert Bloch also developed the humorous vein in his tale "The Living Dead," which begins as a war story set just at the end of World War II in France. A Nazi collaborator Count Borsac has been playing at being a vampire to scare the villagers away from the castle, actually a Nazi stronghold. But the victorious Americans are coming, so the Count reluctantly acknowledges that he must give up his greatest performance. Unfortunately too late. The villagers catch him, carry him back to his coffin, and plunge a pointed stake into his heart: "It was only when the stake came down that he realized there's such a thing as playing a role too well."

Sometimes it is the *over*detailing that forces the reader to distance himself by laughing as in Richard Matheson's story "Drink My Red Blood," when a strange young boy named Jules, fascinated with Dracula, yearns to be a vampire. One day in front of his class he reads his essay in which he states, "When I grow up I want to be a Vampire, I want to have a foul breath and get even with everybody and make all the girls vampires. I want to smell of death . . . I want to sink my terrible white teeth in my victim's neck . . . Then I want to draw my teeth out and let the blood flow easy in my mouth and run hot in my throat . . . And drip off my tongue and run out of my lips down my victim's throat! I want to drink girls' blood! That is my ambition."

In the cultural subfield of comic books the American approach to horror through black humor achieved especial development. It had its origins during the 1950s when E. C. Comics broke with the traditional American format of the superhero—Superman, Batman, Captain Marvel—and featured instead horrible creatures such as vampires and werewolves. But in the aftermath of McCarthyism a 1954 Comic Code Authority was set up to head off public criticism that the comics were undermining "Americanism" among the youth. Section 5, Part B of the Comic Code By-Laws asserted that "Scenes dealing with, or instruments associated with the walking dead, torture, vampires and vampirism, ghouls, cannibals and werewolfism are prohibited." Some comic book publishing firms, Dell for one, did not go along with the prohibition initially, but eventually most of them fell in line, since only comics which adhered to the Comic Code were given wide distribution.

By the 1960s Warren Publishing Company was producing comic books which did not look like the usual colored comics;

they presented horror stories in black and white, in the famous series known as "Creepy" and "Eerie." By 1969 this same publishing company introduced the most successful female vampire in comic history. Her name was Vampirella. Created by the editor of *Famous Monsters of Filmland*, Forrest Ackerman, this very shapely sexy, supernatural *femme fatale*, clad in a scanty skin-tight black outfit (which showed more than it covered), sported a bat-shaped birthmark on her right breast and a golden bat insignia on her costume just below her navel.

In line with the changing American scene, which had gone from McCarthyism of the fifties to the anti-war demonstrations of the late sixties, in 1971 the Comic Code was changed to read: "Vampires, ghouls and werewolves shall be permitted to be used when handled in the classic tradition such as Frankenstein, Dracula, and other high calibre literary works by Edgar Allan Poe, Saki, Conan Doyle and other respected authors whose works are read in schools throughout the country." Marvel comics came up with a Dracula series entitled "The Tomb of Dracula" and "Dracula Lives," which did well throughout the seventies. Even today Vampirella is still going strong.

Shortly before he wrote "Christabel" and "Kublai Khan," Coleridge wrote that he would direct his attention to "persons and characters supernatural, or at least romantic, yet so as to transfer from our inward nature a human interest and a semblance of truth sufficient to procure for these shadows of imagination that willing suspension of disbelief for the moment, which constitutes poetic faith . . ." There is the vampirish Geraldine in "Christabel," and after Coleridge had begun "Christabel" he had an opium-induced dream which resulted in "Kublai Khan;" one fragment of which was rich in eroticism: "A savage place! As holy and enchanted as e'er beneath a waning moon was haunted by a woman wailing for her demon-lover!"

But the author who added the strong sexual tones to the genre was Matthew Gregory Lewis (1773-1818), who wrote the scandalous novel *The Monk*, which was banned by the Society for the Suppression of Vice in England. The Capuchin abbot,

Ambrosio, a foundling raised by the monks, is seduced by the beautiful Matilda who has entered the monastery disguised as a novice. They plunge into one orgy after another. Ambrosio tries to rape an innocent girl Antonia, but Antonia's mother frustrates his effort, so he murders her; then Ambrosio kidnaps Antonia, rapes her and kills her in a vain attempt to avoid discovery—only to discover at the end of the novel that Antonia had been his sister, and so her mother, whom he had murdered, was his very own.

Sexual fear and fear of vampirism both come to the fore in Emily Bronte's novel *Jane Eyre* published in 1847. Rochester's insane wife, Bertha, whom Rochester learns only after his marriage was an older woman and part Creole, is treated like a monster by her husband Rochester because she was "a wife at once intemperate and unchaste . . . at nature the most gross, impure, depraved I ever saw, associated with mine, and called by the law and by society part of me" (Chapter 27). When the governess Jane learns about Bertha's existence on what was to be her own wedding day, she refuses to go on living with Rochester, and only goes back after Bertha has been killed by a timely fire. Her own vision of Bertha is vivid: "Oh, sir, I never saw a face like it! It was a discolored face—it was a savage face. I wish I could forget the roll of the red eyes and the fearful blackened inflation of the lineaments! . . . The lips were swelled and dark, the brow furrowed; the black eyebrows widely raised over the bloodshot eyes. Shall I tell you of what it reminded me? Of the foul German spectre—the Vampire" (Chapter 25). Jane does not know at that time who Bertha is, having seen her only when Bertha burst into her bedroom to tear Jane's wedding veil. Rochester suffers drastic mutilation and Jane returns to take control over the weak, blind Rochester left with only one hand, an easy task.

Algernon Charles Swinburne, who knew the work of De Sade, and after him Charles Baudelaire, brought about the incarnation of the *femme fatale*—pale, bloodthirsty monster of beauty. In *Chastelard*, the first drama of Swinburne's trilogy, Mary Stuart embodies the image; in the third act Chastelard says about Mary: "My blood shed out about her feet—by God, my heart feels drunken when I think of it. See you, she will not rid herself of me, not though she slay me: Her sweet lips and life will smell of my spilt blood. . . ."

In *Balthazar*, the second in a series of novels set in Egypt by Anglo-Irish author Lawrence Durrell, Pursewarden tells the story of Italian poet Carlo Negroponte who at carnival time has met what he calls "the perfect woman" and shows "with exhausted pride that his body was covered with great bites, like the marks of a weasel's teeth." According to Negroponte, "Until you have experienced it . . . you have no idea what it is like. To have one's blood sucked in darkness by someone one adores." In the end Negroponte dies of the bites.

*Interview with a Vampire* by Anne Rice is a special story, one of the most perverse and morbid to come along in a long time. It is a tale about three vampires, Louis, Lestat and Claudia (a five-year old child), who all live together in New Orleans. As vampires they never grow old, but no one in New Orleans seems to notice these two men and a little girl who stay the same ages for sixty-five years. Nor does anyone in New Orleans appear to worry about the number of victims who fall prey to these vampires. Each kills at least one mortal every night. Victims of disease, plague, and other causes may indeed have outnumbered the vampire victims in old New Orleans, but even so! Louis, the head vampire, recounts his life's story to a boy who takes it down on a tape recorder. In the end the boy rushes off wanting to become a vampire himself. There are some lurid scenes which would shock almost anyone. For example, when an old woman dies, one of the male vampires picks up the dead body and dances with it, and their five-year old girl companion sleeps in one of the coffins on top of one of the male vampires!

But not all horror stories depend on humor and eroticism. Stephen King, author of the highly successful *Carrie*, recently published an excellent spine-tingling vampire novel called *Salem's Lot*. He says about it: "When I wrote my own vampire novel, *Salem's Lot*, I decided to largely jettison the sexual angle" (*Danse Macabre*, p. 76). The story tells about the outbreak of vampirism in a small New England town. Gradually the reader comes to realize that the disease is spreading from family to family. The children infect one another and their own parents in an incestuous interplay.

The perfect place to relive one's dreams and fantasies is naturally the silver screen. And the vampiric elements are being stressed more strongly than ever. In 1913 Hollywood introduced the concept of the "vamp." The word was coined deliberately to launch one of the first movie stars to have a career created solely by publicity. Her theatrical name was Theda Bara (an anagram of "Arab Death"). In the film *A Fool There Was* she had the famous line "Kiss me, my fool" and she was photographed crouching over a skeleton with a look of smug conquest in her eyes. The vamp was the definitive *femme fatale*. She was portrayed as wanton, voluptuous, and cruel.

The first Dracula film, *Nosferatu: A Symphony of Horrors* (1922), was by the German director Friedrich Murnau, who had been educated as an art historian. The film is especially erotic during the ending, when the heroine voluntarily sacrifices herself to spend the night in bed with the vampire "until the cock crows" in order to save her husband and fellow villagers. The vampire is shown on his knees at her bedside, sucking her blood.

Lugosi's *Dracula* of 1931 presented the suave continental type with the heavy accent, the slimy sophisticate always wearing evening clothes, kissing ladies' hands—something very un-American (anyone who kissed your hand was thought likely to bite your neck.) But one is indebted not to Bela Lugosi but to the Anglo-Irish actor and playwright Hamilton Deane for this popular image of the vampire Count Dracula: always in tuxedo complete with black cape, Hamilton Deane introduced this style on the stage; Lugosi only imitated it without being fully aware of what he was doing (or saying for that matter—he never learned English, having memorized many of his lines phonetically). One erotic scene in the movie occurs when Renfield, having accidentally cut his finger on a paper clip, squeezes out the blood and sucks it, while Dracula smilingly looks on approvingly as if pleased to see a human imbibing the precious fluid which he himself favors so much.

*The* truly erotic vampire film of 1931 was *M: A City Seeks a Murderer* by the noted Austrian filmmaker Fritz Lang, which was based on a real-life child murderer Peter Kurten, known in the newspapers as the "Vampire of Düsseldorf." (Lang was in fact a spectator at Kurten's court trial which opened in April 1931.) Kurten, a "living vampire," testified that it all started when he was a child, and a beautiful neighbor gave him duck's milk to drink. He said he killed mainly "to see the blood flow," and rebelliously shouted at his judges, "You cannot understand me; no one can understand me." He needed blood as others need alcohol. One witness stated that "he speaks of his need to kill as others talk of their habit of smoking." In the movie Peter Lorre played the child murderer as one who could not help doing it; it was his sexual compulsion. He was more to be pitied than censured.

In 1932 the gifted Danish director Carl Dreyer created a surrealistic film called *Vampyr*, freely adapted from Le Fanu's *Carmilla*. This presented atmospheric rather than visual horror. The horror was evident in the eyes and gestures of the actors. Shot through gauze, it was basically fear-inspiring anticipation.

The surprising thing is that America took so long to develop its own style in the movies. The German Expressionist techniques, which simulated schizophrenia through the hyperbolic use of weird stage sets, lighting, and camera angles, found little echo in the American films, even though during the thirties so many German filmmakers and cameramen flocked to this country.

In *Dracula's Daughter* (1936) the young female vampire made its first appearance, with Gloria Holden playing Countess Marya Zaleska, a daughter of Count Dracula. She believes that the blood-drinking urge had been consumed by the fire that burned her father's body at the outset of the film. Of course, as Shakespeare and the average viewer know, blood is thicker than water—or fire! She is doomed to the blood lust. This film introduces a new tradition: the vampire in spite of herself. Desperately trying to keep her blood lust under control, she is nonetheless compelled to give in to it. Even her attraction to a young doctor is unable to stem the tide.

One show that made a lasting impression in that era was the Orson Welles version of the Dracula story. It was an hour-long radio show, the first presentation of *The Mercury Theatre on the Air* on the Columbia Broadcasting system. The story had incredibly deep impact. Long before others probed the full erotic aspects of the Dracula story, Orson Welles did. Welles read Dracula's lines and spoke in deep, enticing tones: "The one you love is mine already. I have known her. Already my mark is on her throat. Flesh of my flesh, blood of my blood." Welles made Dracula into a believable "demon lover." But none of the movies of the forties took the cue and advanced the genre at all.

When the werewolf made his first screen appearance during the 1930s, unfortunately there was no literary work on this topic to compare with Stoker's *Dracula*. In the film the *Werewolf of London* (1935), the main actor Henry Hull (as Dr. Wilfred Glendon) was bitten in Tibet by Warner Hand (playing the lycanthrope, Dr. Yogami from the University of Carpathia), while both were out in the mountains seeking the *Mariphasa lupino lumino*, a rare flower which bloomed only in moonlight and was considered to be an antidote against lycanthropy. As a result of the bite, Dr. Glendon became a werewolf himself and was so preoccupied with growing his own *Mariphasa lupino* that he literally forgot to have any sexual contact with his wife. In the end Dr. Yogami steals Dr. Glendon's antidote and Glendon is doomed to turn into a wolf and kill.

The most famous American werewolf movie, *The Wolfman* (1941), starred Lon Chaney Jr. as the tormented, guilt-ridden wolfman. The son of the famous silent screen horror film actor, like Gloria Holden in *Dracula's Daughter*, inspired pity with his crazy suffering looks of pain. Universal Pictures was serving at the time as a home away from home for those German filmmakers on the run from Hitler. Curt Siodmak, who had done his apprenticeship in the German theater, wrote the screenplay in which he created lines that were wrongly assumed to have come from authentic folklore such as:

*Even a man pure of heart*
*Who says his prayers by night*
*Can become a werewolf*
*When the autumn moon is full and bright!*

Maria Ouspenskaya, ex-star from the Moscow Art Theater, played the wolfman's surrogate gypsy mother with melodramatic flair. After Claude Raines has unwittingly clubbed his own son to death, she ends the film poetically: "The way you walk is thorny through no fault of your own. For as the rain enters the soil, and rivers enter the sea, so tears run to their predestined end. Your suffering is over. Now find peace for eternity, my son."

The Val (Vladimir) Lewton films acquired a kind of cult following as classic "soft" horror (the horrible is only suggested, not shown on screen). In Lewton's *Cat People*, directed by Jacques Tourneur, the girl with the foreign accent Irena (played by Simone Simon) is shy and reticent especially in the presence of men, because she is convinced that if she becomes sexually aroused, she will turn into a cat—a variation on the werewolf theme. She does her best to try to warn hero Kent Smith, but, of course, he courts her and marries her only to find her distant and cold in his arms.

During the 1940s "serious" vampire and werewolf movies fell on hard times, and, also, as Stephen King puts it, "The eclipse of horror fiction that began in 1940 lasted for twenty-five years" (*Danse Macabre*, p. 41). Pearl Harbor on December 7, 1941, delivered the *coup de grace* to the horror movies and to horror fiction. When faced with *real* horrors, the straightforward horror movie found no audience. (Perhaps this is one reason why horror movies have never been popular in Russia and Eastern Europe; there everyday horror suffices.)

But it is in the movies of the forties that one can detect the emergence of a uniquely American approach to horror through humor. Two examples stand out, both by Frank Capra: *Arsenic and Old Lace* (1944) and *Abbott and Costello Meet the Killer* (1949). These are different from the straight comedies like *Abbott and*

*Costello Meet Frankenstein* in which the monsters are not threatening at all but simply silly. By contrast in both these special cases the horrible characters are presented and portrayed without parody or ridicule. Comic characters are confronted by truly menacing figures. For example, in *Arsenic and Old Lace* the scarfaced homicidal maniac Jonathan Brewster (played by Raymond Massey) and his macabre sidekick (portrayed by Peter Lorre) were truly frightening; and in *Abbott and Costello Meet the Killer* Boris Karloff played the killer as a real murderer. The contrast between the comic and the horrible heightened both. Unfortunately this genre did not develop any further in the movies of the fifties; instead it was dropped as "outmoded" in favor of straight satire.

A decade after the World War II period, the genre got a shot in the arm. Around 1955 Samuel Z. Arkoff and James H. Nicolson decided that it was about time to revive the horror movie. Almost everyone told them that they were crazy and that they would lose money when they launched their American-International Horror Pictures. The critics were wrong! These very successful films such as "I was a Teen-Age Frankenstein" and "I Was a Teen-Age Monster," etc. were not simple remakes, but instead brought horror home to a people fearful about Communist infiltration in that era of McCarthyism. The setting for these films was not Transylvania nor England, as in the thirties and forties, but usually small-town America. Previously the film monsters were foreigners who spoke broken English, but this time they talked "plain American." (Bela Lugosi, Peter Lorre, and Boris Karloff had all spoken with decidedly un-American accents—horror itself was "un-American." Even Irena in Lewton's sophisticated *Cat People* came from Serbia and had a heavy central European accent.)

For the first time the monster was an average American teenager, misunderstood by his parents. The teenager's parents generally thought the protagonist was a hood with his Vitalis-greased hair and a pair of Luckies tucked into the epaulet of his high school Eisenhower jacket. When he changed into a werewolf or a Frankenstein-like creature, he often kept his jacket on; in fact, his face often looked as if he had simply a very bad case of acne. Teenagers could identify with that.

The old Universal horror classics were syndicated in 1957 for late-night showings on TV across the United States. Suddenly millions of people became acquainted with the old monsters, and in California Forrest Ackerman launched his magazine *Famous Monsters of Filmland*. In New York a newspaper called *The Monster Times* (no doubt in competition with *The New York Times*) appeared, as did innumerable fan magazines called "fanzines" put out by the cognoscenti. Various bizarre live hosts appeared on TV shows (called Shock Theater or Creature Feature) to introduce these old films. All this set the stage for a creative turn in horror film history.

A real turning point in portrayal of the *erotic* vampire came only some twenty-five years ago with the successful British Hammer film *Horror of Dracula* (1958). The British actor of Italian-gypsy lineage, tall, imposing Christopher Lee, played a sensual vampire who kissed his women—to their evident delight—before he bit them on the neck. The heroines were not virginal as they had been in the thirties and forties, and in the Mansfield-Monroe tradition, were very generously endowed. Bela Lugosi never wore fangs, but Lee not only showed his homemade fangs but sported large contact lenses that gave his eyes blood-red veins in technicolor. The critics were scandalized, but the films made millions. But by the 1960s the genre declined again in a morass of stupid remakes.

Roger Vadim's films continued to expand on the theme of Le Fanu's lesbian vampires. In his vapid movie *Blood and Roses* (1960) there were close-ups of women's rain-wet faces kissing and in *Terror in the Crypt* (1963) the women strolled hand in hand through the gardens.

But the real erotic shocker in 1960 was Hitchcock's film *Psycho* with its famous shower scene. Some consider it to have been based on the vampire theme and others on the werewolf. Stephen King, referring to the main protagonist Norman Bates, declares: "Norman is the Werewolf" (*Danse Macabre* p. 84). But, in my opinion, Norman is more of a necrophile than a werewolf, having stuffed the body of his dead mother in taxidermist fashion, as he had stuffed his dead birds. And certainly his dead mother functions like a classic legendary vampire—she controls him, gradually sucks his personality away until the dead mother literally takes over Norman's body in the end.

Another well-done film of this period in the tradition of the unseen terror was Robert Wise's *The Haunting* based on the excellent short novel by Shirley Jackson, entitled *The Haunting of Hill House*. The heroine Eleanor (played by Julie Harris) is one of life's losers, a lonely introvert who had to take care of her aging mother whom she hated. Her girlfriend Theo (played by Claire Bloom) has a lesbian yearning for Eleanor. Something horrible knocks on the walls and pushes at the ornate, paneled door until it looks as if the door will burst. But it does not; the horror is never seen. In the end the old house like a vampire absorbs Eleanor.

In 1961 Roger Corman, a native of Los Angeles, brought out his film *Little Shop of Horrors*, made on a shoestring budget. Corman's own account of the film development may be exaggerated: "We were going to play tennis but it was raining." In the film an exotic plant develops a taste for blood, because its breeder, horticulturalist Seymour Mushnick (Jonathan Haze), has accidentally sprinkled it with blood from his cut finger. The plant develops a vampiric appetite and voice, whining, "Feed me!" So Seymour Mushnick is obliged to provide victims—an odd corpse from time to time, some occasional gangsters (the plant sucks up the bodies but regurgitates the guns). In the end, just as Seymour is presented with a prize for this botanical triumph, the plant's buds open to reveal the faces of all of its previously digested human victims.

Mel Brooks' *Young Frankenstein* is in this same tradition of the "sick joke" of magazine cartoonists Charles Addams and Gahan Wilson, mixed with nostalgia. So, one student disputes whether his professor's real name is "Frankenstein" or "Frankensteen." The hunchback has a hump that shifts positions. And the good doctor questions, "Pardon me boy, is this the Transylvania station?" only to be told by the hunchback as he stumbles along, "Walk this way." Frankenstein's creature features zip-fasteners instead of sutures, and the creature learns how to do a dance step with his creator. The horrible elements never get a chance to be menacing. From the beginning such films are destined to be ridiculous.

The Italian director Mario Bava contributed a film based on Nikolai Gogol's short story "Viy," entitled *La Maschera del Demonio* in 1961 (released as *Black Sunday* in America). In it one of the most voluptuous sex goddesses of all time, Barbara Steele, made her appearance: with her hollow, high cheekbones, she looked like everybody's vision of a sexy female vampire.

*Dracula, Prince of Darkness* or *Blood of Dracula* (1965) was the first major British sequel to the 1958 *Horror of Dracula*. The film was notable only for the erotic sucking scene when Dracula exposes his chest for his female victim to drink (only to be interrupted by the sudden arrival of others).

Finally in 1967 came the first successful attempt to make a comic vampire movie, Roman Polanski's *Le Bal des Vampires* (American title *The Fearless Vampire Killers or Pardon Me, but Your Teeth Are in My Neck*). The film satirizes the Hammer-style horror films. The "learned" doctor- vampire hunter was a clumsy bungler; one vampire was gay and went for the young doctor's assistant (played by Roman Polanski) only to have a little Bible shoved between his teeth; a Jewish vampire was not warded off by a Christian cross; and Sharon Tate finished by biting Polanski on the neck.

The major surprise of 1968 was George Romero's *Night of the Living Dead*, filmed in nine months from 1967 to 1968; the naturalness of the dialog and the actors served to heighten the sense of horror; the film also presented erotic scenes that probed basic human family taboos: the daughter plunges a garden spade into her mother and then eats her mother's body; a brother attacks his sister and drags her out to be eaten by the undead.

But it was in the French films far from American eyes that true vampiric eroticism flourished in this period: Jean Rollin's *Le Vol du Vampire* in 1968 showed the sensuous vampire queen surrounded by her young girlfriends, all drinking blood from bowls. Rollin went on to make *La Reine des Vampires, La Vampire Nue, Vierges et Vampire*, and *Lèvres du Sang*. In 1970 came his *Le Frisson des Vampires*, released in English as *Sex and the Vam-*

*pire*, in which the lesbian vampire clad in leather boots is reduced to sucking her own blood. The main vampire was portrayed as a woman with sexual attraction not for men but for other women.

And what a year for lesbian vampires 1970 proved to be. In the film *To Love a Vampire* (1970) the amply endowed Yvette Stensgaard went after the girls in an all-female boarding school. The Spanish-born director Jesus Franco made *Vampyros Lesbos* (1970), in which a countess who claims to be a descendant of Dracula attacks a young girl like an aggressive lesbian lover. In the British Hammer Studio's *The Vampire Lovers* (1970), Ingrid Pitt portrayed a vampire who had lived on for three generations and terrorized her village. The idea of a female vampire with lesbian tendencies was certainly making itself felt in the film industry.

The lesbian trend continued through the mid-seventies. *The Velvet Vampire* (1971) was directed by Stephanie Rothman, the first woman to make a vampire movie; she had worked with Roger Corman before this film. It is the story of a lesbian-type vampire with a liking for velvet. The female vampire meets a young couple at an exhibition in the "Stoker" gallery and takes them back home. There they gradually recognize the real intent of the vampire and a chase scene ensues. Rothman effectively utilized the kinky, fantasy atmosphere of Southern California: a "laid-back" style of life that is suitable for any blood-sucker who sleeps by day and carouses at night. In a feminist twist, the female vampire disposes of a mugger and a potential rapist in the film.

*Vampyres* (1974) by Joseph Larroz shows two lesbian lovers, Fran and Miriam (Mirianna Morris and Anulka) who have been shot dead. They emerge as vampires, luring unsuspecting motorists to their deserted mansion. Fran finds one of her victims, Ted (played by Murray Brown), so appealing that she does not suck his blood completely dry. Ted responds to her affection, and, though he becomes weaker after each nocturnal encounter, he is infatuated with Fran. In the end Fran forcibly wrests her lesbian partner Miriam from Ted and totters blood-inebriated toward her coffin in the cellar, as daylight approaches.

In the movie *Daughters of Darkness* (1971) by the Belgian film director Harry Kumel, Countess Elizabeth Bathory made her first "authentic" screen appearance; unfortunately it was but a pale reflection of the historical countess. However, as a first attempt to translate the image of the Blood Countess artistically to film, it requires special analysis here.

The setting for the film is not Transylvania, nor is the time period the late sixteenth and early seventeenth centuries, nor, for that matter, is the film in a contemporary setting. Instead, the time period is the 1930s and the main place of action a vast hotel in Ostend on the Atlantic coast of Belgium. Two lovers, Valerie and Stefan, check into a resort hotel. There they meet Countess Bathory with her close-fitting curls, pearly white teeth, and enameled red lipstick—straight out of the women's style of the thirties. Countess Bathory shows an unusual interest in this young couple. She gradually succeeds in getting involved in the sexual relationship between the two of them and is able to lure the girl, whom she finds especially attractive, to her side. Stefan is killed and buried by the two women who have entered into a deep lesbian relationship, one in which the countess is in complete control. At the end of the film the two leave the Ostend hotel and have an automobile accident: the countess dies, impaled on the automobile steering mechanism.

In 1972 a full-length period film based (albeit loosely) on the legendary life of Elizabeth Bathory was released by Hammer Films Studio; it had the provocative title *Countess Dracula* and was produced by Alexander Paal and directed by Peter Sasdy. The general setting is a relatively authentic Hungarian/Central European village from the past, but the film itself was not believable. It showed Countess Bathory changing from an aged woman to a young one on the basis of blood treatments in a matter of seconds. A decent horror film must lead one to believe that the impossible is possible; this one made it impossible to take any of it at all seriously. When, at the end of the film the countess, deprived of her blood cosmetics, quickly turns back into an old hag, the viewer simply does not believe it.

*Ritual of Blood* (*Ceremonia Sangrienta*, 1972) is as yet unreleased in the United States: the protagonist, a marquise (based loosely on Elizabeth Bathory), is fixated upon blood for rejuvenation. Her husband Karl dies and comes back from the dead; they share the young woman whom he captures. The marquise eventually destroys him out of jealousy.

The last film to date to incorporate even a vague semblance of Elizabeth Bathory's life, and the best one of them all, was *Contes Immoraux* (*Immoral Tales*), released in France in 1974 and produced by Anatole Dauman with the screen play by Walerian Borowczyk. In one segment of that film Countess Elizabeth Bathory is portrayed rather effectively. She is shown going on a raid for girls with her cohorts. In her entourage is a page who rides close beside her and whom she addresses fondly. When they arrive back at her castle, Countess Elizabeth and her page go together into a room, and the Countess kisses the page. Only at that moment, when the long hair of the page becomes visible, does the viewer know that the page is in fact a girl. It is a great visual moment and sets the atmosphere for the rest of the action. The girls who have been captured from the local village are made to strip and are washed down. They are murdered sadistically and the countess bathes in their blood.

On television during this period a popular afternoon show was "Dark Shadows" by Don Curtis with Jonathan Frid as the vampire, but when it was made into a movie, it failed. The successful TV production "The Night Stalker" (1972), also by Don Curtis with Barry Atwater as vampire, spawned a series entitled "Kolchak: The Night Stalker" which began in 1974 but only lasted a few short seasons.

A made-for-TV *Dracula* (1973) written by Richard Matheson (author of *I am Legend*) starring Jack Palance complete with fangs and cape, contributed very little to the genre. It opens in Bistritz, Hungary, in May 1897 (it was actually filmed in Yugoslavia and England); the actors spoke Russian instead of Hungarian, and the film limped. Jack Palance gave a disappointing performance to boot. Nonetheless, there was a fine scene when Dracula finds that his long-lost beloved has been destroyed, and he groans and grunts like a wild animal as he smashes various funeral urns.

One of the most embarrassing disasters was the film starring

David Niven called *Old Dracula* (after having been titled *Vampirella, Vampira*, etc.). David Niven should have known better. Why the title was chosen becomes clear when one reads the movid ad: "If You Laughed at Young Frankenstein, You'll Howl at Old Dracula." This was one of the grossest attempts ever to cash in on the popularity of another movie. In it David Niven is the owner of an up-to-date horror castle into which tours are booked. But all the guests are examined in their sleep for a rare blood type which Old Dracula needs to revive his wife (played by Teresa Graves). She is indeed revived, but as a black woman, and at the end David Niven goes black-face too on his way back to Transylvania on a jet liner. Not funny.

Andy Warhol's *Dracula*, also called *Blood for Dracula*, which premiered in 1975, was a genre apart. Written and directed by Paul Morrisey, the film starred Joe Dallesandro as the gardener, Udo Kier as Count Dracula, Vittorio de Sica as the nobleman, and Roman Polanski as a villager.

In this film, Dracula, dying from a lack of virgin's blood (due to a shortage of virgins in Transylvania), travels to Italy. There he tries to find virgin's blood but to no avail—the local gardener always manages to be one virgin ahead of Dracula. In the end the gardener pursues Dracula with an axe and hacks him to pieces, bit by bit.

George Romero, creator of *The Night of the Living Dead* (1968), the most original horror movie ever made by an American, made a movie about a living vampire called *Martin* (1977), a Libra Films Release, produced by Richard Rubenstein. The cast included John Amplas as Martin and Lincoln Maazel as Cuda. Martin is a psychopath, a "living vampire," someone who feels compelled to drink human blood. The setting is the dying steel town of Braddock, Pennsylvania, where both young and old are trapped. They are all dying amid the dreary banality of lower middle-class life. Martin injects his female victims with a knockout drug, opens their veins, drinks their blood and has intercourse with the inert bodies. Martin is a necrophile as well as a vampire. The old man in the film, Cuda, uses methods from the Old World to try to deal with the vampire, such as crucifixes, garlic, and mirrors. It is all to no avail. Martin himself has one normal sexual encounter with an older woman played by Elyane Nadeau, but this ends in his own destruction. George Romero and Dario Argento, who did *Suspiria* and *Deep Red*, combined forces to do a sequel to *Night of the Living Dead* entitled *Dawn of the Dead* (1979), with several gross-out scenes in a typical American shopping mall.

A current cult film usually shown at midnight is *The Rocky Horror Picture Show* (1975). Produced by Lou Adler for 20th Century-Fox, it is a kind of rock musical with monsters and homosexuals galore with throwbacks to the classic horror movies of the forties and fifties, plus a transvestite Transylvanian.

The *Count Dracula* (1978) BBC TV production was a valiant try but failed to measure up despite attempts to adhere to Stoker's basic storyline. Yet the film did mark a breakthrough in its use of quality personnel and production. Louis Jourdan as Count Dracula was too cold, too aloof. He was the elegant European aristocrat but had none of the demonic obsessed mystery. The religious theme was highlighted. Renfield loved his "Master" and Jourdan referred to his beloved as "my bountiful wine press." He was indeed a strange lord, the anti-Christ, founder of a new kind of religion. "I seek disciples," he proclaimed, "just as your Master did." His new order seemed closer to redemption than to disease. Jourdan's Dracula was like the Reverend Jim Jones. Unfortunately the electronic device of negative images, video mattes of Jourdan's face, detracted by jarring the viewer out of context. The assorted fangs and gushing blood did not enhance the film.

During the late 1970s word got around Hollywood that vampire and werewolf movies were box office disasters. But the Broadway success of the revived 1927 Dracula play by Hamilton Deane and John Balderston which opened on October 20, 1977, caused Hollywood filmmakers to reassess the situation. As a result, a deluge of horror movies hit in 1979 and one felt like Noah trying to navigate in the pelting rain—except that it was raining blood and gore instead of plain water.

In 1979 John Badham's *Dracula* appeared with Frank Langella trying to repeat his humorously erotic stage performance in the film; his beloved Mina sucked the blood from his chest and was even shown sleeping in a coffin with the count. But the most erotic moment came when Van Helsin (played by Laurence Olivier) discovers that his dead daughter's grave is empty. He descends below it into an underground pool, where his dead daughter surprises him and begs for a kiss from her father. She is a pock-marked, decayed, revolting corpse, so he stakes her out.

Another 1979 critical hit was Werner Herzog's *Nosferatu* in which French actress Isabelle Adjani attracts the horrid count to her bedroom where she enjoys him drinking her blood so much that she pulls him back down when he attempts to leave; he in turn suffers it all because of his deep love for her. Usually at the end of a horror film the humans have confidence that they can win. But this film calls that into question; society is helpless at trying to curb vampirism.

The Mel Simon comedy entitled *Love at First Bite* released in 1979 was directed by Stan Dragoti. It presented Count Dracula (George Hamilton) as someone with a strange social problem; luckily for him his girlfriend (Susan St. James) liked his kinky form of sex. Some of George Hamilton's lines have entered American humor almost as much as Bela Lugosi's old lines. For example, when the Transylvanian peasants arrive with pitchforks to drive out the count, Hamilton as Dracula proclaims: "What would Transylvania be without Dracula" It would be like Monday night in Bucharest!" Or when the mix-up in coffins arriving in New York occurs, Dracula's is mistakenly sent to a funeral home in Harlem. After the count emerges and is walking down the streets of Harlem, he is accosted by a black mugger who says, "Hey, baby, why you all dressed up like that? Hey, honkie!" To which the count, evidently unaccustomed to the language, heatedly states, "I am *not* hunkie, I am Romanian!"

In 1979 an adaptation of Stephen King's superb vampire tale *Salem's Lot* appeared on TV (screenplay by Paul Morosh; starring David Soul, James Mason and Lew Ayres). It was replayed on nationwide TV in September 1981. In the truncated TV version the sex angle, which Stephen King had largely "jettisoned," takes over. In a Hitchcockian deliberate diversion of the audience's attention, the classic subplot of the suspicious husband surprising his wife and her lover with a shotgun is eased into the story. A frightening erotic element occurs when dead Ralph Glick with his strange eyes appears scratching at Danny Glick's window. Danny, as if in a trance, opens the window for his dead brother to enter, and Ralph attacks Danny. When Danny is discovered collapsed the next day, the search for an unknown disease follows lines very reminiscent of Bram Stoker's novel *Dracula*. Is it pernicious anemia? Young Mark Petrice knows that the vampire Barlow is responsible for killing his mother, father and brother. He vows vengeance. In the end the writer Ben and Mark Petrie join forces to eradicate the vampire Barlow. They also eliminate Ben's girlfriend who has become a vampire, and Ben warns, "There will be others!"

Nineteen eighty-one saw the resurgence of the werewolf theme in several films. The Orion Pictures *Wolfen*, which featured superwolves, based on the book by Whitley Strieber, starring a seemingly bored Albert Finney, was merely a dull rehash of trite themes, aside from the American Indian who experienced shape-changing. The film *An American Werewolf in London*, written and directed by John Landis of *Animal House* fame, drew upon the monster movie tradition for purposes of amusing parody and even dared to offer suggestions of cunnilingus. Despite the gore and gross-out scenes, the photography was superb and the script well done. *An American Werewolf in London* begins as all the good horror movies have done, with ordinary dialog and scenes. Two Americans are hiking through the English countryside, they talk jokingly and naturally, nothing supernatural occurs. But there are ominous signs in the local English pub, where the villagers are sullen, grim, and afraid. On the road the two young Americans are attacked by a werewolf. Jack is killed, but he comes back to visit his friend. The unique twist is that Jack speaks naturally as he did in life, and he continues to like his friend. The best scene is in a British porno movie house when the hero, after greeting his ever-natural friend Jack in yet further state of physical decomposition, begins changing into a werewolf, making grunts and groans amusingly similar to those of the porno actors and actresses on the movie house screen. It is the epitome of the American genre, having fun with horror.

Here, in the spirit of the 1936 *Dracula's Daughter* and 1941 *The Wolfman*, we once again see the *reluctant* monster as well: the person doomed to commit evil by fate, not by choice. The hero is a tortured individual who does not want to change into wolf form but is compelled to do so. In the end of the film the average viewer feels sorry for the hero as he reaches out to embrace his beloved, only to be gunned down by the mob as a menace to society.

Today one is struck by the particular *lack* of legendary horror based upon the supernatural. Instead out-and-out psychotic murderers abound. *Halloween* by John Carpenter, released in 1978, set the trend. A knife-wielding psychopath, a fugitive from a mental institution, menaces a typical American suburban neighborhood. The actress Jamie Lee Curtis who played everyone's fantasy of the lovely baby-sitter, was pursued by the maniac and established herself as the new uncrowned queen of the horror movies. The recent movies such as *The Texas Chainsaw Massacre*, *The Hills Have Eyes* continue that trend towards "real," not imaginary horror, as does the British horror film *Raw Meat*, directed by an American, Gary Sherman, and *Frightmare* by Peter Walker in which a seemingly sweet old woman finds that she cannot go on living without eating human flesh, so her dear, devoted husband helps her get it.

One of the prime reasons for the current comic approach is that the horrors of one older generation generally become objects of ridicule for subsequent generations. Count Dracula, the Wolfman, and Frankenstein have become household words in the United States and western Europe. Almost every child knows what they do from TV reruns of the old movies. So, the familiar monsters are set up as prime targets for satire.

Horror stories and films should be funny. A sense of humor is essential. Only the crazies take them seriously. Unfortunately there has been a great deal of sheer exploitation of the genre. As in the case of porno stories and movies, many people have seen a chance to make a quick buck and have thought that it is relatively easy to create a good (i.e., frightening) horror story or movie. Actually it is very difficult to write a good horror story and to create a good horror movie, and a good, *funny* horror story or movie is doubly difficult to execute.

The open question is whether the inherent eroticism and humor in vampire, werewolf and necrophile films can compete with explicit sex movies. Many unsuccessful attempts have been made to combine the inherent eroticism with pornographic explicitness. The results have almost invariably been sexploitation films of the lowest sort. Let me merely cite the worst: *Dracula's Saga* (1972) and *Cannibal Girls* (1974).

The current comic approach as evidenced in *Love at First Bite*, and *An American Werewolf in London* are, I *hope*, the harbingers of things to come. It may be, however, that they are the last gasps of a dying genre. As the Anglo-Irish poet William Butler Yeats put it in his prophetic work entitled "The Second Coming:"

> Turning and turning in the widening gyre
> The falcon cannot hear the falconer;
> Things fall apart; the center cannot hold;
> More anarchy is loosed upon the world,
> The blood-dimmed tide is loosed, and everywhere
> The ceremony of innocence is drowned;
> The best lack all conviction, while the worst
> Are full of passionate intensity.
> And what rough beast, its hour come round at last,
> Slouches towards Bethlehem to be born?

Is one faced with a Yeatsian-like "rough beast" with a smile on its face and wit in its head, slouching towards Bethlehem to be born or merely the decaying pornography of contemporary Sodom and Gomorrah?

# Conclusion

ELIZABETH BATHORY, as vampire, the werewolf, and necrophile, still lies in wait for some artist capable of making her attractive. The recent hit record, Warren Zevon's *The Werewolf of London*, is one example of this renewal. Television has, of course, made it difficult for one to create the fright that the audience can experience in a darkened movie theater. How can one really be afraid of a tiny creature on a small screen, especially when the commercial breaks destroy any belief? How can one be afraid when one is surrounded by a familiar home environment? On TV's "Sesame Street" even the Count is reduced to teaching children their numerals. TV turns monsters into munsters, non-threatening comics.

Still, there are five basic reasons for current serious interest in horror history as exemplified in Elizabeth Bathory with references to vampirism, werewolfism, and necrophilism:

1) *a rejection of getting old and dying.* The Elizabeth Bathory legend highlights the perennial human search for some fountain of youth. Most humans would like to remain young and avoid the rigors of old age when the human body invariably begins to break down. Most people do not want to die and would, like Fausts, grab at the chance for eternal life, provided, of course, that one could remain youthful (like a well-fed vampire). In fact, most people, especially in the Western world and

in the United States, try to appear younger than they really are. Most would even settle for "looking young," if they could not *be* forever young. They jog with intensity and sit in the sun to get their skin tanned, since paleness is associated with old people and corpses. (There is an especial irony in the craze to get a tan: it is well established both in the medical world and the beauty trade that nothing is more damaging to skin and ages it more than exposure to the sun.)

We even fix up our dead to appear youthful and healthy in death. Their faces are heavily brushed with cosmetics, their eyes are dutifully closed, so that they appear to be only having a good night's sleep. It is important that they look good. The decay of death is denied. They are referred to as "the dearly *departed*" who have "*passed away*"—as if they had merely gone on some short vacation. As soon as the cosmetics have done their job and begin to fade, the dead are transported to distant cemeteries, places far out of sight of the living.

To many people, death appears to be the ultimate irrevocable horror to be faced. We are incapable of understanding Count Dracula's admonition that there are "worse things waiting for man than death!" Instead, most humans find themselves literally "hung up" on death. "Death," the boy Mark Petrie says in Stephen King's book *Salem's Lot*, "is when the monsters get you," and the author Stephen King concludes, "if I had to restrict everything I have ever said or written about the horror genre to one statement . . . it would be that one. It is not the way adults look at death; it is a crude metaphor which leaves little room for the possibility of heaven, hell, Nirvanna . . ." (*Danse Macabre*, p. 190). Behind this lies the rejection of the Christian idea of death as an opening to another life as well as rejection of the Oriental notion of eternal return in which nothing really dies but merely comes back in another form. Among those who do not have the traditional religious concept of an afterlife or of rebirth to sustain them are some who appear to have adopted a morality based on gratification of the senses in the here and now. The furthest extension of this can be seen in the legendary vampire and werewolf, who totally reject death.

For them "life beyond the grave" has become the search for the undying body.

Most people have ambivalent attitudes towards death. Some envision death as a natural ending to human life, which must be accepted. Others fear the pain of death and do not wish to go through that mysterious, unknown, final experience. Most people do not want to die but do not know how to live beyond death. The vampire has found a method for life beyond the grave. One twentieth century author, Roger Vadim, has even suggested that there was a group of Jewish cultists who had discovered the secret of Jesus Christ's resurrection from the dead, had been forced out of their homeland, and had sought refuge in the Balkans; hence, the widespread belief in the undead in southeastern Europe. There is no evidence for that claim, however; it goes well with the mistaken belief that Jews use the blood of Christian babies in their Passover ceremonies.

Behind the vampirism concept is the Oriental notion that nothing ever really dies. Life merely changes its form. In the past, people used disguises to try to hide from the returning dead in the hopes that the *revenants* would not find them. The black veil worn traditionally by women at funerals is one surviving way of accomplishing that objective.

Throughout history, in all cultures, human beings have struggled to find a meaning for death. Soothsayers, philosophers, priests, and scientists have all tried their hand at producing a rationale for death—without much success. Today we may smile at the "childish" notions our ancestors had about the meaning of death. Are our notions any better than theirs? Those who come after us will undoubtedly smile at the current "scientific" ideas about death, ideas to which we cling as tenaciously as earlier societies clung to theirs.

2) *a fascination with the attractiveness of "the fix"; a tendency toward addiction within each of us*: Many people spend their lives seeking a quick, easy way to happiness. Some resort to alcohol, others to various drugs in order to "get a high." Elizabeth Bathory and the contemporary vampires, werewolves, and necrophiles are similar to alcoholics and drug addicts. Each is

fixated upon his or her own fetishism. Each goes for "the frosting on the cake" and ignores the cake itself. Once introduced to the practice, some of the victims also become fetishists, like alcoholics and drug addicts, as well.

In the dialog of the classic 1958 movie *Horror of Dracula*, Dr. Van Helsing touches upon that raw nerve when he recites into his recording machine: "Established that victims consciously detest being dominated by vampirism, but are unable to relinquish the practice, similar to addiction to drugs." The victims of the vampire get as hooked on the "drug" as well as the "pusher." In Le Fanu's novel *Carmilla*, the vampiric countess prepares her upcoming "meals," with the refined attentions of a gourmet, and her so-called "victim" Laura responds like a ready and willing sacrifice. As Baudelaire put it: "I am the vampire of my own heart."

In Peter Straub's recent novel, *Ghost Story*, the identity between the average protagonist Don Wanderley and the monster, an eerie little girl, is made frighteningly clear:

> "Okay, let's try again," he said. "What are you?" For the first time since he had taken her into the car, she really *smiled*. It was a transformation, but not a kind to make him feel easier; she did not look any less adult. "You know," she said. He insisted "What are you?" She smiled all through her amazing response, "I am you." "No. I am me. You are you." "I am you."

3) *the breakdown of traditional social values: the violation of taboos*: Elizabeth Bathory and her kind stand against common *family* values. Human mothers should not eat their children, as Elizabeth Bathory ate parts of the young servants in her extended "family." Similarly, children should not devour their parents, like teenaged vampires or werewolves. There is a medical delusion called "the Capgras syndrome," in which the patient believes that his parents or lovers have turned into threatening doubles. This enables the patient to deny his basic hatred of a loved one by splitting the loved one into a "good" side and a "bad" side. It is the "bad" side of the loved one which the patient feels compelled to destroy. For example, in the 1970 movie *Taste the Blood of Dracula*, the children who are domi-

nated demonically by their Victorian fathers are able to unleash their anger against their fathers only after Dracula arrives to help them channel their fury. The daughters murder their three respective fathers, because, although they love the "good" side of their fathers, they hate the "bad." Torture and murder, as practiced by "mother" Elizabeth Bathory, were simply means of disciplining those young females in her household.

4) *a fascination with hostile sexual behavior*: The vampire, the werewolf, and the necrophile, like Elizabeth, attack; they commit acts that are violent and harmful, like a rapist. Most people are interested in watching rape scenes, in which either the male or the female is the aggressor. The voyeuristic mass appeal of the rape scene is, in fact, so powerful that almost all authors of horror stories or films feel obliged to include at least one such scene. There are deep psychological reasons for this. Dr. Robert Stoller put his finger on the nub of the problem printed in the *American Archives of General Psychiatry* (June 1970): "If hostility could be totally lifted out of sexual excitement, there would be no perversions, but would normal sexuality be possible?" Some one has to attack in hopes that the attacked will have sense enough to submit.

5) *an emphasis on sexual ambiguity*: In a society based upon the notion of monogamy and the importance of stable, one-man-to-one-woman sexual relationships, there is bound to be an enormous amount of sexual energy that has to be repressed. This must have been particularly true in Elizabeth's society, and in the past in general. Whatever is strongly repressed usually seeks some sort of outlet. In a male-dominated society, women had to be shielded from oral sex with one another, since the male might not be able to satisfy the yearnings of a girl who had been previously sexually aroused to such forbidden pleasures.

We fear the sexual partner who gets so carried away that he or she loses control and seeks to incorporate parts of the beloved to himself or herself. Biting and maiming, such as practiced by Elizabeth Bathory, as well as by vampires, werewolves and necrophiles, embody the depths of sexual dread. A recent woman's lib cartoon made this point with black humor by depicting a powerful, triumphant woman hovering over a male skeleton with the caption underneath: "He asked me to eat him, so I did!"

In his book *Structural Approach to the Fantastic*, the specialist Tsvetan Todorov says that "it is no longer necessary to resort to the devil in order to speak of an excessive sexual desire." Yet, even today when sexual juggernauts are no longer generally characterized as "possessed by the devil," sexual fantasy and fear have survived in the average bedroom. Even after the psychoanalytical approach has exhausted the deeper meanings behind the horror genre and allowed one seemingly to unmask the sexual motives behind the vampire, werewolf, and necrophile, unanswered questions remain. The supernatural and the unintelligible continue to play roles in the sex lives of most modern people, since human sexual encounters remain essentially mysterious. Things are, after all, rarely what they seem to be.

*Appendices*

# APPENDIX A

# *Old Documentation*

## I. Court of Inquiry, December 1610 (State Archives, Budapest)

At the very end of December 1610, the Hungarian Parliament gave a hearing to the castellan of Bytca, Gaspar Bajaky, who represented the complaints of the villagers, and to Imre Megyery, guardian of Elizabeth's son, Paul. The official report dated January 7, 1611, was kept in the secret Vienna Imperial Archives

## II. Copy of the Trial Report Dated January 2, 1611

(Copy in the Vienna State Archives. Original in the Budapest State Archives.)

This first trial in 1611 began with the recording of the confessions made to Gaspar Bajaky, castellan of Bytca, and Gaspar Kardos, public notary, and duly recorded by Daniel Eördeögh. The same eleven questions in Hungarian were put to the four defendants, Joannes Ujvary, alias Ficzko, Helena Jo, Dorothea Szentes, and Katarina Beneczky (see p. 204).

Summary Translation from the Original
Transcript of the Final Court Decision
in Latin, January 7, 1611

The document states that "upon the initiative of the illustrious Count George Thurzo of Bethlenfalva, the Palatine of the Hungarian King, etc., in the fortress town of the illustrious lord of Bitce (Bytca), a juridical investigation and trial, directed by the chief state attorney, George Zavodszky, was convened against the accused John Ficzko and also Helena, Dorothea, and Catharina, women from Sarvar . . . Whereas His Highness Count George Thurzo of Bethlenfalva, etc., had been unanimously elected to the office of Lord Palatine by the Estates of the Realm, in order to protect all good persons and punish the evil without fear or favor, after God and his King, His Highness, not wishing to close his eyes and turn a deaf ear to the satanic terror against Christian blood and the horrifying cruelties unheard of among the female sex since the world began, which Elizabeth Bathory, widow of the much-esteemed and highly-considered Ferenc Nadasdy, perpetrated upon her serving maids, other women and innocent souls, whom she extirpated from this world in almost unbelievable numbers, had ordered a complete investigation of the accusations leveled against Countess Nadasdy. Those charges of her great and infamous criminal actions have been substantiated by eye-witnesses and those who heard about them, after a series of investigations and the testimonies of her own servants against the widow of Nadasdy, so that her culpability has become manifest.

"His illustrious Highness had formed a committee consisting of the well-known and magnificent Nicholas Zriniy and George Drugeth of Homonna and their faithful servants, and Imre Megyery, guardian of the fatherless Nadasdy, and they in turn had gone to the manor house in the town of Csejthe (Cachtice). At the very entrance to the manor house they came upon things pertinent to this case. There was a certain virgin named Doricza who had been miserably extirpated by pain and torture, two other girls were found murdered in similar agonizing ways within that very manor house in the town of Csejthe (Cachtice), which was under the control of the widow Nadasdy. His illustrious Highness, witnessing this evident and ferocious tyranny, having caught the bloody, and godless woman, the widow Nadasdy, *in flagranti* of her crime, placed her under immediate perpetual imprisonment in Castle Csejthe (Cachtice) and arrested John Ficzko, Helena, Dorothea, and Catharina".

After some lengthy legal language comes the list of thirteen witnesses and their testimonies under oath. The most revealing testimony came from witness number ten, named Susanna (Zsuzanna) who stated that she heard that a certain Jacob Szilvassy had found a list in a box belonging to the Countess which put the total number of girls killed at 650.

"Since the voluntary confession of John Ficzko, Helena, Dorothea and Catharina, as well as the ones made under torture, together with the evidence provided by witnesses under oath, patently proved their guilt, a guilt surpassing all evil and cruelty, namely, murder, butcherings and most horrendous and assorted tortures, and because these grave crimes must be punished with the harshest penalty provided by law, we hereby sentence:

"First of all, Helena (Helena Jo, widow of Istvan Nagy), secondly Dorothea (Dorottya Szentes, widow of Benedek Szeoch), as the foremost perpetrators of this great blood crime, and in accordance with the lawful punishment for murderers, to have all the fingers on their hands, which they used as instruments in so much torture and butcherings and which they dipped in the blood of Christians, torn out by the public executioner with a pair of red-hot pincers; thereafter they shall be thrown alive on the fire.

"As for Fizko (Janos Ujvary), because of his youthful age and complicity in fewer crimes, we sentence him to decapitation. His body, drained of blood, should then be reunited with his two fellow accomplices where we wish that he be burned.

"Concerning Catharina (Katalin Beneczky), as the two accused women exonerated her and on the accusations of Ficzko alone we cannot sentence her; she should be kept in jail until provable charges are brought against her. This sentence was made public and read to the accused and was immediately put into effect and carried out. To testify to this and in order that such things should not happen in the future, we sign this document with our own hands and confirm it with our seal, and permit the same to be handled over to his Highness, the Lord Palatine, to be released to the public. The Year of Our Lord 7 January, 1611, in the market town of Bitce (Bytca)."

The document is signed by sixteen judges under the chairmanship of His Honor Theodaz Szirmai of Szulyo, Royal Judge of the King's Court. Twenty judges had been cited as present in the introductory section of the report, but four of them did not sign the final decree, evidently because those four judges were not actually present at the issuance of the final decree.

## Summary Translation of the Last Will and Testament of Countess Elizabeth Bathory

Shortly before her death in 1614, the Countess summoned two priests from the cathedral chapter of the Esztergom (Gran) Archbishopric, in order for them to witness her last will and testament. The two priests, named Andres Kerpelich and Imre Agriensy, reported that due to "the amicable petition of the illustrious and grand Lady Elizabeth Bathory, the visible widow of the respectable and grand former Lord Nadasdy" they went to Cachtice Castle where the Countess was being held under perpetual house arrest.

Since the Countess was imprisoned and not permitted to come into their presence personally, the priests simply listened to her instructions through her cell door. According to the report of the priests, the Countess formally expressed her last will and testament on July 31, 1614. She stated that she wanted all of her remaining properties to be divided among her surviving children upon her death. The document reveals that she was particularly opposed to the idea of having her son-in-law George Drugeth of Homonna continue to administer some of the properties rightfully belonging to her children. The written text was formally signed on the feast of St. Peter in Chains, i.e., August 3, 1614.

Translation of the questions put to the
defendants and their answers in Hungarian
at the January 2, 1611 trial

QUESTION 1. **The number of years of service in the house of the countess.**
ANSWERS: a) Ficzko: It has been sixteen years or even more. He was forcibly taken into the service of the countess through the wife of Martin Deak who lived in Csejthe [Cachtice].

b) Helena Jo: She lived in the countess's house for the past ten years. She was wet-nurse to the girls and to Paul Nadasdy [Elizabeth Bathory's children].

c) Dorothea Szentes: She has been living at the countess's house already for five years. She was summoned to the castle by Helena Jo on the best of promises that she would be chosen for service with Mrs. Homonnay [Elizabeth's youngest married daughter Katharina].

d) Katarina Beneczky: She has been living at the countess's house already for ten years. The mother of the preacher from Sarvar, Valentin Vargas's spouse, had brought her to the castle to be a washerwoman.

QUESTION 2. **How many persons had the countess had killed?**
ANSWERS: a) Ficzko: He knows of no women; as for girls, some thirty-seven were murdered in the course of his time of service.

b) Helena Jo: The sum total of those killed was fifty-one, perhaps even more.

c) Dorothea Szentes: As far as the young women and seamstresses are concerned, there were about thirty-six whom the countess had killed.

d) Katarina Beneczky: She did not count the victims, because she was only a washerwoman, but she guessed that fifty girls were probably killed during her time of service.

## QUESTION 3. Who and from where were the murdered ones?

ANSWERS: a) Ficzko: He does not know whose daughters they were. Those recently killed were brought from a Croatian village near Rednek. They had been at her Ladyship's place less than a month when they were murdered.

b) Helena Jo: She does not know whose children they were, but she remembers two women from Szittkay. George Janosy brought one of his young sisters; also two aristocratic girls were brought from Besce; in the same way also two from Czegled: one of them was murdered, the other still lives. Someone also murdered Mrs. Szele. One [girl] was acquired from Polany. Janos Barsony's wife had also procured a high-placed girl, born of aristocratic parents. One [girl] who came from the locality where Janos Polannyi lives was also murdered.

c) Dorothea Szentes: She does not know from which families and from where the girls came; she recognizes, as do the above-mentioned, that they came from different places.

d) Katarina Beneczky: She does not know whose children they were or where they came from, because she did not procure any of them; she only knows about the women from Szittkay.

## QUESTION 4. Who enticed the victims into the house?

ANSWERS: a) Ficzko: He went six times to seek girls, in order to please [Dorothea] Szentes; they were recruited in such a way that they were promised work as tavern girls or as servants somewhere. Along with Szentes, the wife of Janos Barsony, who lives not far from Gyöngyös in Taplantalva, went in search of girls; furthermore, a Croatian woman who lives with Matyas Detvös in Sarvar and who also lives across from Mrs. Janos Szalay [went in search of girls]. Janos Szabos's widow also brought a girl, her own daughter. They were also murdered, and, even though the mother knew this precisely, nonetheless she procured and acquired more. The wife of György Szabo gave her daughters over to the countess in Csejthe, who were also murdered, but she [the wife of György Szabo] did not procure any more. The wife of Istvan Szabo brought a great many.

[Helena] Jo also brought quite a few. [Katàrina] Beneczky did not bring many; she only procured those who were murdered by Dorothea [Szentes].

b) Helena Jo: Girls were procured in the following way: Janos Szalay's wife, next a Jewess, and lastly a Slovak woman, all three of whom lived in Sarvar, did it. The wife of Janos Barsony, who lives in Taplantalva, had also brought many. The wife of Janos Liptay had also procured two or three girls, and, although she knew that they would be murdered, she still brought girls, because her Ladyship had threatened her. She [Helena Jo] herself had brought two girls; one is dead, the other, the little Cziglei, still lives. Along with the wife of Janos Barsony, Helena Jo came back and remained behind, but the wife of Janos Barsony had herself brought an aristocratic girl from Polany. Later they went around a great deal with the stablemaster Daniel Vas, in order to seek out a girl servant for Mrs. Homonnay [Elizabeth Bathory's youngest daughter, Katherina, married to Drugeth de Homonnay]; they finally found one, a choice little girl from Becse. The wife of Istvan Szabo, who lives in Vep, had already brought sufficiently many girls. Her Ladyship had given one of them a garment and another a fur piece as gifts. The wife of Balthazar Horvath, who lives near a monastery in a tiny town, also procured very many girls.

c) Dorothea Szentes: The wife of Janos Szilay, who came from Köcs, already widowed and living in Dömölk [enticed victims]; finally, the wife of Liptay brought girls to Csejthe. In general, she supported all the statements by [Helena] Jo.

d) Katarina Beneczky's testimony was similar to that of Szentes, but she added that the wife of Janos Liptay also brought a girl; the wife of Miklos Kardos brought two, and that is why she herself did not dare to leave the village any more. However, Dorka [Szentes] brought the most; she had procured all of those recently dead.

QUESTION 5. In what ways were the victims murdered?

ANSWER: a) Ficzko: They were murdered in the following manner: Darvulia, who lived in Sarvar, bound the arms of the girls with Viennese rope, until their hands, which were tied behind them, became a deadly pale color. The girls would then be beaten so long that the soles of their feet and the surfaces of their hands bristled. They were beaten so long that each one, without interruption, suffered over five hundred blows from the women accomplices. These women had all first learned torturing from Darvulia. The girls were beaten until they died. Dorka [Dorothea Szentes] had the hand of the girl from Csejthe, who was different from the others, cut off with a scissors. When the brushwood was not bound up, the girls would immediately be dragged to the torture chamber. If the folds in the clothing [of the countess] were not smoothed out, or if the fire had not been brought up, or if the outer garments [of the countess] had not been pressed, the recalcitrant girls were at once tortured to death. It happened that the noses and lips of the girls were burned with a flat-iron by her Ladyship herself or by the old women. The countess also stuck her own fingers into the mouths of the girls and ripped their mouths and tortured them in this way. If the girls had not finished their obligatory sewing chores by ten o'clock at night, they were immediately tortured. In one single day they were dragged away like lambs for torturing even ten times . . . once about four or five girls were compelled to stand naked in front of the leering young male servants and to sew or bind up brushwood in this state. When her Ladyship was on a visit here in Bicse [Bytca], near Predmer, her Ladyship had a girl put in water up to her neck and then had water poured over her, the reason being that the girl had escaped by way of Illava, but had later been recaptured. The girl later died at Csejthe.

b) Helena Jo: Her Ladyship with her own hands had keys heated red-hot and then burned the hands of the girls with them. The same thing happened with gold pieces which the girls had found but had not passed on to her Ladyship. By the way, her Ladyship also had a woman named Zichy killed in Ecsed, and with her own hands her Ladyship killed another old woman. At Sarvar during summer his Lordship [Ferenc Nadasdy] had the younger sister [of Helena Jo] undressed until stark naked, while his Lordship looked on with his own eyes; the girl was then covered over with honey and made to stand throughout a day and a night, so that she, due to the great pain which she was forced to endure, got the falling sickness. She fell to the ground. His Lordship taught the countess that in such a case one must place pieces of paper dipped in oil between the toes of the girl and set them on fire; even if she was already half dead, she would jump up.

c) Dorothea Szentes supported the statements of Ficzko and Jo completely and added that the countess often tortured the girls herself. If [Dorothea] could not beat them, her Ladyship did it with a heavy cudgel as thick as the foot of an armchair; moreover, the countess stuck pins into the upper and lower lips of the girls and tortured them in this way.

d) Katarina Beneczky stated the same things and added: When Darvulia later went blind, Jo and Szentes had learned how to torture just as well. Her Ladyship had once sent off the entire household staff up to the castle at the time when Mrs. Zrinyi [the countess's eldest married daughter, Anna] came to Csejthe for a visit. Dorka [Dorothea Szentes] held the girls up there in strict captivity and gave them neither food nor drink. She treated them like slaves; they were not permitted to go anywhere. They were bathed in cold water, and it was poured over them; at the same time they were obliged to stand naked overnight. Dorka [Dorothea Szentes] even said, "Let lightning strike anyone who gives them something to eat!," and she watched over them so carefully that neither the castle bailiff nor anyone else could give them any food. As the countess wanted to travel with her daughter Mrs. Zrinyi [the countess's eldest daughter, Anna] to Pistyan [Piestany], Beneczky was sent up to the castle, in order to see if any one of the girls was in condition to accompany her Ladyship to Pistyan [Piestany]. Beneczky then saw that six were near to death from hunger. Upon her return [from the castle] she informed her Ladyship, "Your Grace, truly not one of them can accompany you." Astonished, her Ladyship clapped her hands together and became enraged at Dorka [Dorothea Szentes]. She said, "She should not have carried things so far!" The girls were brought down [from the castle] and all died in the manor house area in a house; then they were beaten by her Ladyship and also by Dorka. They must have died of hunger, since no one gave them anything to eat.

QUESTION 6. **Who helped the countess?**
ANSWER: a) Ficzko: aside from the three female accomplices, a person at Csejthe, a certain Helena, who was known as the wife of the coachman Kopar, had also killed girls. She is the one who with Mrs. Vai murdered two girls in Pistyan [Piestany]. In union with this Helena the countess had killed the Viennese girl Modly in Keresztur.

b) Helena Jo: When Darvulia became tired, Szentes and Beneczky beat up the girls, also she [Darvulia] did it when she was in good health. She herself beat the girls, because her Ladyship ordered her to do it. It was, however, Darvulia who tortured the most cruelly; she forced girls to stand all night long in cold water; she beat them along with that and poured water on them. [Dorothea] Szentes, moreover, cut the swollen parts of their bodies with scissors. Lastly, the servant Ficzko hit the girls again and again in the face, if her Ladyship ordered him to do it.

c) Dorothea Szentes: She helped her Ladyship torture sometimes one or the other girls, because she was forced to do so by her Ladyship.

d) Katarina Beneczky: [Helena] Jo was the cruelest, as far as issuing instructions goes, even though she could no longer do it with her own hands. She was brought over from Sarvar by the countess with this express view in mind; her Ladyship had even had her [Helena Jo's] two daughters married off and gave them fourteen beautiful gowns. [Helena] Jo was the first adviser. Katalin [Katarina Beneczky] had beaten up girls as [Dorothea] Szentes had, if she was forced to do it. If she did not want to beat the girls, she was herself tortured and beaten. Once, as a result of the beatings she suffered, she lay sick in bed for an entire month. She was taken away by [Helena] Jo and beaten up badly. . . . The last victim, who was newly found dead, was, after she had been beaten half to death, even further mishandled by the countess. The girl died at eleven o'clock.

QUESTION 7. **Where were to bodies buried or hidden?**
ANSWER: a) Ficzko: Besides the ones referred to already, when the Lord Palatine went to Pozsony [Bratislava, Pressburg], five were later tossed into a pit, two in the canal of the little garden, one of which was found there and dragged out, two were brought at night to Leseticz [the town of Pobola not far from Cachtice] and buried in the church; these had been brought down from the castle, where they had been murdered. The old women [Helena Jo, Dorothea Szentes, and Katarina Beneczky] hid and buried the girls. Here at Csejthe he personally helped bury four, two at Leseticz, one at Kereszttur, and one at Sarvar. The others, as in the case of Sarvar, Kereszttur, and Leseticz, were buried with song [a reference to the death ritual chanted over the bodies by students]. The countess praised the old women if they had killed one of the girls.

b) Helena Jo: Where bodies were buried, she does not know; only so much is known to her, that these same ones were thrown in a fruit garden. [Dorothea] Szentes and [Katarina] Beneczky had five bodies buried with song during the day at Sarvar. At Kereszttur they were also buried with students [singing the death ritual]. In one village near Varanno the countess also murdered a girl. Katalin [Katarina Beneczky] was obliged to remain behind, in order to bury [the girl's body].

c) Dorothea Szentes: Within one and a half weeks five girls died at Csejthe; they were tossed into a room under a bed one on top of the other. After that, the countess went to Sarvar. [Katarina] Bene-czky thereafter dragged the bodies off with the help of the entire group of servants into a fruit pit during this time. . . . Other bodies, which one could not hide, were openly buried by the preacher. [Do-rothea] Szentes in league with Ficzko had brought one girl to Leseticz and buried her there.

d) Katarina Beneczky: Two of the murdered girls were buried in Leseticz. As for the five different girls at Csejthe, Szentes knew that, since they were dead, their bodies were put under a bed and were covered with lime; nonetheless, she said, when asked, that the girls were probably still alive. After that, the countess departed for Sarvar. [Katarina] Beneczky was charged with the task of scraping out the floor of the house and hiding the bodies there. However, she did not do it, because the necessary strength failed her. The bodies then began to decay, and they sent forth an ever-so-evil stench through the entire manorhouse, so that everyone there had to smell it. She [Beneczky] had no one to advise her on what to do about it, so she then dragged these same [bodies] in God's name into a fruit pit with the help of Bulia and a maiden. There she buried the bodies together at night with the help of [Dorothea] Szentes, who hid the bodies in the canal. These were the ones which the dogs unearthed, so that the servants of Lord Zrinyi saw them. During the sojourn at Csejthe only eight girls were killed.

### Question 8. Had her Ladyship tortured and killed with her own hands?

Answer: a) Ficzko: The countess stuck needles into the girls, she pinched the girls in the face and in other places, and pierced them under their fingernails. Then she dragged the tortured girls naked out into the snow and had the old women pour cold water over them. She helped them with that until the water froze on the victim, who then died as a result. When she herself did not do the torturing, she entrusted the task to the old women. She then had them [servant girls] put in the coal-house. For a week long she gave the girls no food, and whoever got food secretly to them was punished at once.

b) Helena Jo: Her Ladyship beat the girls and murdered them in such a way that her clothes were drenched in blood. She often had to change her shirt . . . she also had the bloodied stone pavement washed. If [Dorothea] Szentes began to beat the girls, her Ladyship stood alongside. She had the girls undress stark naked, thrown to the ground, and she began to beat them so hard that one could scoop up the blood from their beds by the handfuls. Then she had ashes strewn around. It also happened that she bit out individual pieces of flesh from the girls with her teeth. She also attacked the girls with knives, and she hit and tortured them generally in many ways. Katalin [Katarina Beneczky] knows and has seen herself how her Ladyship singed the private parts of a girl with a burning candle.

c) Dorothea Szentes' testimony was similar to that of the two before her. One time her Ladyship lay sick and therefore could not beat anyone herself, so [Dorothea] Szentes was compelled to bring the victims to the bed [of the countess], whereupon a piece of flesh from a girl's face or from her shoulders was bitten off. Her Ladyship stuck needles into the girls' fingers and then said to them, "If it hurts, you old whores, then simply pull them out!" But if the girls pulled the needles out, then she [the countess] beat them immediately and cut off their fingers.

d) Katarina [Beneczky] testified to the same things as the others.

QUESTION 9. **Where were they tortured?**
ANSWER: a) Ficzko: In Beczko [Beckov] torturing took place at night in a room of the wash-house; at Sarvar inside the castle, where no one was permitted access; at Keresztur in the lavatory; at Csejthe in the wash-house. If we were on the road, however, her Ladyship would torture the girls with her own hands in her carriage; she beat them, pinched, them, and stuck needles into their lips.

b) Helena Jo: Wherever her Ladyship found herself, she sought out a suitable place where she could torture girls. In Vienna the monks hurled their pots against the windows, when they heard the lamentations [of the girls being tortured]. In Pozsony [Pressburg, Bratislava] she had Szentes do the beatings.

c) Dorothea Szentes: Everywhere her Ladyship stayed, she tortured. In general, she testified as the others.

d) Katarina Beneczky: She testified similarly and added: In Vienna her Ladyship tortured the daughter of Ilona Harczy. A girl from Dömölk, who had sat with Katalin [Katarina Beneczky], died on the way from Pistyan [Piestany] to Csejthe. The girl was like the one who had been beaten half to death at Pistyan [Piestany] . . . and ripped up by her Ladyship and so killed.

QUESTION 10. **Who among the staff of servants was present or knew or saw the crimes of her Ladyship?**
ANSWERS: a) Ficzko: The court master Benedikt Desö knew above

all about most of the occurrences. . . . In general, the servants and also the serfs saw everything, especially a certain Vasfejü, whom her Ladyship recently released from service on this side of Danube, knew everything better and more than Katalin [Katarina Beneczky]. Each had free access to her Ladyship and also buried many. . . .

b) Helena Jo: She knew in that regard Balthazar Pobi, Istvan Vagi, the steward, the servants, and the serfs. Kozma also knew about the horrible deeds. Similarly, the steward Szilvassy had seen how her Ladyship tortured girls who were compelled to stand stark naked before them.

c) Dorothea Szentes expressed herself in similar fashion.

d) Katarina Beneczky testified in similar fashion.

**QUESTION 11. Since what time had her Ladyship begun to commit these atrocities?**

ANSWERS: a) Ficzko: Already during the lifetime of the deceased lord [Count Nadasdy] she began to torture in this way, but then she did not strive for a death, as she did later, because his Lordship would have censured that, even though he tried not to get involved in anything she did. However, after Darvulia came to the house, the slaughter of the girls began; her Ladyship became more cruel. She owned a mirror, which had a frame running around it in the form of a pretzel; in front of this [mirror] she would gaze at herself with her arms supporting her head for as long as two hours straight. [Erzsi] Majorova [a peasant woman] from Miava prepared some water and brought it to the manorhouse at four o'clock one morning. It was poured into a bread trough. Her Ladyship herself bathed in it. After that, the water was poured into the river stream. From the other dough left in the trough they wanted to make a cake, because her Ladyship wanted to poison the King, the Lord Palatine, and Imre Megyery with it.

b) Helena Jo: She does not know when her Ladyship began her atrocities, because by the time she came into the house they were already well established. But her Ladyship learned these cruelties from Darvulia, since that one [Darvulia] was her intimate confidante.

c) Dorothea Szentes: She does not know when the cruelties began, since she has lived only five years at her Ladyship's house.

d) Katarina Beneczky: Her Ladyship is supposed to have learned her horrible tortures from Darvulia; Katalin [Katarina Beneczky] asserted that she had heard this.

# New Documentation

I. Report in Latin in the case of Countess Elizabeth Bathory at an inquiry held under orders from King Matthias II at Bratislava dated September 16, 1610 (original in the State Archives, Budapest under Thurzo, F.28, no. 19). "Domina Elizabeth Bathory" is accused of cruelly torturing and killing "many girls and virgins"; thirty-four witnesses testified in support of the accusations.

II. Report in Latin on the case of Countess Bathory under order from King Matthias II at Bratislava, dated July 26, 1611 (original in the State Archives, Budapest under Thurzo, f.28, 2.19). The countess is accused of having, under "diabolical impulse," cruelly mutilated and killed "many innocent virgins of noble and non-noble birth"; 224 witnesses testified.

In this document it is stated that "almost forty testified under oath" to "Elizabeth Bathory's atrocities." Some girls had been "submerged in a frozen river during the winter," some "were scorched in the shoulder with a fiery sword," others had "scalding water poured upon them" and then "their skin was torn off," others had been so "horribly beaten by rods that they were full of black and blue marks." One girl had "quite large wounds on her shoulders and scorched hands" inflicted by her Ladyship "with tongs." Some of the witnesses claimed that they knew nothing about the case, but most others supported the testimonies of previous witnesses concerning various atrocities attributed to Countess Elizabeth Bathory.

Benson, E. F. "And No Bird Sings," in the Haining anthology.

———. "Mrs. Amworth" (first published in 1920), in the Collins, Shepard, and Volta and Riva anthologies.

———. "The Room in the Tower," in *The Room in the Tower and Other Stories*. London: Mills and Boon, 1912. Also in the Dickie, Shepard, and Collins anthologies.

Bischoff, D. and Lampton, C. "Feeding Time," in Elwood R. (ed.), *The Fifty Meter Monsters, and Other Horrors*. New York: Pocket Books, 1976.

Blackwood, Algernon. "The Transfer" (first published in 1912), in the Parry anthology.

Bloch, Robert. "The Bat Is My Brother." *Weird Tales* (Nov. 1944). Also in the Parry anthology.

———. "The Bogey Man Will Get You" (first published in 1946), in the Carter anthology.

———. "The Cloak." *Unknown* (May 1931). Also in the Volta and Riva anthology.

———. "Hungarian Rhapsody," in *Pleasant Dreams*. New York: Jove, 1979.

———. "The Living Dead," in the Haining and McNally anthologies.

Bradbury, Ray. "Homecoming," in Daniels, Les (ed.), *Dying of Fright: Masterpieces of the Macabre*. New York: Scribner, 1976.

———. "The Man Upstairs," in the Bradbury and the Volta and Riva anthologies.

———. "Pillar of Fire," in the Haining anthology.

———. "Skeleton," in the Bradbury anthology.

Braddon, M. E. "Good Lady Ducayne," *The Strand Magazine* (Feb. 1896). Also in the Shephard anthology.

Caldecott, Sir Andrew. "Authorship Disputed," in *Fires Burn Blue*. New York: Longmans, Green & Co., 1948.

Calvino, Italo. "The Tale of the Vampires' Kingdom," in *The Castle of Crossed Destinies*. New York: Harcourt, 1977.

Campbell, Ramsey. "Conversion," in the Parry anthology.

Capuana, Luigi. "A Vampire," in the Volta and Riva anthology.

Carr, Terry. "Sleeping Beauty." *New Worlds of Fantasy* No. 3.

Chesterton, G. K. "Vampire of the Village," in *Father Brown Omnibus*. New York: Dodd, Mead & Co., 1951.

Clark, Dale. "Peace Denied," in the Resch anthology.

Copper, Basil. "Dr. Porthos," in the Haining anthology.

Cowles, Frederick. "The Vampire of Kaldenstein" (first published in 1938), in the Parry anthology.

# Bibliography/Filmography

I. Elizabeth Bathory

Baring-Gould, S. "A Hungarian Bather in Blood," *The Book of Werewolves*. London: 1865; New York: Causeway Books 1973, pp. 139–141.

Elsberg, R. von. *Elizabeth Bathory (Die Blutgräfin)*. Breslau: 1904.

Penrose, Valentine. *Erzsebet Bathory, La Comtesse Sanglante*. Paris, 1962; Eng. trans. *The Bloody Countess*. London: 1970.

Périsset, Maurice. *La Comtesse de Sang. Erzsebeth Bathory*. Paris: Pygmalion, 1975.

Rexa, Dezsö. *Bathory Erzsebet Nadasdy Ferencne*. Budapest: 1908.

Ronay, Gabriel. *The Truth About Dracula*. 1972; London: Gallancz, New York: Stein and Day, 1972.

Seabrook, William. "World Champion Lady Vampire of All Time," *Witchcraft*. New York: Hartcourt, Brace & Co., 1940; New York: Lancer Books, 1968, pp. 101–112.

Turoczi, Laszlo. *Bathory Erzsebet*. Budapest: 1744.

———. *Ungaria suis cum regibus compendio data*. Nagyszombat: 1729.

Wagener, Michael. *Beiträge zur Philosophischen Anthropologie*. Vienna: 1796.

II. Vlad Dracula, The Impaler

Bentley, Juliette. "Vlad Voivode Dracula." *Supernatural* 2 (1969).

Constantiniu, Florin. "Vlad Tepes." *Romanian Bulletin* (Oct. 1977).

Czabai, Stephen. "The Real Dracula." *The Hungarian Quarterly* (Autumn 1941): 327–32.

Florescu, Radu, and McNally, Raymond T. *Dracula: A Biography of Vlad the Impaler, 1431–1476*. New York: Hawthorn Books, 1973.

Kirtley, Basil F. "Dracula, the Monastic Chronicles and Slavic Folklore." *Midwest Folklore* 6, 3 (1956): 133–39.

MacKenzie, Andrew. *Dracula Country*. London: Arthur Barker, 1977.

McNally, Raymond T. and Florescu, Radu. *In Search of Dracula*. Greenwich, Conn.: New York Graphic Society, 1972. New York: Warner Paperback Library, 1973. New York: Galahad Books, 1975.

Nandris, Grigore. "The Dracula Theme in the European Literature of the West and of the East," in Edel, Leon (ed.), *Comparative Literature: Matter and Method*. Urbana, Ill.: University of Illinois, 1969.

———. "A Philological Analysis of Dracula and Rumanian Place-names and masculine Personal Names in a/ea." *Slavonic and East European Review* 37 (1959): 321–27.

### III. Biographies

Browne, Nelson. *Sheridan Le Fanu*. New York: Roy Publishers, 1951; London: A. Barker, 1951.

Farson, Daniel. *The Man Who Wrote Dracula*. London: M. Joseph, 1976; New York: St. Martin's Press, 1976.

Godwin, George. *Peter Kurten: A Study in Sadism*. London: Heinemann Medical Books, 1938, 1945.

Ludlam, Harry. *A Biography of Dracula—The Life Story of Bram Stoker*. London: Fireside Press, W. Foulsham & Co., 1962.

*The Trial of John George Haigh*. Dunboyne, Lord (ed.). London: William Hodge & Co., 1953.

Wagner, Margaret Seaton. *The Monster of Düsseldorf: The Life and Trial of Peter Kürten*. London: Faber and Faber, 1932.

### IV. Anthologies

Blaisdell, Elinore. *Tales of the Undead, Vampires and Visitants*. London: Crowell, 1947.

Bradbury, Ray. *October Country*. New York: Ballantine, 1955.

Carter, N. L. *The Curse of the Undead*. Greenwich, Conn.: Fawcett Gold Medal Books, 1970.

Collins, Barnabas and Quentin. *The Dark Shadows Book of Vampires and Werewolves*. New York: Paperback Library, 1970.

Collins, Charles M. *A Feast of Blood*. New York: Avon Books, 1967.

Dickie, James. *The Undead*. London: Pan Books, 1973; New York: Pocket Books, 1976.

Frayling, Christopher. *The Vampyre: A Bedside Companion*. New York: Charles Scribner's Sons, 1978.

Glut, Donald F. *True Vampires of History.* New York: 1971.

Haining, Peter. *The Dracula Scrapbook.* New York: Bramhall House, 1977.

———. *Tales of Unknown Horror.* London: New England Library, 1978.

———. *The Ghouls.* New York: Stein and Day, 1971; New York: Pocket Book, 1972 (includes "Dracula's Guest" under the title "Dracula's Daughter").

———. *The Midnight People.* New York: Popular Library, 1968; London: Frewin, 1968; New York (as *Vampires at Midnight*): Grosset and Dunlap, 1970; London (as *Vampires at Midnight*): Everest Books, 1975.

———. *Gothic Tales of Terror.* Maryland: Penguin, 1973 (includes Polidori's "Vampyre").

Howard, Robert Errin. *Skull-Face and Others.* Sauk City, Wisc.: Arkham House, 1974.

Hunt, William. *Chosen Haunts.* North Riverside, Ill.: Pandora Publications, 1981.

McNally, Raymond T. *A Clutch of Vampires.* Greenwich, Conn.: New York Graphic Society, 1973; New York: Warner Paperback Library, 1974.

Moskowitz, Sam. *Horrors Unknown.* New York: Walker & Co., 1971.

Norton, Alden H. *Masters of Horror.* New York: Berkeley Medallion Books, 1968 (includes Stoker's "Dracula's Guest" and Clemence Houseman's "The Werewolf").

Parry, Michel. *The Rivals of Dracula.* London: Corgi Books, 1977.

Resch, Kathy. *Decades.* Santa Clara, Calif.: Pentagram Publications, 1977.

Robinson, Richard. *The Best of the World of Dark Shadows.* Dardanelle, Ariz.: Imperial Press, 1979.

Shepard, Leslie. *The Dracula Book of Great Vampire Stories.* Secaucus, New Jersey: Citadel Press, 1977; New York: Jove, 1978.

Stevens, Austin N. *Mysterious New England.* Dublin, N.H.: Yankee, 1979 (includes Nancy Kinder's "The Vampires of Rhode Island").

Stoker, Bram. *Dracula's Guest.* London: 1914; New York: 1937; London: Arrow Books, 1966, 1974; London: Jarrolds, 1966; New York: Zebra, 1978.

Tolstoy, Alexei, R., *Vampires: Stories of the Supernatural.* Harmondsworth, Middlesex, Great Britain: Penguin Books, 1946; New York: Hawthorn Books, 1969.

Underwood, Peter. *The Vampire's Bedside Companion.* London: Leslie Frewin, 1975.

Volta, Ornella, and Riva, Valeria (foreword by Roger Vadim). *The Vampire: An Anthology*. London: Neville Spearman, 1963; London: Pan Books, 1965.

Winfield, Chester; Hemp, Roy; and McDonly, Dudley. *Monster Sex Stories*. New York: Gallery Press, 1972.

## V. Works on Literature, Psychology and Anthropology.

Bierman, J. S. "Genesis and Dating of Dracula from Bram Stoker's Working Notes." *Notes and Queries* 24 (Feb. 1977) 25.

Black, George. *A List of Works Relating to Lycanthropy*. New York: Public Library; 1920.

Bonaparte, Marie. *The Life and Works of Edgar Allan Poe*. London: Imago, 1949.

Bonewits, Wanda. "Dracula, the Black Christ." *Gnostica* 4, 7 (March 1975) 1, 28–29.

Brokaw, Kurt. *A Night In Transylvania: The Dracula Scrapbook*. New York: Grosset & Dunlap, 1976.

Burton, Sir Richard. *Vikram the Vampire*. London: 1870; New York: Dover, 1969.

Calmet, Don Augustin. *Traité sur les Apparitions des Esprits et sur les Vampyres*. Paris: 1751. Parts in the Frayling, McNally and Volta and Riva anthologies.

Carden, Philip, with Ken Mann. *Vampirism: A Sexual Study*. San Diego, Calif. 1969.

Carter, Margaret L. *Vampirism in Literature: Shadow of a Shade*. New York: Gordon Press, 1975.

Copper, Basil. *The Vampire in Legend, Fact and Art*. London: Hale, 1973; Secaucus, N. J.: The Citadel Press, 1974.

Daniels, Les. *Living in Fear: A History of Horror in the Mass Media*. New York: Charles Scribner's Sons, 1975.

Dunn, Dennis. "The Vampire as Addict." *Journal of Vampirism* II, 3 (Fall 1979) 10–13.

Ellis, Havelock. *Studies in the Psychology of Sex*. New York: Random house, 1936.

Epaulard, Alexis. *Vampyrisme, nécrophile, nécrosadisme & nécrophages*. Lyons: 1901.

Faivre, Tony. *Les Vampires*. Paris, 1962.

Farson, Daniel. *Vampires, Zombies and Monster Men*. London: Aldus Books, 1975; Garden City, N.Y.: Doubleday, 1976.

Frazer, James G. *The Fear of the Dead in Primitive Religions*. London: 1934.

Gerard, Emily de Laszowska. *The Land Beyond the Forest*. London, 1888. Of especial value is the chapter "Transylvanian Superstitions," which had first appeared in *The Nineteenth Century*, Vol. 18, London: 1885, pp. 135–50. Also in the Haining anthology.

Hare, Augustus. "The Vampire of Croglin Grange," *The Story of My Life*. London: 1900. Also in the Glut, McNally, Summers, Copper, and Masters anthologies.

Hennelly, M. M., Jr. "Dracula: The Gnostic Quest and Victorian Wasteland." *English Literature in Transition* 20, 1 (1977) 13–26.

Hernaudey, A. M. "Vampires and Vampiresses: A Reading of 62." *Books Abroad* 50 ( Summer 1976) 570–6.

Herz, Wilhelm. *Der Werwolf*. Stuttgart. 1862.

Hill, Douglas. *Return from the Dead*. London. 1970.

———. *The History of Ghosts, Vampires and Werewolves.*: Harrow, 1973.

Hurwood, Bernhardt J. *Monsters and Nightmares*. New York: Belmont Productions, 1967.

———. *Monsters Galore*. New York: 1965.

———. *Passport to the Supernatural*. New York: Taplinger, 1972.

———. *Terror by Night*. New York: Lancer, 1963; New York (as the *Monstrous Undead*): Lander, 1969; New York (as *The Vampire Papers*): Pinnacle, 1976.

———. *Vampires*. New York: Quick Fox, 1981.

———. *Vampires, Werewolves and Ghouls*. New York: Ace Books, 1968, 1973.

Illis, L. "On Porphyria and the Aetiology of Werewolves." *Section of the History of Medicine*. Vol. 57 (Jan. 1964) 23–26.

Jones, Ernest. *On the Nightmare*. Chapter IV, "The Vampire," pp. 98–130. New York: Liveright Publishing Corp., 1951, 1971. "The Vampire" also appears in the Frayling anthology.

Karp, W. "Dracula Returns; or Vampirism as an Antidote to the Blues." *Horizon* 18 (Autumn 1976) 40–41.

Kayton, Lawrence. "The Relationship of the Vampire Legend to Schizophrenia." *Journal of Youth and Adolescence* 1, 4 (1972) 303–14.

King, Stephen. *Danse Macabre*. New York: Everest House, 1981.

Krafft-Ebing, Richard von. *Psychopathia Sexualis*. New York: Pioneer, 1950; New York: Bell, 1962.

Kriss, Marika. *Werewolves, Shapeshifters and Skinwalkers*. Los Angeles: 1979.

Lefebure, Charles. *The Blood Cults*. New York: Ace, 1969.

Lewis, Paul. "Laughing at Fear: Two Versions of the Mock Gothic." *Studies in Short Fiction*. Vol. 15 (Fall 1978) 411–14.

Marystone, Cyril, *The Shepherds are Lost*. McLaughlin, S. D.: Peter Knowles Smith, 1975.

Masters, Anthony. *The Natural History of the Vampire*. New York: G. P. Putnan's Sons, 1972; New York: Berkeley Medallion Books, 1976.

Masters, R. E. L. and Edward Lea. *Perverse Crimes in History: Sadism, Lust-Murder, Necrophilia—Ancient to Modern Times*. New York: Julian Press, 1963; New York (as *Sex Crimes in History*): Matrix House, 1966.

McCully, Robert. "Vampirism: Historical Perspective and Underlying Process in Relation to a Case of Auto-Vampirism." *The Journal of Nervous and Mental Disease* 139, 5 (Nov. 1964) 440–51.

———. "The Laugh of Satan: A Study of Familial Murder." *Journal of Personality* 42, 1 (1978) 81–91.

Miller, Beverly. *Blood Lust*. Reseda, Calif.: Academy Press, 1974.

Murgoci, A. "The Vampire in Rumania." *Folklore* XXXVII, 4 (Dec. 31, 1926).

Murphy, P. J. *Ghouls: Studies and Case Histories of Necrophilia*. London: J. R. Grant, 1965.

O'Donnell, Elliott. *Werewolves*. London: Methuen, 1912.

———. "The Vampire Society." *Occult Review* (1934). Also in the Haining anthology.

Perkowski, Jan L. (ed.). *Vampire of the Slavs*. Cambridge, Mass.: Slavica Publishers, 1976.

Raible, Christopher Gist. "Dracula: Christian Heretic." *The Christian Century* 96 (Jan. 31, 1979) 103–104.

Ronay, Gabriel. *The Truth About Dracula*. New York: St. Martin's Press, 1972; London (as *The Dracula Myth*): W. H. Allan, 1972; New York: Stein and Day, 1974: London (as *The Dracula Myth*): Pan Books, 1975.

Seabrook, Wm. *Witchcraft: Its Power in the World Today*. New York: Harcourt, Brace & Co., 1940; New York: Lancer, 1968.

Senn, Harry. "Some Werewolf Legends and the Calusari Ritual in Rumania." *East European Quarterly* XI, No. 1 (19–)–.

Steiner, Rudolf. *The Occult Significance of Blood*. Boston: Occult and Modern Thought Book Centre, 1912; London: Anthroposophical Publishing Co., 1926; Makelumne Hill, Cal Health Research, 1972.

Sturm, Dieter and Volker, Klaus. *Von Denen Vampiren oder Menschensäugern*. Munich: Hanser, 1968.

Summers, Montague. *The Vampire: His Kith and Kin*. London: 1928; New York: 1929; New Hyde Park, N. Y.: University Books, 1961.

————*The Werewolf*. London: Keogh Paul, 1933.

Todorov, Tsvetan *The Fantastic*. Cleveland: Case Western Reserve University, 1973.

Tondriau, J. and Villeneuve, R. *Devils and Demons: A Dictionary of Demonology*. New York: Pyramid Special, 1972.

Trigg, Elwood B. *Gypsy Demons and Divinities*. Secaucus, N. J.: Citadel Press, 1972.

Trodahl, Schwartz & Goslin. "The Pigmentation of Dental Tissues in Erythropoietic (Congenital) Porphyria." *Journal of Oral Pathology*, Vol. I (1972) 159–171.

Twitchell, James, B. *The Living Dead: A Study of the Vampire in Romantic Literature*. Durham, N. C.: Duke University Press, 1981.

Van Over, Raymond. "Vampire and Demon Lover," in Ebon, Martin (ed.), *The Satan Trap: Dangers of the Occult*. Garden City, N. J.: Doubleday and Co., 1976, pp. 108–111.

Vanden Bergh, R. L., and Kelly, J. F. "Vampirism: A Review with New Observations." *Archives of General Psychiatry* 11, 5 (1964) 543–547.

Varma, Devendra P. *The Gothic Flame*. London: A. Barker, 1957.

Villeneuve, Roland. *Loups-garoux et Vampires*. Paris and Geneva, 1963.

Volta, Ornella. *The Vampire*. London: Tandem, 1965, 1970.; New York: Award Books.

Wallace, Bruce. "Vampires Revamped." *Omni* (June 1979) p. 146.

Weissman, J. "Women and Vampires: Dracula as a Victorian Novel." *Midwest Quarterly* 18 (July 1977) 392–405.

Wolf, Leonard. *A Dream of Dracula*. New York: Little, Brown & Co., 1972.; New York: Popular Library, 1973.

Wright, Dudley. *Vampires*. London: 1914; New York: Gordon Press, 1970; New York: Gale, 1973; New York: Causeway Books, 1973.

Zinck, K. Charles and Myrna. *Psychological Studies on the Increase of Lycanthropy and Vampirism in America; 1930–1941*. New Orleans: Zachary Ken, 1952.

## VI. Vampire Novels in a Series

Daniels, Les

*The Black Castle*. New York: Charles Scribner's Sons, 1978; New York: Berkley Books, 1979.

*The Silver Skull*. New York: Charles Scribner's Sons, 1979.

*Citizen Vampire*. New York: Charles Scribner's Sons, 1981.

Goulart, Ron. The Vampirella Series.

*Bloodstalk*. London: Sphere Books, 1975; New York: Warner Paperback, 1975.

*On Alien Wings*. London: Sphere Books, 1975; New York: Warner Paperback, 1975.

*Deadwalk*. London: Sphere Books, 1976; New York: Warner Paperback, 1976.

*Blood Wedding*. London: Sphere Books, 1976; New York: Warner Paperback, 1976.

*Death Game*. London: Sphere Books, 1976; New York: Warner Paperback, 1976.

*Snakegod*. London: Sphere Books, 1976; New York: Warner Paperback, 1976.

Graham, Jean
  *Dark Angel*. Santa Clara, Calif.: Pentagram Publications, 1977.
  *Dark Lord*. San Diego, Calif.: Peacock Press, 1980.

Lory, Robert. The Dracula Horror Series
  *Dracula Returns!*. New York: Pinnacle Books, 1973.
  *The Hand of Dracula*. New York: Pinnacle Books, 1973.
  *Dracula's Brothers*. New York: Pinnacle Books, 1973.
  *Dracula's Gold*. New York: Pinnacle Books, 1973.
  *The Drums of Dracula*. New York: Pinnacle Books, 1974.
  *The Witching of Dracula*. New York: Pinnacle Books, 1974.
  *Dracula's Disciple*. New York: Pinnacle Books, 1975.
  *Challenge to Dracula*. New York: Pinnacle Books, 1975.

Ross, Marilyn. The Dark Shadows Series
  *Barnabas Collins*. New York: Paperback Library, 1968.
  *The Secret of Barnabas Collins*. New York: Paperback Library, 1969, 1970.
  *The Demon of Barnabas Collins*. New York: Paperback Library, 1969.
  *The Foe of Barnabas Collins*. New York: Paperback Library, 1969.
  *The Phantom and Barnabas Collins*. New York: Paperback Library, 1969.
  *Barnabas Collins Versus the Warlock*. New York: Paperback Library, 1969.
  *The Peril of Barnabas Collins*. New York: Paperback Library, 1969.
  *Barnabas Collins and the Mysterious Ghost*. New York: Paperback Library, 1969.
  *Barnabas Collins and Quentin's Demon*. New York: Paperback Library, 1969.
  *Barnabas Collins and the Gypsy Witch*. New York: Paperback Library, 1969.

*Barnabas, Quentin and the Mummy's Curse.* New York: Paperback Library, 1970.

*Barnabas, Quentin and the Avenging Ghost.* New York: Paperback Library, 1970.

*Barnabas, Quentin and the Nightmare Assassin.* New York: Paperback Library, 1970.

*Barnabas, Quentin and the Crystal Coffin.* New York: Paperback Library, 1970.

*Barnabas, Quentin and the Witches Curse.* New York: Paperback Library, 1970.

*Barnabas, Quentin and the Haunted Cave.* New York: Paperback Library, 1970.

*Barnabas, Quentin and the Frightened Bride.* New York: Paperback Library, 1970.

*Barnabas, Quentin and the Scorpio Curse.* New York: Paperback Library, 1970.

*Barnabas, Quentin and the Serpent.* New York: Paperback Library, 1970.

*Barnabas, Quentin and the Magic Potion.* New York: Paperback Library, 1970.

*Barnabas, Quentin and the Body Snatchers.* New York: Paperback Library, 1971.

*Barnabas, Quentin and Dr. Jekyll's Son.* New York: Paperback Library, 1971.

*Barnabas, Quentin and the Grave Robbers.* New York: Paperback Library, 1971.

*Barnabas, Quentin and the Sea Ghost.* New York: Paperback Library, 1971.

*Barnabas, Quentin and the Mad Magician.* New York: Paperback Library, 1971.

*Barnabas, Quentin and the Hidden Tomb.* New York: Paperback Library, 1971.

*Barnabas, Quentin and the Vampire Beauty.* New York: Paperback Library, 1972.

Saberhagen, Fred

*The Dracula Tape.* New York: Warner Paperback Library, 1975; New York: Ace Books, 1980.

*The Holmes-Dracula File.* New York: Ace Books, 1978.

*An Old Friend of the Family.* New York: Ace Books, 1979.

*Thorn.* New York: Ace Books, 1980.

Tremayne, Peter

*Dracula Unborn*. London: Bailey Brothers and Swinfen, 1977; London: Corgi Books, 1977; New York (as *Bloodright: Memoirs of Mircea— Son to Dracula*): Walker and Co., 1979; New York (as *Bloodright*, etc.): Dell, 1980.

*The Revenge of Dracula*. New York: Walker and Co., 1979.

*Dracula, My Love*. London: Magnum Books, 1980.

Yarbro, Chelsea Quinn
*Hotel Transylvania*. New York: St. Martin's Press, 1978; New York: Signet, 1979.

*The Palace*. New York: St. Martin's Press, 1978; New York: Signet, 1979.

*Blood Games*. New York: St. Martin's Press, 1979; New York: Signet, 1980.

*Path of the Eclipse*. New York: St. Martin's Press, 1981.

## VII. Individual Novels

*The Adult Version of Dracula*. Calga Publishers, 1970.

Ascher, Eugene. *To Kill a Corpse*. London: World Distributors, 1955.

Barling, Tom. *Dracula*. New York: Grosset & Dunlap, 1976.

Bischoff, David. *Vampires of Nightworld*. New York: Ballantine/ Del Rey, 1981.

Bond, Edlyne. *Miranda*. Lawndale, Calif.: Phantom Press, 1982.

Brett, Stephen. *The Vampire Chase*. New York: Manor Books, 1979.

Brown, Carter. *So What Killed the Vampire?* New York: Signet, 1966.

Butler, Octavia E. *Mind of My Mind*. New York: Doubleday, 1977.

Carr, John Dickson. *The Three Coffins*. New York: Harper & Brothers, 1935; Boston: Gregg Press, 1979.

Charnas, Suzy McKee. *The Vampire Tapestry*. New York: Simon and Schuster, 1980.

Clark, Dale. *Resolutions in Time*. North Riverside, Ill.: Pandora Publications, 1980.

Coffman, Virginia. *The Vampyre of Moura*. New York: Ace Books, 1970.

Combs, David. *The Intrusion*. New York: Avon, 1981.

Dear, Ian. *Village of Blood*. London: NEL, 1975.

Dobbin, Muriel. *A Taste for Power*. New York: Richard Marek, 1980.

Drake, Asa. *Crimson Kisses*. New York: Avon Books, 1981.

Dreadstone, Carl. *Dracula's Daughter*. New York: Berkley Medallion, 1977.

Endore, Guy. *The Werewolf of Paris*. Paris: 1933.

Estleman, Loren D. *Sherlock Homes vs. Dracula*. New York: Doubleday, 1978; New York and Harmondsworth, England: Penguin, 1979.

Ewers, Hans-Heinz. *Vampire*. New York: The John Day Company, 1934; London (as *Vampire's Prey*): Jarrolds, 1937.

Farrar, Stewart. *The Dance of Blood*. London: Arrow Books, 1977.

Fleming, Nigel. *To Love a Vampire*. Encino, Calif.: World-Wide Publishing Co., 1980.

Fortune, Dion. *The Demon Lover*. London: Aquarian Publishing Co., 1931; London: Star Books/Wyndham, 1976.

Frederick, Otto. *Count Dracula's Canadian Affair*. New York: Pageant Press, 1960.

Gardine, Michael. *Lamia*. New York: Dell, 1981.

Giles, Raymond. *Night of the Vampire*. New York: Avon Books, 1969; London: NEL, 1970.

Glut, Donald F. *Frankenstein Meets Dracula*. London: NEL, 1977.

Hall, Angus. *The Scars of Dracula*. New York: Beagle Books, 1971; London: Sphere Books, 1971.

Horler, Sidney. *The Vampire*. London: Hutchingson & Co., 1935; New York: Bookfinger, 1974.

Houseman, Clemence. *The Werewolf*. London: John Lane, 1896; Chicago, Williams, 1896 (first pub. in the London magazine, *Atlanta* 1896).

Hughes, William. *Lust for a Vampire*. New York: Beagle Books, 1971; London: Sphere Books, 1971.

Hurwood, Bernhardt, J. *By Blood Alone*. New York: Charter Books, 1979.

Jennings, Jan. *Vamphr*. New York: Pinnacle Books, 1981.

Johnson, Ken. *Hounds of Dracula*. New York: Signet Books, 1977; London (as *Dracula's Dog*): Everest Books, 1977.

Johnstone, William W. *The Devil's Kiss*. New York: Zebra, 1980.

Kearny, Maxwell. *Dracula Sucks*. New York: Zebra, 1981.

Kerruish, Jessie Douglas. *The Undying Monster*. London: Phillip Allan, 1968; New York: Award Books, 1970; London: Tandem Books, 1970.

Kimberly, Gail. *Dracula Began*. New York: Pyramid, 1976.

King, Stephen. *Salem's Lot*. New York: Doubleday, 1975; New York: Signet, 1976.

Knight, Mallory T. *Dracutwig*. New York: Award Books, 1969.

Lee, Tanith. *Sabella of the Blood Stone*. New York: Daw Books, 1980.

Lortz, Richard. *Children of the Night*. New York: Dell, 1974.

*Love at First Bite*. Los Angeles: Fotonovel Publications, 1979.

Lovell, Marc. *An Enquiry into the Existence of Vampires*. Garden City, N. Y.: Doubleday, 1974; London: Coronet Books.

Madison, J. J. *The Thing*. New York: Belmont Tower Books, 1971.

Matheson, Richard. *I Am Legend*. New York: Fawcett Publications, 1954; New York: Berkley Medallion, 1971.

McCammon, Robert R. *They Thirst*. New York: Avon Books, 1981.

McDaniel, David. *The Vampire Affair*. New York: Ace, 1966.

Monette, Paul. *Nosferatu: The Vampyre*. New York: Avon Books, 1979.

Myers, Robert J., *The Virgin and the Vampire*. New York: Pocket Books, 1977.

Nile, Dorothea. *The Vampire Cameo*. New York: Lancer Books, 1968.

Owen, Dean. *The Brides of Dracula*. New York: Monarch, 1960.

Parry, Michel. *Countess Dracula*. New York: Beagle Books, 1971; London: Sphere Books, 1971.

Paul, F. W. *The Orgy at Madame Dracula's*. New York: Lancer Books, 1968.

Randolphe, Arabella. *The Vampire Tapes*. New York: Berkley Medallion, 1977.

Raven, Simon. *Doctors Wear Scarlet*. London: A. Blond, 1960; New York: Simon and Schuster, 1961.

Rechy, John. *The Vampires*. New York: Grove Press, 1973, 1977.

Rice, Anne. *Interview with the Vampire*. New York: Alfred A. Knopf, 1976; New York: Ballantine, 1977, 1978, 1979.

Rice, Jeff. *The Night Stalker*. New York: Pocket Books, 1973, 1974.

Romero, George, and Sparrow, Susan. *Dawn of the Dead*. New York: St. Martin's Press, 1978.

Ronson, Mark. *Bloodthirst*. London: Hamlyn, 1980.

Rudorff, Raymond. *The Dracula Archives*. New York: Arbor House (World), 1971; New York: Pocket Books, 1972.

Samuels, Victor. *The Vampire Women*. New York: Popular Library, 1973.

Savory, Gerald. *Count Dracula*. London: Corgi, 1977.

Saxon, Peter. *Vampire's Moon*. New York: Unibook, 1970.

Scram, Arthur N. *The Werewolf vs. the Vampire Woman*. Beverly Hills, Calif.: Guild-Hartford publishing Co., 1972.

Selby, Curt. *Blood County*. New York: Popular Library, 1976.

Sherman, Jory. *Vegas Vampire*. Los Angeles: Pinnacle Books, 1980.

Shirley, John. *Dracula in Love*. New York: Zebra Books, 1979.

Smith, Guy N. *Bats out of Hell*. New York: Signet Books, 1979.

Smith, Martin Cruz. *Nightwing*. New York: Norton, 1977; New York: Jove, 1977.

Stewart, Desmond. *The Vampire of Mons*. New York: Harper & Row, 1976; London: Hamilton, 1976; New York: Avon Books, 1977.

Stockbridge, Grant. *Death Reign of the Vampire King.* (Spider Series, No. 1) New York: Pocket Books, 1976.

Stoker, Bram. *The Lady of the Shroud.* London: W. Heinemann, 1909; London: Arrow Books, 1962, 1963, 1974.

Straub, Peter. *Ghost Story.* New York: Coward, McCann & Geoghegan, 1978; New York: Pocket Books, 1980.

Streiber, Whitley. *The Wolfen.* New York: Wm. Morrow, 1978; New York: Bantam, 1979.

Sturgeon, Theodore. *Some of Your Blood.* New York: Ballantine, 1961, 1977.

Tignor, Beth. *Tryst of Dark Shadows.* North Riverside, Ill.: Pandora Publications, 1981.

*Varney the Vampire: or the Feast of Blood,* by James Malcolm Rymer or Thomas Peckett Prest. London: E. Lloyd, 1840 (§71847 in "Penny Numbers" installments); New York: Arno Press, 1970; New York: (in two volumes) Dover Publications, 1972.

Veley, Charles. *Night Whispers.* Garden City, N. Y.: Doubleday, 1980; New York: Ballantine, 1981.

Viereck, George Sylvester. *The House of the Vampire.* New York: Moffat, Yard & Co., 1908, 1912.

Williamson, J. N. *Death-Coach.* New York: Zebra, 1981.

Wilson, Colin. *The Space Vampires.* New York: Random House, 1976; London: Hart-Davis and Mac Givvon, 1976; New York: Pocket Books, 1977.

Wilson, F. Paul. *The Keep.* New York: Morrow, 1981.

Winston, Daoma. *The Vampire Curse.* New York: Warner Paperback, 1971, 1975.

## VIII. Short Stories

Aickman, Robert. "Pages from a Young Girl's Journal," in *Cold Hand in Mine; Strange Stories.* New York: Scribner, 1977.

Allan, Peter. "Domdaniel," in the Underwood anthology.

Allen, Woody. "Count Dracula," in *Getting Even.* New York: Random House, 1971.

Apuleius, Lusius. "The Vampire," in Wolfe, Leonard (ed.), *Wolf's Complete Book of Terror.* New York: Crown, 1979.

Arsenault, Jeff and Resch, Kath. "Blood in the Night." *World of Dark Shadows* 28 (Feb. 1981).

Beaumont, Charles. "Blood Brother" (first published in 1963), in *The Playboy Book of Science Fiction and Fantasy.* New York: Playboy Press, 1966.

Benson, E. F. "And No Bird Sings," in the Haining anthology.
———. "Mrs. Amworth" (first published in 1920), in the Collins, Shepard, and Volta and Riva anthologies.
———. "The Room in the Tower," in *The Room in the Tower and Other Stories*. London: Mills and Boon, 1912. Also in the Dickie, Shepard, and Collins anthologies.
Bischoff, D. and Lampton, C. "Feeding Time," in Elwood R. (ed.), *The Fifty Meter Monsters, and Other Horrors*. New York: Pocket Books, 1976.
Blackwood, Algernon. "The Transfer" (first published in 1912), in the Parry anthology.
Bloch, Robert. "The Bat Is My Brother." *Weird Tales* (Nov. 1944). Also in the Parry anthology.
———. "The Bogey Man Will Get You" (first published in 1946), in the Carter anthology.
———. "The Cloak." *Unknown* (May 1931). Also in the Volta and Riva anthology.
———. "Hungarian Rhapsody," in *Pleasant Dreams*. New York: Jove, 1979.
———. "The Living Dead," in the Haining and McNally anthologies.
Bradbury, Ray. "Homecoming," in Daniels, Les (ed.), *Dying of Fright: Masterpieces of the Macabre*. New York: Scribner, 1976.
———. "The Man Upstairs," in the Bradbury and the Volta and Riva anthologies.
———. "Pillar of Fire," in the Haining anthology.
———. "Skeleton," in the Bradbury anthology.
Braddon, M. E. "Good Lady Ducayne," *The Strand Magazine* (Feb. 1896). Also in the Shephard anthology.
Caldecott, Sir Andrew. "Authorship Disputed," in *Fires Burn Blue*. New York: Longmans, Green & Co., 1948.
Calvino, Italo. "The Tale of the Vampires' Kingdom," in *The Castle of Crossed Destinies*. New York: Harcourt, 1977.
Campbell, Ramsey. "Conversion," in the Parry anthology.
Capuana, Luigi. "A Vampire," in the Volta and Riva anthology.
Carr, Terry. "Sleeping Beauty." *New Worlds of Fantasy* No. 3.
Chesterton, G. K. "Vampire of the Village," in *Father Brown Omnibus*. New York: Dodd, Mead & Co., 1951.
Clark, Dale. "Peace Denied," in the Resch anthology.
Copper, Basil. "Dr. Porthos," in the Haining anthology.
Cowles, Frederick. "The Vampire of Kaldenstein" (first published in 1938), in the Parry anthology.

Crawford, F. Marion. "For the Blood Is the Life" (first published in 1911), in the Carter, Collins, Dickie, and Shepard anthologies.

D'Eath, Mark. "Vampyr: And May Your God Go With You." *Erotic Science Fiction Stories*, No. 1.

De Maupassant, Guy. "The Horla" (first published in 1887), in the Shepard and the Volta and Riva anthologies.

Derby, Crispin. "To Claim His Own" in the Underwood anthology.

Derleth, August. "Bat's Belfry." *Weird Tales* (May 1926). Also in the Haining anthology.

Derleth, August (as Stephen Grendon). "The Drifting Snow," in the Haining and McNally anthologies.

Derleth, August, and Schorer, Mark. "The Occupant of the Crypt," in *Colonel Markesan and Less Pleasant People*. Sauk City, Wis.: Arkham House, 1966.

Drake, David. "Something Had to Be Done," in the Parry anthology.

Durrell, Lawrence. "Carnival," in the Volta and Riva and the McNally anthologies.

Evans, E. Everett. "The Undead Die" (first published in 1948), in the Parry anthology.

Farley, Ralphe Milne. "Another Dracula." *Weird Tales* (Sept. and Oct. 1930).

Gautier, Theophile. "The Beautiful Vampire," in the Volta and Riva anthology.

Gogol, Nicolai. "Viy," in the Volta and Riva anthology and (as "Black Sunday") in the Haining anthology.

Greene, Vince. "One Man's Meat," in Oberfirst, R. (ed.), *1955 Anthology of Best Original Short Stories*. Ocean City, N. Y.: Oberfirst Publications, 1955.

Heron E. and Heron, H. "The Story of Baelbrow" (first published in 1898), in the Parry anthology.

Hoffman, E. T. A. "Aurelia," in the Frayling anthology.

Horler, Sydney. "The Believer," in the Haining anthology.

Howard, Richard. "Dies Irae," in the Underwood anthology.

Howard, Robert Ervin. "Hills of the Dead," in the Howard anthology.

———. "Horror from the Mound" in the Howard anthology.

Jacobi, Carl. "Revelations in Black," in *Revelations in Black*. Sauk City, Wis.: Arkham House, 1947. Also in the Collins and the Dickie anthologies.

James, M. R. "Count Mahnus," in *The Collected Ghost Stories of M. R. James*. London: Edward Arnold, 1904. Also in the Collins and the Parry anthologies.

Johnstone, David A. "Mr. Alucard," in Derleth, August (ed.), *Over the Edge*. Sauk City, Wis.: Arkham House, 1964.

King, Stephen. "One for the Road." *Maine Magazine* (March/April 1977). Also in *Night Shift*. New York: Doubleday, 1978.

Knight, Damon. "Eripmav," in Asimov, Isaac, et al. (eds.), *100 Great Science Fiction Short Stories*. New York: Doubleday, 1978.

Kornbluth, C. M. "The Mindworm," in Silverberg, Robert (ed.), *Mind to Mind; Nine Stories of Science Fiction*. Nashville, Tenn.: Thomas Nelson, 1971.

Lach, Jane. "The Stranger." *World of Dark Shadows* 28 (Feb. 1981).

Lee, Tanith. "Red as Blood." *The Year's Best Fantasy Stories. No. 6* (1980).

Le Fanu, Sheridan. "Carmilla," *The Dark Blue* (London, 1871). Also in *In a Glass Darkly*. London: Bentley, 1872; Le Fanu, Sheridan, *Carmilla and the Haunted Baronet*. New York: Warner Paperback, 1970, 1974. Also in the Carter, McNally, Shepard and the Volta and Riva anthologies.

Lehti, Teve. "With the Rising of the Morning Sun." *World of Dark Shadows* Issue 14.

Leiber, Fritz. "Ship of Shadows," in Asimov, Isaac, *The Hugo Winners Vol. 3; The Best from Fantasy and Science Fiction*. New York: Doubleday, 1977.

Leitch, Lavinia. "A Vampire," in *A Vampire and Other Stories*. Boston: Christopher Publishing House, 1927.

Malzberg, Barry N. "Trial of the Blood," in *The Best of Barry N. Malzberg*. New York: Pocket Books, 1976.

Matheson, Richard. "Drink My Red Blood." *Imagination* (April 1951). Also in the McNally, Collins, and Haining anthologies.

———. "No Such Thing as a Vampire," in Pickersgill, Frederick (ed.), *No Such Thing As A Vampire*. London: Corgi Books, 1964.

McClusky, Thorp. "Loot of the Vampire" (first published in 1936), in *Loot of the Vampire*. Oak Lawn, Ill.: Robert Weinberg, 1975.

Miller, P. Schuyler. "Over the River," in the Haining anthology.

Morrow, Sonora. "Hare Times." *Ellery Queen's Mystery Magazine* 64, 6 (Dec. 1974). "The Mysterious Stranger" (first published in 1860), in the Collins and Parry anthologies.

Neruda, Jan. "The Vampire," in Hrbkova, Sara B. (ed.), *Czechoslovak Stories*. London: Duffield, 1920. Also in Busch, Marie, and Pick,

Otto (eds.), *Selected Czech Tales*. Cambridge: England, 1928. Also in the Shepard anthology.

Norris, Frank. "Grettir at Thorhall-stead," in the Moskowitz anthology.

Nuetzel, Charles and Vesperto, Viktor. "Count Down to Doom." *Monster World* 8 (May 1966).

O'Donnell, K. M. "Trial of the Blood," in Goldberg, G. et al. (eds.), *Nighttouch*. New York: St. Martins, 1978.

O'Keefe, M. Timothy. "Blood Money," in Hitchcock, Alfred (ed.), *Alfred Hitchcock's Witch's Brew*. New York: Random House, 1977.

Polidori, John. "The Vampyre." *New Monthly Magazine* (London: April 1819). Also in Bleiler, E. F. (ed.), *Three Gothic Novels*. New York: Dover Publications, 1966 and in the Carter, Collins, Frayling, Haining and McNally anthologies.

Quinn, Seabury, "Body and Soul," in the Moskowitz anthology.

Ray, Jean. "The Guardian of the Cemetery" (first published in 1934), in the Perry anthology.

Reeves, Peter. "Web," in the Hunt anthology.

Resch, Kathy. "Edge" in the Resch anthology.

———. "Kitt's Choice." *World of Dark Shadows*, Issues 1 & 2. Also in the Robinson anthology.

Ritchie, Jack. "Kid Cardula," in Hitchcock, Alfred (ed.), *Alfred Hitchcock's Tales to Take Your Breath Away*. New York: Random House.

Robin, Marcy. "Cursed." *World of Dark Shadows*, Issue 19.

———. "Eternity Now," in the Bond anthology.

———. "The Final Truth." *World of Dark Shadows*, Issue 24/25 (Feb. 1980).

———. "In the Light of a Candle." *World of Dark Shadows*, Issue 13.

———. "Premonition," in the Resch anthology.

———. "Purgatory." *World of Dark Shadows*, Issue 16/17.

———. "Shadowed Soul," in the Hunt anthology.

———. "The Taste of Death." *World of Dark Shadows*, Issue 9. Also in the Robinson anthology.

———. "The Time for Grief," in the Resch anthology.

———. "Transition." in the Resch anthology.

Roditi, E. "The Vampires of Istanbul: A Study in Modern Communications Methods," in *The Delights of Turkey*. New York: New Directions, 1977.

Rogers, Wayne. "Dracula's Brides." *Horror Stories*. (Feb. 1941).

Roman, Victor. "Four Wooden Stakes," in Thomson, Christine Campbell (ed.), *Not at Night Omnibus*. London: Selwyn and Blount, 1925; New York: Vanguard, 1928. Also in the Shepard anthology.

Rutter, Owen. "The Vampires of Tempassuk." In Hoke, Helen (ed.), *Monsters, Monsters, Monsters*. New York: F. Franklin Watts, 1975.

Scott-Moncrieff, D. "Schloss Wappenburg," in *Not for the Squeamish*. London: Background Books, 1948. Also in the Collins anthology.

Smith, Clark Ashton, "The Death of Ilalotha" (first published in 1937), in the Dickie anthology.

————. "The End of the Story" (first published in 1930), in the Dickie Anthology.

————. "A Rendezvous in Averoigne" (first published in 1961), in the Collins anthology.

Smith, Evelyn E. "Softly While You're Sleeping" (first published in 1961), in the Carter anthology.

Smith, Sandy. "Home to Collinwood." *World of Dark Shadows*, Issue 19.

Starkie, Walter. "The Old Man's Story," in *Raggle Taggle*. London: John Murray, 1933. Also in the Dickie anthology.

Stenbock, Count (as Stanislaus Eric). "The Sad Story of a Vampire" (first published in 1894), in the Shepard and Dickie anthologies.

Stoker, Bram. "Dracula's Guest," in the Stoker, Collins, Dickie, McNally, and Shepard anthologies.

Straum, Niel. "Vanishing Breed," in the Carter anthology.

Tieck, Johann Ludwig. "Wake Not the Dead" (first published in English in 1823), in the Collins, Frayling and Haining anthologies.

Tolstoy, Alexis. "The Family of a Vourdalak," in the Tolstoy, Frayling, and Perkowski anthologies.

————. "The Vampire," in the Tolstoy anthology.

Trevisan, Dalton. "The Vampire of Curitiba," in *The Vampire of Curitiba and Other Stories*. New York: Knopf, 1972.

Tubb, E. C. "Fresh Guy," in the Volta and Riva anthology.

Turner, James. "Mirror Without Image," in the Underwood anthology.

Utley, Steven. "Night Life" in the Parry anthology.

Van Vogt, A. E. "Asylum," in *Away and Beyond*. New York: Jove/HBJ Books, 1977.

Wellman, Manly Wade. "The Devil Is Not Mocked." *Unknown Worlds*. (June 1943). Also in Zacherley John (ed.) *Zacherley's Vulture Stew*. New York: Ballantine, 1960.

————. "The Horror Undying." *Weird Tales* (May 1946). Also in the Parry anthology.

————. "The Two Graves of Lilly Warran," in Parry, Michel (ed.), *The Supernatural Solution*. London: Panther Books, 1976.

———. "The Vampire of Shiloh." *Weird Tales* (July 1942). Also in the Haining anthology.

———. "When It Was Moonlight," in *Unknown Worlds*. New York: Wellman, 1940. Also in the Dickie and Haining anthologies.

Worrell, Everil. "The Canal" (first published in 1927), in the Dickie anthology.

Wyndham, John. "Close Behind Him," in Haining, Peter (ed.), *Nightfrights; Occult Stories for All Ages*. New York: Taplinger, 1972.

## IX. Studies of Movies, Theater, and Television

Armstrong, Michael. "Some Like It Chilled — Part 3 — The Undead." *Films and Filming* (April 1971), 37ff.

Bean, Robin. "Dracula and the Mad Monk." *Films and Filming* (August 1965), 55ff.

Borst, Ron. "The Vampire in the Cinema." *Photon* 18 (1970).

Butler, Evan. *Horror in the Cinema*. New York: Paperback Library Edition,1971.

Byrne, Richard B. *Films of Tyranny*. Madison, Wis.: College Printing & Typing Co., 1966, pp. 97–148.

Carroll, Noel. "Nightmare and the Horror Film: The Symbolic Biology of Fantastic Beings." *Film Quarterly* Vol. 34, No. 3 (Spring 1981), pp. 16–24.

Coulteray, George De. *Sadism in the Movies*. New York: Medical Press, 1965.

Cutts, John. "Vampyr." *Films and Filming* (Dec. 1960), 17ff.

Ebert, Roger. "Martin: A Vampire or Mixed-up Kid?" *Chicago Sun Times* (May 27, 1977).

Eisner, Lotte H. *The Haunted Screen: Expressionism in the German Cinema and the Influence of Max Reinhardt*. Berkeley, Calif.: University of California Press, 1969.

———. *Murnau*. Berkeley, Calif.: University of California Press, 1973.

Finocchio, Robert V., and Fister-Liltz, Barbara. *Without Makeup*. North Riverside, Ill.: Pandora Publications, 1980.

Fisher, Terrence. "Horror Is My Business." *Films and Filming, X* (July 1964), pp. 7–8.

Frank, Alan G. *Horror Movies: Tales of Terror in the Cinema*. London: Octopus Books, 1974, 1976; Secaucus, N. J.: (as *Monsters and Vampires*): Derbibooks, 1975.

Geduld, Harry M. "Malign Fiesta: Reflections on the Humor of Horror." Film Section, *Humanist* Vol. 35 (August 1975), p. 45.

Gifford, Denis. *Movie Monsters*. London: 1969.

Glut, Donald F. *The Dracula Book*. Metuchen, N. J.: The Scarecrow Press, 1975.

Halliwell, Leslie. "The Baron, The Count, and Their Ghoul Friends." *Films and Filming* SV (June 1969) pp. 12–16; (July 1969) pp. 13–16.

Kahan, Saul. "Transylvania—Polanski Style." *Cinema* 3, 4; 7ff.

Kelly, Bill. "Salem's Lot." *Cinefantastique* 9, 2 (undated), pp. 9–13.

Losano, Wayne A. "The Vampire Rises Again in the Films of the 70's." *The Film Journal* 2, 2; 60ff.

Majeski, Bill. "Dracula Returns." *Plays* 36 (May 1977), 25–36.

Michel, Jean-Claude. "Les Vampires a l'écran," *L'Ecran Fantastique,* 2 Serie, no. 2. Paris, 1971.

Murphy, Michael J. *The Celluloid Vampires: A History and Filmography, 1897–1979*. Ann Arbor, Mich.: Press, 1979.

Pattison, Barrie. *The Seal of Dracula*. New York: Bounty Books, 1975; London: Lorrimer, 1975.

Perlmutter, Ruth. "The Cinema of the Grotesque." *Georgia Review,* Vol. 33 (Spring 1979), pp. 168–193.

Pirie, David. "New Blood." *Sight and Sound* (Spring 1971), 73ff.

———. *The Vampire Cinema*. New York: Crescent Books, 1977; London: Hamlyn, 1977.

Reed, Donald. *The Vampire on the Screen*. Inglewood, Calif.: Wagon and Star Publishers, 1965.

Resch, Kathy. *The Dark Shadows 1795 Concordance*. Dardanelle, Ariz.: Imperial Press, 1977.

Silver, Alain, and Ursini, James. *The Vampire Film*. Cranbury, N.J. A. S. Barnes and Co., 1975.

Steiger, Brad. *Monsters, Maidens, and Mayhem*. New York: Camerarts Publishing, 1965.

Stout, Tim. "The Vampire in Films," in the Haining anthology.

White, Timothy. "Dracula: The Warmblooded Revival of the Debonaire King of the Undead." *Crawdaddy* (June 1978), pp. 16–33.

Wood, Robin. "Return of the Repressed." *Film Comment* Vol. 14, No. 4, (July–August 1978), pp. 25–32.

## X. Filmography

*Abbott and Costello Meet Frankenstein* (Charles T. Baron, USA, 1948). Bela Lugosi as Dracula.

*An American Werewolf in London* (John Landis, USA, 1981). David Naughton, Jenny Agutter, Griffin Dune and John Woodvine.

*Andy Warhol's Dracula* (Paul Morrisey, USA/Italy, 1974). Udo Kier as Dracula. Also titled: *Blood for Dracula.*

*Billy the Kid vs. Dracula* (William Beaudine, USA, 1966). John Carradine as Dracula.

*Black Sabbath* (Mario Bava, Italy, 1963). Boris Karloff as the *wurdalak* (vampire) in the last of three stories. Italian title: *I Tre Volti della Paura.*

*Black Sunday* (Mario Bava, Italy, 1960). Barbara Steele as the vampire. Italian title: *La Maschera del Demonio.* Also titled: *Revenge of the Vampire.*

*Blacula* (William Crain, USA, 1972). William Marshall as Mamuwalde (Blacula); Charles McCauley as Dracula.

*Blood* (Andy Milligan, USA, 1973). Hope Stransbury as the vampire.

*Blood and Roses* (Roger Vadim, France, 1960). Annette Vadim as Carmilla Von Karnstein. French title: *Et Mourir de Plaisir.*

*The Blood Demon* (Jarald Reinl, West Germany, 1967). Christopher Lee and Lex Barker. German title: *Die Schlangengrube und das Pendel.* Also titled: *The Torture Chamber of Dr. Sadism.*

*Blood of Dracula* (Herbert L. Strock, USA, 1957). Sandra Harrison as a teenage vampire. Also titled: *Blood Is My Heritage.*

*Blood of Dracula's Castle* (Al Adamson and Jean Hewitt, USA 1969). Alex D'Arcy as Dracula; John Carradine as his butler.

*Blood of Frankenstein* (Tulio Demicheli, Spain/West Germany/Italy, 1970). Michael Rennie and Paul Naschy. Spanish title: *El Hombre Que Vino del Ummo.* Also titled: *Dracula vs. Frankenstein.*

*Blood of the Vampire* (Henry Cass, England, 1958). Sir Donald Wolfit as Dr. Callistratus. Also titled: *The Demon with Bloody Hands.*

*Bloodsuckers* (Mel Welles, Spain/West Germany, 1966). Also titled: *Island of the Doomed; Man Eater of Hydra.*

*Bloodsuckers* (Robert Hartford-Davis and Michael Burrowes, England, 1970). Peter Cushing and Patrick MacNee. Also titled: *Incense for the Damned.*

*The Body Beneath* (Andy Milligan, England, 1970). Gavin Reed, Jackie Skarvellis, and Emma Jones.

*Brides of Dracula* (Terence Fisher, England, 1960). David Peel as vampire Baron Meinster; Peter Cushing as Van Helsing.

*Captain Kronos, Vampire Hunter* (Brian Clems, England, 1972). Horst Janson. Also titled: *Kronos: Vampire Castle.*

*Carry on Screaming* (Gerald Thomas, England, 1966). Fenella Fielding as a vampire. Also titled: *Screaming.*

*The Case of the Full Moon Murders* (Joseph Brad Talbort, USA, 1974). Sheila Stuart as the vampire.

*Castle of Blood* (Anthony Dawson, Italy, 1963). Barbara Steele as the vampire. Italian title: *La Danza Macabra*.

*The Castle of the Living Dead* (Lusiano Ricci, Italy/France, 1964). Christopher Lee. Italian title: *Il Castello Dei Morti Vivi*. French title: *Le Château des Morts Vivants*.

*Cemetery Girls* (Javier Aguirra, Spain, 1972). Paul Naschy as Dracula. Spanish title: *El Gran Amor del Conde Dracula*.

*Count Dracula* (Jesus Franco, Spain/Italy/West Germany/England, 1970). Christopher Lee as Dracula. Spanish title: *El Conde Dracula*. Also titled: *Bram Stoker's Count Dracula*.

*Count Dracula* (Phillip Saville, England, 1978 for BBC Television). Louis Jourdan as Dracula; Frank Finlay as Van Helsing.

*Count Dracula and His Vampire Bride* (Alan Gibson, England, 1973). Christopher Lee as Dracula; Peter Cushing as Van Helsing. Also titled: *The Satanic Rites of Dracula*.

*Count Dracula, the True Story* (Yurek Filjalkowski, Canada, 1979). Documentary on Vlad Tepes, filmed in Romania.

*Count Erotica, Vampire* (Tony Teresi, USA, 1971). John Peters and Mary Simon.

*Count Yorga, Vampire* (Bob Kelljan, USA, 1970). Robert Quarry as Count Yorga.

*Countess Dracula (Peter Sasdy, England, 1972)*. Ingrid Pitt as Countess Elizabeth Bathory.

*The Curse of Dracula* (USA, 1979). Weekly serial episodes that appeared on NBC-TV show "Cliffhangers" on American television with Michael Nouri as Dracula.

*Curse of the Undead* (Edward Dein, USA, 1959). Michael Pate as Drake Robey.

*Curse of the Vampires* (Gerardo De Leon, Philippines/USA, 1970). Also titled: *Creatures of Evil*; *Blood of the Vampire*.

*The Curse of the Werewolf* (Terence Fisher, Britain, 1961). Oliver Reed as the Werewolf.

*Dark Vengeance* (Jack Snyder, USA, 1980). Rebecca Wright and Mark Rudolph.

*Daughters of Darkness* (Harry Kumel, Belgium/France/West Germany/Italy, 1970). Delphine Seyrig as Countess Elizabeth Bathory. French title: *Le Rouge aux Lèvres*.

*Dawn of the Dead* (George Romero and Dario Argento, USA, 1979). David Emge and Ken Foree.

*Dead of the Night* (USA, 1977 for ABC-TV). Patrick MacNee. "No Such Thing as a Vampire" is one of the stories in this film.

*Deafula* (Peter Wicksberg, USA, 1975) (in sign language). Peter Wechsberg as Steve Adams/Deafula; Gary Holstrom as Count Dracula.

*The Deathmaster* (Ray Danton, USA, 1971). Robert Quarry as Khorda, a vampire.

*The Devil's Mistress* (Orville Wanzer, USA, 1966). Arthur Resley and Jean Stapleton.

*The Devil's Wedding Night* (Paul Solvay, Spain, 1973). Mark Damon, Sara Bay, and Miriam Barrios. Also titled: *Countess Dracula.*

*Devils of Darkness* (Lane Comfort, England, 1965). William Sylvester and Hubert Noel.

*Disciples of Dracula* ((USA, 1975). Ervin Cartwright, Phil Souza, and Linda Hinds.

*Dr. Terror's Gallery of Horrors* (David Hewitt, USA, 1967). Lon Chaney, Jr., John Carradine, and Rochelle Hudson. Also titled: *Gallery of Horrors; The Witch's Clock; The Blood Suckers; The Blood Drinkers; Return from the Past.*

*Dr. Terror's House of Horrors* (Freddie Francis, England, 1964). Donald Sutherland, Christopher Lee, and Peter Cushing.

*Dracula* (Tod Browning, USA, 1931). Bela Lugosi as Dracula, Edward Van Sloan as Van Helsing; Dwight Frye as Renfield.

*Dracula* (Patrick Dromgoole, England, 1969 for British BBC Television). Dehnolm Elliott as Dracula.

*Dracula* (Dan Curtis, USA, 1973 for CBS Television). Jack Palance as Dracula; Nigel Davenport as Van Helsing.

*Dracula* (Jack Nixon Browne, Canada, 1973 for the Canadian Broadcasting Co.). Norman Welsh and Blair Brown.

*Dracula* (John Badham, USA, 1979). Frank Langella as Dracula; Sir Laurence Olivier as Van Helsing.

*Dracula A.D. 1972* (Alan Gibson, England, 1971). Christopher Lee as Dracula; Peter Cushing as Van Helsing; Christopher Neame as Johnny Alucard. Also titled: *Dracula Today.*

*Dracula and the Boys* (Laurence Merrick, USA, 1969). Also titled: *Does Dracula Really Suck?; Dracula . . . Does He?*

*The Dracula Business* (Anthony de Latbiniere, England, 1974 for BBC Television). Documentary.

*Dracula Exotica* (USA, 1981). Vanessa del Rio and Samantha Fox.

*Dracula, Father and Son* (Edward Molinaro, France, 1976. Christopher Lee and Bernard Menez. French title: *Dracula, Père et Fils.*

*Dracula Has Risen from the Grave* (Freddie Francis, England, 1968). Christopher Lee as Count Dracula.

*Dracula in Istanbul* (Mehmet Muhtar, Turkey, 1952). Atif Kaptan as Dracula. Turkish title: *Drakula Istanbulda.*

*Dracula, Prince of Darkness* (Terence Fisher, England, 1965). Christopher Lee as Dracula. Also titled: *Blood of Dracula.*

*Dracula Saga* (Leon Klimovsky, Spain, 1972). Tina Sainz and Tony Isbert. Spanish title: *La Saga de los Draculas.* Also titled: *Vampires' All Night Orgy.*

*Dracula Sucks* (USA, 1979) Jamie Gillis as Dracula; with Annette Haven.

*Dracula—The Dirty Old Man* (William Edwards, USA, 1969). Vince Kelly as Dracula; with Ann Hollis.

*Dracula vs. Frankenstein* (Al Adamson, USA, 1971). Zandor Vorkov as Dracula; J. Caroll Nash as Dr. Frankenstein.

*Dracula's Daughter* (Lambert Hillyer, USA, 1936). Gloria Holden as Countess Marya Zaleska; Irving Pichel as Sandor.

*Dracula's Dog* (Albert Band, USA, 1977). Frank Ray, Jose Ferrer, Michael Pataki, and Reffie Nalder.

*Dracula's Last Rites* (Dominic Paris, France, 1980). Patricia Lee Hammond and Gerald Fielding.

*Dracula's Vampire Lust* (Mario D'Alcala, Switzerland, 1970). Des Roberts and Alon D'Armand. Also titled: *Dracula's Lusterne Vampire.*

*Dragula* (James Moss, USA, 1973). Casey Donovan and Walter Kent.

*Dragula, Queen of Darkness* (USA, 1979, made for cable TV).

*Every Home Should Have One* (Jim Clark, England, 1970). Marty Feldman and Shelly Berman.

*Fangs of the Living Dead* (Amando de Ossorio, Spain/Italy, 1969). Anita Ekberg and Julian Ugarte. Spanish title: *Malenkala Vampira.* Italian title: *La Nipote del Vampiro.*

*The Fearless Vampire Killers or Pardon Me, But Your Teeth Are in My Neck* (Roman Polanski, England, 1967). Roman Polanski as Alfred; Fredy Mayne as Count Krolock. French title: *Le Bal des Vampires.* Also titled: *Dance of the Vampires.*

*Frankenstein's Bloody Terror* (Enrique Equilez, Spain, 1968). Paul Naschy as the Wolfman. Spanish title: *La Marca del Hombre Lobo.* Also titled: *Mark of the Wolfman.*

*Frankenstein Meets the Wolfman* (Roy Wm. Neil, USA, 1943). Lon Chaney, Jr., as the Wolfman.

*Ganja and Hess* (Bill Gunn, USA, 1973). Duane Jones and Marlene Clark. Also titled: *Blood Couple.*

*Garu, the Mad Monk* (Andy Milligan, England, 1970). Neil Flanagan and Jacqueline Webb.

*Goliath and the Vampire* (Giacomo Gentilmo and Sergio Corbucci, Italy, 1961). Gordon Scott and Gianna Maria Canale. Italian title: *Maciste Control il Vampiro.*

*Grave of the Vampire* (John Patrick Hayes, USA, 1972). William Smith and Michael Pataki.

*Guess What Happened to Count Dracula?* (Laurence Merrick, USA, 1969). Des Roberts and Claudia Barron.

*Hannah, Queen of the Vampires* (Ray Danton, Turkey/USA, 1972). Andrew Prine, Mark Damon, and Therese Gimpera.

*The Hardy Boys and Nancy Drew Meet Dracula* (USA, 1977 for Universal Television). Parker Stevenson, Shaun Cassidy, Pamela Sue Martin, Paul Williams; Lorne Greene as the alleged Dracula.

*Hercules in the Haunted World* (Mario Bava, Italy, 1969). Reg Park and Christopher Lee. Italian title: *Ercole al Centro della Terra.*

*The Historical Dracula—Facts Behind the Fiction* (Ion Bostan, USA/Romania, 1976). An educational documentary film.

*The Horrible Sexy Vampire* (Jose Luis Madrid, Spain, 1970). Waldemar Wohlfart and Patricia Loran. Spanish title: *El Vampiro de la Autopista.*

*Horror of Dracula* (Terence Fisher, England, 1958). Christopher Lee as Dracula; Peter Cushing as Dr. Van Helsing. Also titled: *Dracula.*

*House of Dark Shadows* (Dan Curtis, USA, 1970). Jonathan Frid as vampire Barnabas Collins; Grayson Hall as Dr. Julia Hoffman; Kathryn Leigh Scott as Maggie Evans; Thayer David as Prof. T. Eliot Stokes.

*House of Dracula* (Erle C. Kenton, USA, 1945). John Carradine as the vampire, Baron Latoes; Lon Chaney, Jr.; Lionel Atwill; and Glenn Strange.

*House of Frankenstein* (Erle C. Kenton, USA, 1944). John Carradine as Dracula; Lon Chaney, Jr., as the Wolfman; J. Carrol Naish; and Lionel Atwill.

*The House That Dripped Blood* (Peter Dufell, England, 1971). Peter Cushing, Christopher Lee, Denholm Elliott, Ingrid Pitt; John Pertwee as vampire Paul Henderson.

*House on Bare Mountain* (R. L. Frost, USA, 1962). Bob Cresse and Laura Eden.

*I, Desire* (John L. Moxey, USA, 1982 for ABC Television), David Naughton, Marilyn Jones, Barbara Stock.

*I Was A Teenage Werewolf* (Gene Fowler, USA, 1957). Michael Landon as the werewolf.

*Immoral Tales* (Walerian Borowczyk, France, 1974). One sequence is based very loosely on Countess Elizabeth Bathory. French title: *Contes Immoraux.*

*In Search of Dracula* (Calvin Floyd, Sweden, 1971). Christopher Lee as narrator Vlad Tepes and Dracula. A Documentary.

*Isle of the Dead* (Mark Robson, USA, 1945). Boris Karloff and Ellen Drew.

*It Lives by Night* (Jerry Jameson, USA, 1973). Stewart Moss and Marianne McAndrew. Also titled: *The Bat People*.

*It! The Terror from Beyond Space* (Edward L. Cann, USA, 1958). Marshall Thompson and Sharon Smith.

*Jonathan* (Hans Geissendorfer, West Germany, 1970) with Jergen Jung as Jonathan; Paul Albert Krumm as the Count.

*Kiss Me Quick* (Russ Meyer, USA, 1963). Jackie De Witt and Althea Currier. Also titled: *Dr. Breedlove*.

*Kiss of the Vampire* (Don Sharp, England, 1963). Noel Willman and Jacquie Wallis as vampires.

*Kuroneko* (Kaneto Shindo, Japan, 1968). Kichiemon Nakamura and Nobuko Otowa.

*Lake of Dracula* (Michio Yamamoto, Japan, 1971). Midori Fujita and Sanae Emi. Japanese title: *Chiosu Me*.

*The Last Man on Earth* (Sidney Salkow, Italy, 1964). Vincent Price and Franca Bettoia. Italian title: *L'Ultimo Uomo della Terra*.

*The Leech Woman* (Edward Dein, USA, 1960). Coleen Gray and Phillip Terry.

*Legacy of Satan* (Gerard Damiano, USA, 1973). Lisa Christian as the vampire.

*Legend of Blood Castle* or *Ritual of Blood* (Jorge Grau, Spain/ Italy, 1972). Lucia Bose as Elizabeth Bathory. Spanish title: *Ceremonia Sangrienta*.

*The Lemon Grove Kids Meet the Green Grasshopper and the Vampire Lady from Outer Space* (Ted Rotter, USA, 1963). R. D. Steckler and Carolyn Brandt.

*Lemora: A Child's Tale of the Supernatural* (USA). Also titled: *Lemora, Lady Dracula*.

*Lips of Blood* (Ken Ruder, France, 1972). Michael Flynn and Richard Vitz. French title: *Les Chemins de la Violence*.

*The Living Dead at the Manchester Morgue* (Jorge Grau, England, 1974). Christian Galbo and Raymond Lovelock.

*London After Midnight* (Tod Browning, USA, 1927). Lon Chaney as the fake vampire.

*Love at First Bite* (Stan Dragoti, USA, 1979). George Hamilton as Dracula; Arte Johnson as Renfield; with Susan Saint James and Richard Benjamin.

*Love Making Vampire Style* (Helmut Forenbacher, West Germany, 1970). Eva Renzi and Patrick Jordan. German title: *Beiss Mich, Liebling*.

*Mad Monster Party* (Jules Bass, England, 1967). The voices of Boris Karloff, Alan Swift, Phyllis Diller, and Gale Garnett (an animation film).

*Mama Dracula* (Boris Szulinger, France, 1978). Louise Fletcher, Maria Schneider, and the Wajnberg brothers.

*Mark of the Vampire* (Tod Browning, USA, 1935). Bela Lugosi as Count Mora; Carole Borland as Luna; with Lionel Barrymore and Lionel Atwill.

*Martin* (George Romero, USA, 1977). John Amplas as the vampire; with Elyane Nadeau.

*The Monster Club* (Roy Ward Baker, England, 1982). Vincent Price as a vampire; with John Carradine, Donald Pleasance, Richard Johnsonn, and Britt Eklund.

*Munster, Go Home* (Earl Bellamy, USA, 1966). Fred Gwynne, Al Lewis, Yvonne De Carlo, and Terry Thomas.

*My Son, the Vampire* (John Gilling, England, 1952). Bela Lugosi and Arthur Luncan. Also titled: *Old Mother Riley Meets the Vampire*.

*Night of the Living Dead* (George Romero, USA, 1968). Duane Jones and Judith O'Dea.

*The Night Stalker* (John L. Moxey, USA, 1972 for ABC-TV). Darren McGavin as Karl Kolchak; Barry Atwater as vampire Janos Skorzeny.

*Nightwing* (Arthur Hiller, USA, 1978). Nick Mancuso, Kathryn Harrold, and David Warner.

*Nocturna* (Arthur Hiller, USA, 1979). Nai Bonet as Nocturna; John Carradine as Dracula; with Yvonne de Carlo.

*Nosferatu* (Friedrich Wilhelm Murnau, Germany, 1922). Max Schreck as Count Orlof/Nosferatu. German title: *Nosferatu, Eine Symphonie des Grauens*.

*Nosferatu, the Vampire* (Werner Herzog, West Germany, 1970). Klaus Kinski as the vampire count; with Isabelle Adjani. German title: *Nosferatu, Phantom der Nacht*.

*Old Dracula* (Clive Donner, England, 1974). David Niven as Dracula; with Teresa Graves. Also called: *Vampira*.

*Omega Man* (Boris Segal, USA, 1971). Charleton Heston and Rosalind Cash.

*Playgirls and the Vampire* (Pierre Regnoli, Italy, 1960). Walter Brandi and Lyla Rocca. Italian title: *L'Ultima Preda del Vampiro*.

*Queen of Blood* (Curtis Harrington, USA, 1966). John Saxon, Basil Rathbone, and Florence Marly. Also titled: *Planet of Blood*.

*Requiem for a Vampire* (Jean Rollin, France, 1972). Marie Pierre Castel and Mirelle D'Argent. French titles: *Requiem pour un Vampire; Vièrges et Vampires.* Also titled: *Caged Virgins.*

*Return of Count Yorga* (Bob Kelljan, USA, 1971). Robert Quarry as Count Yorga; with Mariette Hartley.

*The Return of Dracula* (Paul Landres, USA, 1957). Francis Lederer as Dracula/Bellac; with Norma Eberhardt.

*Return of the Vampire* (Lew Landers, USA, 1943). Bela Lugosi as the vampire Armand Tesla; with Roland Varno.

*Revenge of the Munsters* (USA, 1980). Fred Gwynne, Al Lewis, and Yvonne De Carlo.

*Salem's Lot* (Tobe Hooper, USA, 1980 for CBS Television). Reggie Nalder as the vampire Barlow; with David Soul, Lance Kerwin, and James Mason.

*Saturday the 14th* (Howard Cohen, USA, 1981). Richard Benjamin and Paula Prentiss.

*Scars of Dracula* (Roy Ward Baker, England, 1970). Christopher Lee as Dracula; with Jim Hanley.

*Scream, Blacula, Scream* (Bob Kelljan, USA, 1973). William Marshall as Mamuwalde/Blacula; with Pam Grier.

*The Seven Brothers Meet Dracula* (Roy Ward Baker, Hong Kong/England, 1974). Peter Cushing as Van Helsing; with Julie Ege. Also titled: *The Legend of the Seven Golden Vampires.*

*Sex and the Vampire* (Jean Rollin, France, 1970). Sandra Julien, Jean-Marie Durand, and Dominique. French title: *Le Frisson des Vampires.*

*Slaughter of the Vampires* (Robert Mauri, Italy, 1962). Walter Brandi as the vampire; with Graziella Granata. Italian title: *La Strage dei Vampiri.* Also titled: *Curse of the Blood Ghouls.*

*Son of Dracula* (Robert Siodmak, USA, 1943). Lon Chaney, Jr. as Count Alucard; with Louise Allbritton.

*Son of Dracula* (Freddie Francis, England, 1973). Harry Nilsson as Dracula; Ringo Starr as Merlin. Also titled: *Count Downe.*

*Spermula* (Charles Matton, France, 1976).

*A Taste of Blood* (Herschell Gordon Lewis, USA, 1967). Bill Rogers and Elizabeth Wilkinson.

*Taste the Blood of Dracula* (Peter Sasdy, England, 1970). Christopher Lee as Dracula; with Linda Hayden.

*Tender Dracula* (Alain Robbe Grillet, France, 1973). Peter Cushing as an actor of vampire roles. French title: *Tendre Dracula.*

*Terror Creatures from the Grave* (Massimo Pupillo, Italy/USA, 1965). Barbara Steele and Walter Brandi. Italian title: *Cinque Tombe per un Medium.*

*Terror in the Crypt* (Thomas Miller, Camillo Mastrocinque, Italy/ Spain, 1963). Christopher Lee and Adriana Ambisi. Spanish title: *La Maldicion de los Karnsteins*. Italian title: *La Cripta e l'Incubo*.

*The Theatre of Death* (Samuel Gallu, England, 1966). Christopher Lee and Julien Glover. Also titled: *Blood Fiend*.

*The Thing from Another World* (Christian Nyby, USA, 1951). James Arness as the Thing; with Kenneth Tobey.

*To Love A Vampire* (Jimmy Sangster, England, 1970). Yvette Stensgaard as vampiress Mircalla. Also titled: *Lust for a Vampire*.

*Track of the Vampire* (Jack Hill and Stephanie Rothman, USA, 1966). William Campbell as an artist vampire. Also titled: *Blood Bath*.

*Twins of Evil* (John Hough, England, 1972). Peter Cushing as Gustav Weil; Madeleine and Mary Collinson as Frieda and Maria Gelhorn.

*The Undying Monster* (John Brahm, USA, 1942).

*Uncle Was a Vampire* (Pio Angeletti, Italy, 1959). Christopher Lee as the vampire. Italian title: *Tempi Duri per i Vampiri*.

*Valley of the Zombies* (Phillip Ford, USA, 1946). Robert Livingston and Adrian Booth.

*Vampire* (USA, 1979 for ABC-TV). Richard Lynch as vampire Voytek; with John Rawlins, Kathryn Harrold, and E. G. Marshall.

*The Vampire* (Paul Landres, USA, 1957). John Beals and Coleen Gray.

*The Vampire and the Ballerina* (Renato Polselli, Italy, 1961). Walter Brandi and Helen Remy. Italian title: *L'Amante del Vampiro*.

*The Vampire Bat* (Frank Strayer, USA, 1922). Lionel Atwill, Fay Ray, Melvyn Douglas, and Dwight Frye.

*Vampire Circus* (Robert Young, England, 1971). Robert Tayman as Count Mitterhouse; with Adrienne Corro and Laurence Paine.

*The Vampire Happening* (Freddie Francis, West Germany, 1971). Ferdy Mayne as Dracula, with Pia Degermark. German title: *Gibissen Wird Nur Nachts*.

*Vampire Hookers* (USA, 1979). John Carradine.

*Vampire Lovers* (Roy Ward Baker, England, 1970). Ingrid Pitt as Carmilla Karnstein; with Peter Cushing and Madeline Smith.

*Vampire Men of the Lost Planet* (Al Adamson, USA, 1970). John Carradine, Robert Dix, and Vickie Volante. Also titled: *Horror of the Blood Monsters; Creatures of the Prehistoric Planet*.

*The Vampire's Ghost* (Lesley Selander, USA, 1945). John Abbot as vampire Webb Fallon; with Julie Vance.

*Vampyr* (Carl Theodor Dreyer, France, 1932). Julian West, Maurice Schultz, and Sybille Schmitz.

*Vampyres* (Joseph Larroz, England, 1974). Marianna Morris and Anulka as a female vampire couple.

*Vault of Horror* (Roy Ward Baker, England, 1973). Daniel Massey and Anna Massey. Also titled: *Tales from the Crypt*.

*The Velvet Vampire* (Stephanie Rothman, USA, 1971). Celeste Yarnall as vampire Diane Le Fanu.

*The Werewolf of London* (Stuart Walker, USA, 1935). Henry Hull as the first werewolf on film.

*The Werewolf* (Fred Sears, USA, 1956).

*The Werewolf vs. the Vampire Woman* (Leon Klimovsky, Spain/West Germany, 1970). Paul Naschy, Gaby Fuchs, and Barbara Copell. Spanish title: *La Noche de Walpurgis*. German title: *Nacht der Vampir*. Also titled: *Shadow of the Werewolf*.

*Wolfen* (Michael Wadleigh, USA, 1981). Albert Finney.

*The Wolfman* (George Waggner, USA, 1941). Lon Chaney, Jr., as the wolfman.

# Index